LIBRARY OF HEBREW BIBLE/OLD TESTAMENT STUDIES

679

Formerly Journal for the Study of the Old Testament Supplement Series

Editors
Claudia V. Camp, Texas Christian University
Andrew Mein, Westcott House, Cambridge

Founding Editors
David J. A. Clines, Philip R. Davies and David M. Gunn

Editorial Board
Alan Cooper, Susan Gillingham
John Goldingay, Norman K. Gottwald, James E. Harding,
John Jarick, Carol Meyers, Daniel L. Smith-Christopher,
Francesca Stavrakopoulou, James W. Watts

DRESS AND CLOTHING IN THE HEBREW BIBLE

"For All Her Household Are Clothed in Crimson"

Edited by
Antonios Finitsis

LONDON • NEW YORK • OXFORD • NEW DELHI • SYDNEY

T&T CLARK
Bloomsbury Publishing Plc
50 Bedford Square, London, WC1B 3DP, UK
1385 Broadway, New York, NY 10018, USA
29 Earlsfort Terrace, Dublin 2, Ireland

BLOOMSBURY, T&T CLARK and the T&T Clark logo
are trademarks of Bloomsbury Publishing Plc

First published in Great Britain 2019
This paperback edition published in 2021

Copyright © Antonios Finitsis and contributors, 2019

Antonios Finitsis has asserted his right under the Copyright,
Designs and Patents Act, 1988, to be identified as Editor of this work.

For legal purposes the Acknowledgments on p. xii constitute
an extension of this copyright page.

All rights reserved. No part of this publication may be reproduced or
transmitted in any form or by any means, electronic or mechanical,
including photocopying, recording, or any information storage or retrieval
system, without prior permission in writing from the publishers.

Bloomsbury Publishing Plc does not have any control over, or responsibility for,
any thirdparty websites referred to or in this book. All internet addresses given
in this book were correct at the time of going to press. The author and publisher
regret any inconvenience caused if addresses have changed or sites have
ceased to exist, but can accept no responsibility for any such changes.

A catalogue record for this book is available from the British Library.

Library of Congress Cataloging-in-Publication Data
Names: Finitsis, Antonios, editor.
Title: Dress and clothing in the Hebrew Bible: for all her household are
clothed in crimson / edited by Antonios Finitsis.
Description: 1 [edition]. | New York: T&T Clark, 2019. |
Series: Library of Hebrew Bible/Old Testament studies, 2513-8758; volume 679 |
Includes bibliographical references and index.
Identifiers: LCCN 2019016125 | ISBN 9780567686404 (hardback) |
ISBN 9780567686411 (epdf)
Subjects: LCSH: Biblical costume. | Clothing and dress–Middle East. |
Bible. Old Testament–Criticism, interpretation, etc.
Classification: LCC BS680.C65 D74 2019 | DDC 221.8/391–dc23
LC record available at https://lccn.loc.gov/2019016125

ISBN: HB: 978-0-5676-8640-4
PB: 978-0-5677-0036-0
ePDF: 978-0-5676-8641-1
ePUB: 978-0-5676-8976-4

Series: Library of Hebrew Bible/Old Testament Studies, volume 679

ISSN 2513-8758

Typeset by Integra Software Services Pvt. Ltd.

To find out more about our authors and books visit
www.bloomsbury.com and sign up for our newsletters.

To all Women of Substance and to Polyxeni Finitsi and Evaggelia Passali, illustrative examples of the Woman of Substance in rural Greece, circa 1940s.

CONTENTS

List of Illustrations	ix
Foreword	x
Acknowledgments	xii
Abbreviations	xiii
List of Contributors	xvi

Introduction
"FOR ALL HER HOUSEHOLD ARE CLOTHED IN CRIMSON"
    Antonios Finitsis   1

Chapter 1
YHWH'S CLOTHING, KINGSHIP, AND POWER: ORIGINS AND VESTIGES IN COMPARATIVE ANCIENT NEAR EASTERN CONTEXTS
    Shawn W. Flynn   11

Chapter 2
BETWEEN TWO WORLDS: THE FUNCTIONAL AND SYMBOLIC SIGNIFICANCE OF THE HIGH PRIESTLY REGALIA
    Carmen Joy Imes   29

Chapter 3
APOTROPAIC ACCESSORIES: THE PEOPLE'S TASSELS AND THE HIGH PRIEST'S ROSETTE
    Joshua Joel Spoelstra   63

Chapter 4
TAMAR AND TAMAR: CLOTHING AS DECEPTION AND DEFIANCE
    Sara M. Koenig   87

Chapter 5
IS SAUL AMONG THE PHILISTINES? A PORTRAYAL OF ISRAEL'S FIRST AND FLAWED KING
    Sean E. Cook   109

Chapter 6
THE EMPEROR AND HIS CLOTHING: DAVID ROBED AND UNROBED BEFORE THE ARK AND MICHAL
    Ian D. Wilson   125

Chapter 7
DISROBING AN ISAIANIC METAPHOR מְעִיל צְדָקָה (*MĚ'ÎL ṢĔḎĀQÂ* "ROBE OF RIGHTEOUSNESS") AS POWER TRANSFER IN ISAIAH 61:10
    Scott R.A. Starbuck   143

Chapter 8
WERE YHWH'S CLOTHES WORTH REMEMBERING AND THINKING ABOUT AMONG THE LITERATI OF LATE PERSIAN/EARLY HELLENISTIC JUDAH/YEHUD? OBSERVATIONS AND CONSIDERATIONS
    Ehud Ben Zvi   161

Select Bibliography   183
Index of Primary Sources   187
Index of Subjects   190

LIST OF ILLUSTRATIONS

Figures

2.1	Priestly garments	31
2.2	Pharaoh Rameses III (Necropolis, Thebes)	40
2.3	Pharaoh Rameses III (Medinet Habu, Thebes)	41
2.4	Pharaoh Seti I with the goddess Maat (Abydos)	42
2.5	Babylonian king Marduk-Nadin-Akhe	44
2.6	Assyrian king Ashur-nasir-pal	45
2.7	Court musician for Ashur-nasir-pal	46
2.8	Unknown nationality before Assyrian king Sargon II	47

Tables

2.1	Haran's levels of fabric styles	32
2.2	A comparison of lists of priestly garments	36
2.3	Stated purposes for the high priestly garments in Exodus 28	55

FOREWORD

Alicia J. Batten
Conrad Grebel University College, University of Waterloo

Every day we engage with dress, whether it is through our own perplexity about what to wear, the fashion images we see plastered on billboards, or perhaps a news item about a dress scandal. Dress seems as basic as food, and as far as we know, humans have "dressed" in some form at least since they have walked upright. Dress serves practical purposes, such as protection from the elements, but it is also a central means of expressing and identifying ourselves, both individually and collectively, and can serve as a tool of accommodation or resistance. As a form of materiality, dress is sensory and as such is a fundamental means through which our bodies experience the world.

"Dress studies" has become an interdisciplinary field in which one finds historians, anthropologists, sociologists, art historians, and many others trained in a range of disciplines. It is still a reasonably "young" field although we find references to dress, as well as strong moral and philosophical opinions about it, throughout a range of ancient and contemporary literature. Given that self-presentation is often subject to the scrutiny of the group, dress figures centrally as people in various societies and cultures navigate their way through everyday life. Dress is not only a sign of status, for many, but sometimes, in its arrangement, an indicator of character. Comparable to an argument, dress can possess rhetorical functions and serve, perhaps even more effectively than language, to convince or dissuade.

Based upon a range of evidence, dress was also very significant for the cultures of antiquity. References to dress are plentiful throughout ancient literature; and the Bible is no exception. Both the Hebrew Bible and the New Testament feature dress in a variety of ways. Sometimes the shedding or donning of a dress item can signal a transition point within a narrative and have a literary function. At other moments dress—or the lack of it—has theological significance; or, dress images function metaphorically to assist in concretizing specific ideas. There are elaborate descriptions of dress in the Bible as well as clear and explicit guidelines as to what should or should not be worn. In addition, there are many fleeting references to dress which are easy to miss. By using dress as a lens for reading, therefore, we notice things that previously may have gone under the radar, for presumably the authors included every reference to dress for a reason.

Given the import of dress for many biblical texts, it is wonderful to see a group of scholars come together to discuss the importance of dress, in this case within the context of the Hebrew Bible. The topic has not received much sustained attention;

and biblical scholarship in this area is in its beginning stages. These studies not only assist us in understanding the functions of dress within ancient cultures but also deepen our appreciation for the meanings of the biblical texts. By focusing upon dress, as this scholarship does, we are able to see new dimensions within Hebrew narrative and poetry. In their diversity and range, these essays are witness to the myriad of ways that dress can function in literature. I congratulate the editor and authors for their work. The book will contribute to a growing and welcome body of scholarship on dress in the ancient world and more specifically, advance scholarship on dress, the Hebrew Bible, and related ancient literature.

ACKNOWLEDGMENTS

It might be the case that only in quantum physics one can make something out of nothing. This is certainly not the case for the present volume. This book is a testament of the strength found in unity and of collegial collaboration among senior and junior colleagues in Hebrew Bible. Thus, I would like to offer gratitude to a constellation of people who were incredibly helpful toward the completion of the present work. Alicia Batten is an excellent scholar and a delightful human being to whom I will be perpetually grateful for her mentorship and inspiration. Katherine Wiley offered sage advice on the topic of dress, and I am appreciative for her guidance. My friend and colleague Agnes Choi read my introduction and offered key feedback for which I am thankful. I would also like to mention first Ardy Bass and then Mari Kim for their work as Executive Secretaries/Regionally Elected Directors for the Pacific Northwest region of the AAR/SBL and for their encouragement toward our research group. My appreciation toward John J. Collins is unwavering for teaching me lessons that last a lifetime.

Special acknowledgment goes to all the scholars who worked and contributed to this volume. Ehud Ben Zvi for suggesting the research topic and Sara M. Koenig and Scott Starbuck for enthusiastically supporting it. Shawn W. Flynn was the first to submit a research proposal once the call for papers went out. Sara, Scott, and Shawn were the first to submit their papers and commit their energies toward the research group in 2014. The following year, the next wave of scholars joined and enriched our deliberations. Ian D. Wilson, Carmen Joy Imes, Sean Cook, Joshua Joel Spoelstra, and Ehud Ben Zvi catapulted the level of our research to unprecedented heights. They all brought their best game, and I cannot put in words the gratification and exhilaration that characterized our meetings. It would not have happened without their formidable expertise and disarming openness to constructive criticism. I admire them for their achievements and commend them for their intellectual generosity and work ethic. I am proud to have worked by their side; I could not have asked for better research partners.

Each year numerous colleagues from the Pacific Northwest region attended our meetings and participated in our conversations. We only benefited from their recommendations. I would like to recognize all of you formally here. At the moment, there is in development the work of a second research group in dress. Thank you for your diligence and I look forward to the continuation of our work together.

Lastly, I would like to thank my family away from home and my colleagues in the Religion Department at PLU. You are a true community of scholars with whom I am happy to work.

ABBREVIATIONS

AB	Anchor Bible
ABC	Anchor Bible Commentary
ABD	*Anchor Bible Dictionary*
ACJ	*Acta Sumerologica Journal*
AJA	*American Journal of Archaeology*
AJSL	*American Journal of Semitic Languages and Literature*
ALUOS	Annual of Leeds University Oriental Society
ANEP	James B. Pritchard (ed.), *Ancient Near East in Pictures Relating to the Old Testament* (Princeton: Princeton University Press, 1954)
ANET	James B. Pritchard (ed.), *Ancient Near Eastern Texts Relating to the Old Testament* (Princeton: Princeton University Press, 1950)
AOAT	Alter Orient und Altes Testament
ASV	American Standard Version
AYBRL	The Anchor Yale Bible Reference Library
BA	*Biblical Archaeologist*
BAR	*Biblical Archaeology Review*
BASOR	*Bulletin of the American Schools of Oriental Research*
BBRSup	Bulletin for Biblical Research Supplements
BCMA	*The Bulletin of the Cleveland Museum of Art*
BDB	Francis Brown, S.R. Driver and Charles A. Briggs, *A Hebrew and English Lexicon of the Old Testament* (Oxford: Clarendon Press, 1907)
BFAM	*Bulletin of the Fogg Art Museum*
BMMA	*Bulletin of the Metropolitan Museum of Art*
BRLAJ	The Brill Reference Library of Ancient Judaism
BTB	*Biblical Theology Bulletin*
BZAW	Beihefte zur Zeitschrift für die alttestamentliche Wissenschaft
CAD	Ignace I. Gelb et al. (eds), *The Assyrian Dictionary of the Oriental Institute of the University of Chicago* (Chicago: Oriental Institute, 1956)
CBET	Contributions to Biblical Exegesis and Theology
CBQ	*Catholic Biblical Quarterly*
CEB	Common English Bible
CoBOT	Coniectanea biblica, Old Testament
COS	*The Context of Scripture*. Edited by W. W. Hallo. 3 vols. (Leiden: Brill, 1997–)

DCH	*Dictionary of Classical Hebrew*. Edited by David J. A. Clines. (Sheffield: Phoenix, 1993)
ECC	Eerdmans Critical Commentary
ESV	English Standard Version
FAT	Forschungen zum Alten Testament
FOTL	Forms of Old Testament Literature
HAL	The Hebrew and Aramaic Lexicon of the Old Testament
HALOT	Ludwig Koehler and Walter Baumgartner. *The Hebrew and Aramaic Lexicon of the Old Testament*. Translated and edited by M. E. J. Richardson. (Leiden: Brill, 2001)
HCOT	Historical Commentary on the Old Testament
HCSB	Holman Christian Standard Bible
HS	*Hebrew Studies*
HSM	Harvard Semitic Monographs
HTR	*Harvard Theological Review*
HUCA	*Hebrew Union College Annual*
ICC	International Critical Commentary
IEJ	*Israel Exploration Journal*
JAOS	*Journal of the American Oriental Society*
JANER	*Journal of Ancient Near Eastern Religions*
JARCE	*Journal of the American Research Center in Egypt*
JBL	*Journal of Biblical Literature*
JCS	*Journal of Cuneiform Studies*
JE	Jewish Encyclopedia
JETS	*Journal of the Evangelical Theological Society*
JTS	*Journal of Theological Studies*
JNES	*Journal of Near Eastern Studies*
JPS	The Jewish Publication Society
JQR	*Jewish Quarterly Review*
JRAS	*Journal of the Royal Asiatic Society*
JRitSt	*Journal of Ritual Studies*
JSS	*Journal of Semitic Studies*
JSOT	*Journal for the Study of the Old Testament*
JSOTSup	*Journal for the Study of the Old Testament, Supplement Series*
KB	Ludwig Koehler and Walter Baumgartner (eds), *Lexicon in Veteris Testamenti libros* (Leiden: E.J. Brill, 1953)
KJV	King James Version
LHBOTS	Library of the Hebrew Bible, Old Testament Studies
LXX	Septuagint
LXX^B	Septuagint, Codex Vaticanus
LXX^L	Septuagint, Codex Vienna Genesis
MT	Masoretic Text
NASB	New American Standard Bible
NET	New English Translation
NETS	New English Translation of the Septuagint

NICOT	New International Commentary on the Old Testament
NIDOTTE	Willem A. VanGemeren (ed.), *New International Dictionary of Old Testament Theology and Exegesis* 5 vols. (Grand Rapids: Zondervan, 1997)
NIV	New International Version
NLT	New Living Translation
NJPS	*Tanakh: The Holy Scriptures: The New JPS Translation according to the Traditional Hebrew Text*
NKJV	New King James Version
NSRV	New Revised Standard Version
OBO	Orbis biblicus et orientalis
OEAE	Oxford Encyclopedia of Ancient Egypt
OTL	Old Testament Library
OTS	Oudtestamentlische Studiën
PAPS	*Proceedings of the American Philosophical Society*
PEQ	*Palestine Exploration Quarterly*
PSBA	*Proceedings of the Society of Biblical Archaeology*
RA	Revue d'assyriologie et d'archaeologie orientale
RSV	Revised Standard Version
SAA	State Archives of Assyria
SAALT	State Archives of Assyria Literary Texts
SAK	Studien zur Altägyptichen Kultur
SBLWAW	Sup Society of Biblical Literature, Writings from the Ancient World Supplements
SJOT	*Scandinavian Journal of the Old Testament*
StR	Studia Reliogiologica
SPAA	Selected Papers on Ancient Art and Architecture
TNK	Tanakh
TDOT	G.J. Botterweck and H. Ringgren (eds), *Theological Dictionary of the Old Testament*
UF	*Ugarit-Forschungen*
VT	*Vetus Testamentum*
VTSup	Vetus Testamentum, Supplements
WBC	*Word Biblical Commentary*
WUNT	Wissentschaftliche Untersuchungen zum Neue Testament
WZKM	*Wiener Zeitschrift für die Kunde des Morgenlandes*
ZAW	Zeitschrift für die Altentestamentliche Wissenschaft

LIST OF CONTRIBUTORS

Alicia Batten, Associate Professor of Religious Studies and Theological Studies
Conrad Grebel University College, University of Waterloo, Waterloo, Ontario

Sean E. Cook, Lecturer in Biblical/Religious Studies
Mount Royal University, St. Mary's University, Calgary, Alberta

Antonios Finitsis, Associate Professor of Hebrew Bible
Pacific Lutheran University, Tacoma, Washington

Shawn W. Flynn, Associate Professor of Hebrew Bible and Academic Dean
St. Joseph's College, University of Alberta, Edmonton, Alberta

Carmen Joy Imes, Associate Professor in Old Testament, Program Coordinator for Biblical Studies
Prairie College, Three Hills, Alberta

Sara M. Koenig, Associate Professor of Biblical Studies
Seattle Pacific University, Seattle, Washington

Joshua Joel Spoelstra, Research Associate
Stellenbosch University, Stellenbosch, South Africa

Scott R.A. Starbuck, Lecturer of Religious Studies
Gonzaga University, Spokane, Washington

Ian D. Wilson, Assistant Professor of Religious Studies, Director of the Chester Ronning Centre
Augustana Campus, University of Alberta, Camrose, Alberta

Ehud Ben Zvi, Professor Emeritus
University of Alberta, Edmonton, Alberta

INTRODUCTION: "FOR ALL HER HOUSEHOLD ARE CLOTHED IN CRIMSON"

Antonios Finitsis

The chapters in this volume are the outcome of a research group that formed in 2014 under the auspices of the Hebrew Bible (HB) unit in the Pacific Northwest region of the Society of Biblical Literature. In an effort to build on the signature collegiality of the Pacific Northwest, I put out a call for proposals on the topic of "Clothing." Interested scholars would need to work together in the manner of a think tank over the period of three years in order to produce new scholarship on the topic. Proposals kept coming in and participants, as well as observers, contributed to unprecedented levels of energy and constructive dialogue during our meetings each year. As our research changed and evolved so did the name of the group. The first fruits of our truly collaborative work matured into the eight following chapters.

A change in dress

"Clothing" was the term we used initially to frame the topic of discourse for the emerging research group. Our choice was deliberate yet not fully informed. The goal was to articulate a theme that would allow broad flexibility in terms of scholarly interest, textual selection, historical period, and methodological approach and we were successful in that endeavor. However, during our deliberations we came to see that the selected *terminus technicus* had been surpassed in the field; thus, our original terminology was revised and the research group was modified to "Dress."

The consensus around the term "dress" emerged from the seminal work of Joanne B. Eicher and Mary Ellen Roach-Higgins. Their goal was to develop an unambiguous and inclusive definition, free of personal or social valuing or bias, that was usable across national and cultural boundaries. Thus, they defined dress as the "assemblage of body modifications and/or supplements displayed by a person in communicating with other human beings."[1] They argued that this definition is

---

1. Joanne B. Eicher and Mary Ellen Roach-Higgins, "Definition and Classification of Dress: Implications for Analysis of Gender Roles," in *Dress and Gender: Making Meaning*

successful because it "includes a long list of possible direct modifications of the body such as coiffed hair, colored skin, pierced ears, and scented breath, as well as an equally long list of garments, jewelry, accessories, and other categories of items added to the body as supplements."[2] Their emphasis on dress as a means of communication directs attention to the content and implications of such communication.

The red thread

This volume cannot and does not aspire to be a comprehensive discussion of dress in the HB. As Alicia Batten aptly states in her foreword to this volume, "dress studies" is a reasonably young field and it is still developing in a range of disciplines. In the study of the HB, it is even younger and we are excited to discover where it may lead us as the number of conversation partners grows and the investigation advances. Even as we began our analysis, we were well aware that dress items are tailored to fit multivalent purposes and thus, cover a wide array of communication. Ostensibly, they serve a wide range of heuristic objectives while, simultaneously, they divulge the details of a profoundly symbolic world. Among others, they communicate messages, define identities, express aspirations, reflect values, and create a coherent and culture-specific visual language. Roach-Higgins and Eicher offer a compelling point when they state "the list of possible meanings communicated by type of dress is seemingly endless."[3]

In the study of HB, there is an additional consideration. This embodied language suits equally well both physical and meta-physical considerations, proving to be particularly articulate toward religious concerns. Indeed, at a time when reading and writing were the select privilege of a small minority, dress was the widely understood form of language.[4] It is no wonder then, that it figures prominently in both ancient narratives and art. The *locus classicus* for dress and its importance in the discipline of religion has been the communication of different

---

in Cultural Contexts, ed. Ruth Barnes and Joanne B. Eicher. Cross-Cultural Perspectives on Women, Vol. 2 (Oxford: Berg, 1993), 15.

2. Mary Ellen Roach-Higgins and Joanne B. Eicher, "Dress and Identity," *Clothing and Textiles Research Journal* 10 (1992): 1. As they explained, "The word clothing is most frequently used to emphasize enclosures that cover the body and generally omits body modifications. In addition, the word clothing, like adornment, almost inevitably introduces personal or social values." Ibid., 3.

3. Ibid., 4.

4. Mary Ellen Roach-Higgins and Joanne B. Eicher have concluded "dress has a certain priority over verbal discourse in communicating identity since it ordinarily sets the stage for subsequent verbal communication." Ibid., 7.

identities.⁵ Nevertheless, I agree with the conclusion that Laura Gawlinski draws in her research. She declares: "Opening a dialogue between theoretical approaches to dress and religion encourages a cross-pollination of ideas beyond the trappings of 'difference.'"⁶ Thus, the scholarly work presented here attempts to move beyond the use of dress to communicate different identities.

This volume fixes its analytical gaze on the primary evidence of the ancient Near East (ANE) and the HB and attempts to achieve two goals. First, it straddles the divide between the material and the ideological and second, it lends shape and texture to the developing implications of this interconnection. The red thread running through the chapters is the power communicated by dress in all its forms, generative and destructive, real, perceived, and projected.

The color purple

The subtitle of our volume is intended to call attention to the topic of power. It comes from the ode to the woman of substance in Prov 31:10–31, a complete sequential alphabet acrostic poem in twenty-two verses that concludes the book of Proverbs. The protagonist, an idealized patriarchal projection is, אֵשֶׁת חַיִל, *ēšet ḥayil*, the woman of substance. This term has alternatively been variously translated as "the good wife," "virtuous woman," "capable wife," "noble woman," or more literally and to-the-point, "woman of strength."⁷ As Michael V. Fox explains the word *ḥayil* means "strength, whether in wealth, physical power, military might, practical competencies, or character."⁸ It would seem, then, that the goal of Prov 31:10–31 is to explore power in conjunction with the female gender.⁹ It is interesting that in a

---

5. Laura Gawlinski reports: "Scholarship on dress in living religions has emphasized ... how it can be used to show religious identity physically. The focus tends to be on dress as a means for communities or individuals to show their separation." She further clarifies: "Dress in the context of religious practice marks identity, communicates personal characteristics and community ideals, and negotiates hierarchy. Its close relationship to the body makes it suited to participate in the construction of gender as well as in the performance of authority and belief." Laura Gawlinski, "Theorizing Religious Dress," in *What Shall I Say of Clothes? Theoretical and Methodological Approaches to the Study of Dress in Antiquity*, ed. Megan Cifarelli and Laura Gawlinski. Selected Papers on Ancient Art and Architecture, Vol. 3 (Boston, MA: Archaeological Institute of America, 2017), 161.

6. Ibid., 175.

7. Cf. L. Juliana Claassens, "The Woman of Substance and Human Flourishing: Proverbs 31:10–31 and Martha Nussbaum's Capabilities Approach," *Journal of Feminist Studies in Religion* 32.1 (2016): 7.

8. Michael V. Fox, *Proverbs 10–31: A New Translation with Introduction and Commentary*, AYB, Vol. 18B (New Haven, CT: Yale University Press, 2009), 891.

9. M. Beth Szlos notices that this poem employs four separate literary devices in order to depict a physically powerful woman: (a) action verbs; (b) words that mean "power"

poem set firmly in a harsh agrarian setting, there are seven separate references to literal and metaphorical dress (Prov 31:10, 13, 19, 21, 22, 24, and 25). The first metaphorical reference (31:10) alludes to the pricelessness yet attainability of rubies, that is, the power of acquiring jewels and the second reference (31:25) points to the defining power of dress.[10] The literal references concern the power that comes from the total control of a mode of production in which agriculture is the sustaining foundation.[11] According to these verses, the woman of substance is responsible for the entire process, from seeking and securing raw materials, to dress manufacturing, and finally to its commercial distribution.[12] The number of verses that refer to dress becomes even more pronounced when one takes into account that the poem is only twenty-two verses in length. Fully, one-third of the poem deals with aspects of dress. Therefore, dress emerges as one of the ways in which this poem constructs the profile of a powerful woman.[13] I would contend that the coup de grâce regarding dress and power is dealt with the remark in 31:21b: "For all her household are clothed in crimson."

In the biblical context, crimson refers to expensive articles of clothing worn by the rich (cf. 2 Sam 1:24; Isa 1:18; Jer 4:30). Thus, the color itself is an allusion to affluence and financial power. In the context of Prov 31:21 it poses something of an exegetical crux when read with the first part of the verse: "She is not afraid for her household when it snows, for all her household are clothed in crimson."

---

or "strength"; (c) body parts referred to as "hers"; and (d) commercial vocabulary that emphasizes her industriousness. M. Beth Szlos, "A Portrait of Power: A Literal-Critical Study of the Depiction of the Woman in Proverbs 31:10–31," *Union Seminary Quarterly Review* 54.1 (2000): 97–103.

10. I consider rubies here as a supplement used by a person for the purpose of communication with others, thus, a dress item.

11. Specifically, Prov 31:13 refers to the search of wool and flax and her manual labor; 31:19 mentions her use of the distaff and spindle; 31:23 brings up the production of coverings as well as fine articles of clothing; 31:24 calls attention to her selling and trading activities; and in 31:25 the vehicle reference is to clothing while the tenor points to the communication of defining character traits.

12. Gale A. Yee, following Jobling, designates the mode of production characteristic of pre-state Israel as "familial" because it allows the integration of the critical roles that women played in the Israelite family household. Gale A. Yee, *Poor Banished Children of Eve: Woman as Evil in the Hebrew Bible* (Minneapolis: Fortress, 2003), 31–32.

13. I concur with Julia A. Hendon's definition of power: "Rather than construe power as something certain people have or as a particular capacity, practice or political economy perspectives start from the premise that 'power is an effect of the operation of social relations.'" Julia A. Hendon, "The Engendered Household," in *Women in Antiquity: Theoretical Approaches to Gender and Archaeology*, ed. S.M. Nelson (Lanham, MD: Alta Mira Press, 2007), 156. Particularly, I want to call attention to Hendon's insight: "Women's autonomy seems to decrease as social hierarchies become more entrenched; thus, some women were of high status but had relatively less autonomy." Ibid., 157.

Some commentators have questioned the ways in which crimson garments could keep her family warm in cold weather. Thus, influenced by the translation "two-ply" in the LXX and Vulgate (δισσὰς; duplicus), they vocalize the word שָׁנַיִם, šānîm, scarlet as šᵉnayim instead and understand it to mean "double."[14] Fox astutely observes, however, that šᵉnayim means "two," not "double" so the emendation is not successful. Furthermore, there is no reason to assume that the MT text is wrong.[15] The problem is solved once we grasp the connection between the color and the financial power of this woman. Arjun Appadurai provides the needed theoretical underpinning when he writes: "Even though from a *theoretical* point of view human actors encode things with significance, from a *methodological* point of view, it is the things-in-motion that illuminate their human context."[16] Thus, I agree with Fox that it is not the crimson dye that provides warmth, but the clothing itself. The point is that "so sumptuously does she provide for her family that even clothes meant for warmth are luxurious."[17] The crimson color indicates that she is a lavish provider for her family. The broader context of her manufacturing and trading activities, however, reveal the source of her power. Her economic power has enabled such prosperity that the members of her household enjoy the privileges of royalty.

Crimson as a symbol of royalty has strong roots in the ANE. As I. Irving Ziderman reports "the first written records of purple dyeing, from Nuzi, Mesopotamia, are about 3,500 years old" and they are followed by texts in Akkadian, Ugaritic, and Hebrew.[18] The earliest material archaeological evidence of purple dyeing is found in Leuke (a small island southeast of Crete) and dates to the seventeenth century BCE. Crimson dye was included among the prestige goods that ancient Cretans would have traded with their eastern Mediterranean and western Asiatic partners.[19] Reportedly, the value of the dye was equal to that of gold. There were three factors that drove the value of the dye so high: its manufacturing process, its scarcity, and its colorfast properties. The dye was made from certain types of shellfish—*muricidae*, more commonly called *murex*—that

---

14. Cf. Roland E. Murphy, *Proverbs*, WBC (Nashville, TN: Thomas Nelson, 1998), 244. Also, Richard J. Clifford, *Proverbs*, OTL (Louisville, KY: Westminster John Knox, 1999), 276.

15. William Mc Kane comments: "Is this the way in which the ēšet ḥayil would keep her family warm in winter? Would they have to put two of everything? It could be argued that this is just a way of saying that there is no shortage of good clothing in her household." William Mc Kane, *Proverbs*, OTL (Philadelphia, PA: Westminster, 1970), 669.

16. Arjun Appadurai, *The Social Life of Things: Commodities in Cultural Perspective* (Cambridge: Cambridge University Press, 1988), 5, italics in the original.

17. Fox, *Proverbs 10–31*, 896.

18. I. Irving Ziderman, "Seashells and Ancient Purple Dyeing," *Biblical Archaeologist* 53.2 (1990): 98.

19. A. Bernard Knapp, "Bronze Age Mediterranean Island Cultures and Ancient Near East, Part 1," *Biblical Archaeologist* 55.3 (1992): 65.

lived in shallow shore waters around the Mediterranean Sea. Their yellowish white mucus turned reddish-purple after being exposed to oxygen and sunlight. Subsequently, the shellfish needed to be boiled in order to extract the dye. Pliny details the ancient manufacturing process in his *Natural History*.[20] We know that thousands of shells were needed to yield just a few ounces of this dye.[21] Thus, the manufacturing process was expensive, time-consuming, and labor intensive. These qualities alone would be enough to place the dye in high demand. However, there are additional traits that made this dye irresistible. The crimson color was brighter than most natural dyes and it did not require the use of a dye fixative in order to keep it stable.[22] As Amanda H. Podany underlines: "Murex-dyed fabric kept its startling color even when washed or left in the sun."[23] In other words, the dye was a symbol of permanence, rarity, and opulence, while its background was marked by cosmopolitan trade. It is no wonder then, that it became synonymous with royalty and emblematic of power.

Vestments of power

The book begins with a chapter by Shawn W. Flynn. He explores the religious and cross-cultural significance of divine dress in order to examine the system of meanings and types of power which it evoked in the ANE. He shows that dress played an important role in determining divine power and establishing hierarchies of power. Lastly, he uncovers the points of contact between Mesopotamia and ancient Israel in order to demonstrate how the Israelite tradition found a unique expression of YHWH's power and stability while avoiding the negative implications of a clothed cultic statue.

In Chapter 2 Carmen Joy Imes examines the active and transformational power of dress. Her findings underline the performative aspect of religion by

---

20. Pliny the Elder, *The Natural History*, ed. John Bostock and H. T. Riley, in Perseus Digital Library, Book 9, Chap. 62, http://www.perseus.tufts.edu/hopper/text?doc=Perseus:text:1999.02.0137:book=9:chapter=62 (accessed September 3, 2018).

21. Ziderman reports: "An enormous amount of Phoenician banded dye murex shells was found near Sidon in 1864. This mound of shells, all broken above the chromogenic gland, revealed the species from which blue-purple was manufactured." Ziderman, 99.

22. I should specify that the Phoenicians were producing both a purple and a crimson color shade from different species of *murex* shells. Ziderman elaborates they "produced two distinct purple products, a blue-purple, hyacinth, and a red-purple, Tyrian purple." Ibid., 98. Both hues were in demand and had different uses in the fabrication of priestly vestments and tabernacle furnishings. For details on that see the chapter by Carmen Imes "Between Two Worlds: The Functional and Symbolic Significance of the High Priestly Regalia," in this volume, 61–64.

23. Amanda H. Podany, *Brotherhood of Kings: How International Relationships Shaped the Ancient Near East* (Oxford: Oxford University Press, 2010), 274.

demonstrating that religious authority does not stem from who somebody is but rather what somebody does. She argues that Aaron's official garments authorized him to act as YHWH's representative to the people and the people's representative to YHWH. Aaron's priestly vestments distinguished him from the people and also established his identity as the intermediary between two worlds. Not only were the high priestly garments symbolic of the role he played, but they were also constitutive of that role. As Marie Louise Stig Sørensen has shown, ritual practices transform through action, thus, "It is … not a matter of belief enacted but rather a belief becoming and being constituted through the action. In the most literal sense, the belief is experienced and fulfilled in the action."[24]

In Chapter 3 Joshua Joel Spoelstra examines the ways in which form and function of amuletic accessories intersect with covenantal theology in ancient Israel and thus, are imbued with meaning. Specifically, he discusses the purpose and intentionality of adornment articles. He posits that the people's tassels, as an extension of the high priest's rosette, have apotropaic powers. They guard a person from menacing spiritual forces and empower human flourishing. He uncovers the achievement of the aforementioned goal through homophonic linguistic connections and a convergence between signal and signifier. In this sense, the accessories are formed by covenantal theology and in return they participate in its recreation and perpetuation.[25]

In Chapter 4 Sara M. Koenig focuses on the communicative aspect of getting dressed and shows the ways in which it has empowered women in two distinct cases.[26] She argues that for Tamar in Genesis 38 and Tamar in 2 Samuel 13 clothing goes beyond symbolic markers of status to characterize their respective actions, deception, and defiance. For both women dress communicates their identity and carries expectations for behavior appropriate to that identity. They both defy the expectations their dress communicates. Both are entrapped, and the action they undertake with their garments yields a level of liberation.

In Chapter 5 Sean E. Cook examines the way in which dress can be used to disempower, more so the way in which it can be used to ascribe alterity. Cook argues that by means of Saul's garments, Saul is shown to appear more like a

---

24. Marie Louise Stig Sørensen, "Introduction to Part 1: Belief as Practice," in *Embodied Knowledge: Historical Perspectives on Belief and Theology*, ed. M. L. S. Sørensen and Katharina Rebay-Salisbury (Oxford: Oxbow Books, 2013), 13.

25. Cf. Laura Gawlinski: "Dress does not simply reflect social forces, but it is a participant in their creation and recreations." Gawlinski, "Theorizing Religious Dress," 172.

26. Marie Louise Stig Sørensen maintains that it is analytically helpful to distinguish between "the composition of dress from the act of wearing it. The composition of a dress is about decisions and the negotiation of possibilities within available resources, while the wearing of it involves primarily performance of the body and social communication rather than further manipulation of the material possibilities." Marie Louise Stig Sørensen, "Gender, Things, and Material Culture," in *Women in Antiquity: Theoretical Approaches to Gender and Archaeology*, ed. S.M. Nelson (Lanham, MD: Alta Mira Press, 2007), 90.

foreigner than an Israelite. While Saul is among the elect, God's chosen people of Israel, Saul is progressively "Othered" via his dress in the narratives of 1 Samuel and in the end he is presented as a Philistine. Mary Ellen Roach-Higgins and Joanne B. Eicher explain: "Identities are communicated by dress as it announces social positions of wearer to both wearer and observers within a particular interaction situation."[27]

In Chapter 6 Ian D. Wilson considers the ways in which the memory of dress can provide critique and political commentary. He looks at the way in which dress functions as a system of communication akin to Terence S. Turner's "social skin" and to the ways in which dressed individuals are presented and interpreted by others.[28] Specifically, he examines the famous story of David dancing before YHWH's Ark as it enters Jerusalem. It exists in two distinct versions (2 Sam 6 and 1 Chr 15) that differ remarkably in many of their details. One such detail is the king's clothing. Drawing on research in cognitive psychology, Wilson argues that the existence of two different versions would function to partially warrant Michal's distaste for David's dressing down, while still maintaining a critical stance toward the queen.

In Chapter 7 Scott R.A. Starbuck analyzes dress as a manner to reappropriate and communalize power. The author argues that the phrase "robe of righteousness" was used to envision a positive reversal of social status likely contributing to attempts toward a sociopolitical reorganization in the post-exilic community. As such, it illustrates the power of imagined clothing for political and sacerdotal agendas. Dress reflects and encodes societal values, as such, it can be used to manipulate, rearrange, and even subvert these values.[29]

Ehud Ben Zvi provides the concluding chapter. He explores the curious discursive omission of YHWH's clothing and its concomitant implications for the power of divine dress. Ben Zvi notes the existence of an underlying, but strong tendency to dis-prefer depictions and imaginative exercises involving YHWH's clothes, even in the absence of an alternative. He argues that a constellation of factors rendered YHWH's clothes not much worth remembering or thinking about in Judah/Yehud during the Late Persian/Early Hellenistic period, if at all. As Karen Tranberg Hansen has argued dress prompts recognition and identification by association: "Even when they do not dress bodies, cloth and clothing contribute to new ways of thinking and being."[30]

---

27. Roach-Higgins and Eicher, "Dress and Identity," 5.
28. Terence S. Turner, "The Social Skin," *Journal of Ethnographic Theory* 2.2 (2012): 486–504.
29. Cf. Terence S. Turner: "The system of bodily adornment as a whole (all the transformations of the 'social skin' considered as a set) defines each class in terms of its relations with others. The 'social skin' thus becomes, at this third level of interpretation, the boundary between social classes." Terence S. Turner, "The Social Skin," 503.
30. Karen Tranberg Hansen, "The World in Dress: Anthropological Perspectives on Clothing, Fashion, and Culture," *Annual Review of Anthropology* 33 (2004): 381.

Introduction

The chapters in this volume provide more than a collection of case studies on dress and the HB. Examined together, they offer an illustration of the power inhabiting dress, as well as the dynamic forms and expressions with which this power can manifest. We are aware that this volume only scratches the surface of an exciting and promising field of study and our goal is simply to serve as the catalyst for a robust future study and analysis.

To conclude, I feel compelled to return to the shellfish at the root of this particular construction of power and shed light to a human crime that widens the chasm between the modern and the ancient worlds. It also happens to create a rich irony around the semiotic permanence that so many ancient cultures ascribed to the crimson color. Marine biologists report that *murex* shellfish are disappearing from the eastern Mediterranean coast falling victim to an ongoing multi-species collapse attributed to global rises in sea temperatures.[31] As humans, we are ever aware of our ephemeral nature and we have attempted to use dress to prevail upon the passage of time. The ode to the woman of substance illustrates this very point in Prov 31:25 with the comment: "Strength and dignity are her clothing, and she laughs at the time to come." The inherent impermanence of humanity explains our infatuation with and pursuit of power. History has shown time and again that this pursuit has come about in largely destructive ways. Not surprisingly, then, in our relentless attempts to achieve—mostly material—transcendence, we deal death to the organisms that we have used in the past to color our aspirations of indelible power. Is this a side effect of our attempt to assert our will over nature or a condemnation of our quest to secure power? Dressing up or down our endeavors to harness power will require further interpretation.

---

31. Peter Meaumont, "Ancient Shellfish Used for Purple Dye Vanishes from Eastern Med" Environment, *The Guardian*, US Edition, Mon 5 Dec, 2016, 10:24 EST, https://www.theguardian.com/environment/2016/dec/05/ancient-shellfish-red-mouthed-rock-shell-purple-dye-vanishes-eastern-med (accessed September 3, 2018).

1

YHWH'S CLOTHING, KINGSHIP, AND POWER: ORIGINS AND VESTIGES IN COMPARATIVE ANCIENT NEAR EASTERN CONTEXTS

Shawn W. Flynn

The rhetorical function of dress in the Israelite religion and the HB is difficult to capture. Yet the perspectives of colleagues in this volume identify multiple types and uses of dress. These gradients of dress, and identifying their different functions, no doubt help in the task of reading and interpretation, thus changing our expectations and opening integrative possibilities when dress is referenced. Let us consider three main categories operative in this volume and situate the approach here accordingly. At times dress is referenced in the HB with no intention or meaning behind the physical reference. One ought to allow that this occurs and need not force additional meaning onto dress in those texts. At other times dress is a metaphor and, as such, holds a communicative function in the narrative.[1] As Imes notes in this volume, the priestly garment "provides a visual lexicon that partly explains the absence of an image in the Israelite cult."[2] One can easily determine this second category if the question of the function of dress in a narrative contributes something to the text's meaning. Consider Koeing and Starbuck as examples of this category. A final possible category is a constitutive

---

With thanks to Ehud Ben Zvi's response to an earlier form of this chapter. He helped emphasize the lack of reference to YHWH's clothing and the importance of wrestling with that gap. Also thanks to Sara Koenig, Antonios Finitsis, Scott Starbuck, Carmen Imes, and all the participants for their feedback during the PNWSBL Hebrew Bible Research Group on Clothing 2014–2016.

1. For the common use of "vehicle" and "tenor" in literary circles when discussing metaphor, see Chris Baldick, ed., "Metaphor," in *The Oxford Dictionary of Literary Terms* (3rd edition; New York: Oxford University Press, 2008), 206. For example, the out of the ordinary clothing in 2 Samuel 6 comes to mind, as discussed by Ian Wilson, "The Emperor and His Clothing: David Robed and Unrobed before the Ark and Michal," in this volume, 208–36.

2. See Carmen Imes, "Between Two Worlds: The Functional and Symbolic Significance of the High Priestly Regalia," in this volume, 47–96.

function of dress.³ Like the second category, this third one has all the features of communicative power, but the dress itself moves beyond the symbolic to hold its own power. As readers engage with this volume, it is helpful to ask which of these three categories are being discussed and when the authors are moving between them in a single study. In this chapter, the question of dress for deities oscillates between the second and third categories. Here the ANE function of divine dress has a constitutive role, and the HB echoes some of that function in expressions of YHWHism while strategically moving YHWH's clothing from the third category into the second category.

The communicative power of dress in ancient texts is evident not only for humans but also for deities. For example, in Mesopotamian ritual and mythological texts, divine dress plays an important role that solidifies a deity's power and sphere of authority. The temple statue was always dressed and accompanied by ritualistic ceremony for the needs of the god incarnated in that divine statue.⁴ Comparatively, YHWH is expressed with clothing only in rare cases, and there is neither a corresponding statue nor ritual texts to illuminate the function of that dress.⁵ Thus, how does one understand the rare references to YHWH's clothing in

---

3. With thanks to Carmen Imes for this term to capture a category I was attempting to describe.

4. Nadav Na'aman, "No Anthropomorphic Graven Image. Notes on the Assumed Anthropomorphic Cult Statues in the Temples of YHWH in the Pre-Exilic Period," *UF* 31 (1999): 391–415; and see Tryggve N. D. Mettinger, *No Graven Image?: Israelite Aniconism in Its Ancient Near Eastern Context* (CoBOT, 42; Stockholm: Almqvist & Wiksell International, 1995). This is not surprising in light of the prophetic tradition's admonition of these statues (Jer 10:3–15; Isa 40:18–20; 41:6–7; 44:9–22). For an analysis of these passages, see Michael B. Dick, "Prophetic Parodies of Making the Cult Image," in *Born in Heaven, Made on Earth: The Making of the Cult Image in the Ancient Near East*, ed. M. Dick (Winona Lk: IN Eisenbrauns, 1999), 1–54.

5. There are of course various proposals that YHWH was represented as a cult image. This is possible especially in popular religion of the domicile and perhaps evident at Kuntillet 'Ajrud. If this is a representation of YHWH and his consort, YHWH in this text wears the horned cap of divinity, similar to the Naram-Sin relief (2296–2240 BCE). Likewise in the Hammurabi stele the god Shamash is represented with the horned cap of divinity. For discussions arguing that YHWH was represented in a cult image, consider Herbert Niehr, "In Search of YHWH's Cult Statue in the First Temple," in *The Image and the Book: Iconic Cults, Aniconism, and the Rise of Book in Israel and the Ancient Near East*, ed. Karel van der Toorn; Contributions to Biblical Exegesis and Theology 21 (Leuven: Peeters, 1997), 73–96; or consider Christoph Uehlinger, "Anthropomorphic Cult Statuary in Iron Age Palestine and the Search for Yahweh's Cult Images," in *The Image and the Book: Iconic Cults, Aniconism, and the Rise of Book in Israel and the Ancient Near East*, ed. Karel van der Toorn; Contributions to Biblical Exegesis and Theology 21 (Leuven: Peeters, 1997), 97–156. For a broader Levantine perspective, see Theodore J. Lewis, "Syro-Palestinian Iconography and Divine Images," in *Cult Image and Divine Representation in the Ancient Near East*, ed. N.H. Walls (Boston, MA: American Schools of Oriental Research 10, 2005), 102–03.

the HB? Despite this obvious gap there are important points of contact between the Israelite and Mesopotamian use of divine garments and how each tradition relates the garment to divine power and divine kingship. These points of contact elucidate the function of YHWH's clothing in the HB and demonstrate one of the ways YHWH's kingship and power was expressed, albeit rarely.

This study addresses three areas to better understand the origins of YHWH's clothing and what impact divine dress had for ancient Israelites. First, we study the semantic ranges of different terms for clothing in Hebrew and Akkadian; a linguistic discussion both contributes to this volume and helps envision what type of divine garment (thanks to the iconographical material) is intended in both the Israelite and Mesopotamian contexts. Second, we explore instances in Mesopotamian ritual and mythological texts where divine clothing is connected to divine power. The narrative poem the Descent of Ištar and the mīs pî ritual texts both develop important connections between divine dress and power relevant for understanding a similar connection in the HB. Third, by comparing what deities wear between Marduk, YHWH in Isaiah 6, and selected Psalms, it becomes evident that the rare Israelite use of divine clothing connects clothing to power and at the same time moves away from a reliance on cultic clothing while retaining all the necessary expressions of power and kingship. One might call this a "grammar of dis-preference."[6] In this particular study, I argue that the points of contact across Israel and Mesopotamia show how the Israelite tradition found a unique expression of YHWH's power and stability while avoiding the negative implications of the clothed cultic statue common in the ANE.

Clothing in Akkadian and Hebrew

To understand YHWH's specific garment in texts like Isaiah 6 and other texts of the HB, a comparison of Hebrew and Akkadian lexemes distinguishes general/common garments from specific/important garments, the latter more relevant for this study. Foster has summarized different types of clothing in the Sargonic period (2334–2154 BCE) and, while this time period is much earlier than ours, his comprehensive discussion provides usefully broad categories.[7] This introduces how Akkadian expresses different types of clothing, thus informing the same distinctions in Hebrew. In that discussion, Foster also shows that studying clothing

---

6. For a fuller discussion of why the ancient Israelites and the HB had a "grammar of dis-preference" for YHWH's clothing, see Ehud Ben-Zvi's study in this volume, 266–303.

7. For a specific discussion of Neo-Assyrian dress of the gods, see Kiersten Neumann, "Gods among Men: Fashioning the Divine Image in Assyria," pages 3–24 in *"What Shall I Say of Clothes?": Theoretical and Methodological Approaches to the Study of Dress in Antiquity*, ed. Megan Cifarelli and Laura Gawlinski; Archaeological Institute of America (Boston, MA, 2017). This essay also offers a representative collection of images helpful for the topic.

and textile terminology is very complex since the connection of the lexeme to its actual textile is often ambiguous.⁸ Therefore, while one must be cautious connecting a lexeme to a specific artifact/image, we can form a general picture of the divine garment.

Foster's data set shows that the folded, ruffled, or flounced garment always has a body in repose; it is the most commonly used one in divine contexts.⁹ Known as the *pala*, and used often with nobility, the human king, or the divine king, this type of garment is recognizable in reliefs and is easily distinguished by its lines. The Nabu-apla-iddina stone tablet provides an accessible image of an enthroned deity with this flounced garment.¹⁰ The tablet describes a rededication ceremony of the god Shamash. The corresponding image shows two deities on the relief, one deity enthroned and the smaller deity leading the worshipper to the head deity. Each deity wears some form of the flounced garment. Thus, it is no surprise the corresponding text under the image explains the restoration of the cult statue and as part of that ritual describes a variety of garments offered to the god.¹¹ By undergoing this cultic restoration, the human king participates in an Ebabbar *lubuštu* ceremony where the gods receive their garments.¹² The ritual use of the flounced garment solidifies the cult statue in their temple and communicates the kingship of the particular deity over their specific sphere of authority and, by extension, the human king's authority and favor with that god.¹³ Further, the

---

8. For example, Vita surveys 56 different terms in Ugarit and some Hittite loanwords for textiles and clothing. Many meanings are uncertain. Juan-Pablo Vita, "Textile Terminology in the Ugaritic Texts," in *Textile Terminologies in the Ancient Near East and Mediterranean From the Third World to the First Millennia BC*, ed. C. Michel and M.-L. Nosch; Ancient Textiles Series 8 (Oxbow Books, 2013), 328–34.

9. See the discussion in Benjamin Foster, "Clothing in Sargonic Mesopotamia: Visual and Written Evidence," pages 110–45 in *Textile Terminologies in the Ancient Near East and Mediterranean from the Third World to the First Millennia BC*, ed. C. Michel and M.L. Nosch; Ancient Textiles Series 8 (Oxbow Books, 2013), 123–25. For images in both Mesopotamia and Egypt, see in this volume Imes, "Between Two Worlds: The Functional and Symbolic Significance of the High Priestly Regalia."

10. Stone tablet from Sippar with inscription of Nabu-apla-iddina (885–850 BCE) BM 91000 ANEP, 529. L.W. King, ed., *Babylonian Boundary Stones and Memorial Tablets in the British Museum* (London: Oxford University Press, 1912), 121.

11. King, *Babylonian Boundary Stones*, lines 42–54.

12. For the divine clothing of the *lubuštu* ceremony, see Eiko Matsushima, "On the Material Related to Clothing Ceremony-lubustu in the Later Periods in Babylonia," *Acta Sumerologica Journal* 16 (1994): 177–200; Eiko Matsushima, "Some Remarks on the Divine Garments: kusitu and nahlaptu," *Acta Sumerologica Journal* 17 (1995): 233–49.

13. The *lubuštu* ceremony is not as widely attested as some of the others we will discuss here. For a discussion of their use in the context of some boundary stones, see also Christopher E. Woods, "The Sun-God Tablet of Nabû-apla-iddina Revisited." The scarcity of this ceremony is exemplified by the represented examples in Marc J. H. Linssen, *The*

flounced garment on a deity in a cultic context is not limited to a small subset of texts. The connection between divine clothing and the rededication ceremony was widely prevalent. Such ceremonies have a consistent usage, primarily from the 800 BCE, and were still a reference point in later administrative texts until the time of Darius I (550–486 BCE). This provides a consistent reference point within the broader cultural matrix of the biblical authors regardless of when we date the biblical texts.[14]

Comparing the flounced *pala* to more common garments clarifies the *pala's* unique use. Unlike the *pala*, the kilt (*ibbaru*) allows freedom of movement for farmers, workers, or warriors. The exposed seam of the kilt was usually worn on the right side and was secured by a cord along the waist. Since this was a more common garment, the linguistic connection to this textile is likely *ib-ba-ru* (worn at the waist)[15] with its corresponding tie known as the *iblal* or the *niglal*. This garment did not function to distinguish human from deity since we know warrior gods like Baal also wear the kilt.[16]

In this same category one could place the Akkadian *šakattu*. This was an extended form of the kilt worn in open and closed manners as a longer garment wrapped around the entire body. This is further distinguished by a fringed rectangular piece of cloth that was wrapped around the first piece[17] and possibly an early form of the cloak (*kusītu*).[18] For example, we see this garment in the Shalmaneser III inscription (black obelisk), the Neo-Assyrian king who wears a form of this garment as does the Israelite king Jehu on the same obelisk. Thus, a

---

Cults of Uruk and Babylon: The Temple Ritual Texts as Evidence for Hellenistic Cult Practice (Leiden: Brill/Styx, 2004), 51–55. A possible parallel in Ugaritic texts is *mazru*. Perhaps more relevant is *kupšu* which in Mari is a garment decorated with fine gems belonging to the king. For discussion, see Vita, "Textile Terminology in the Ugaritic Texts," 328–34.

14. Woods, "The Sun-God Tablet of Nabû-apla-iddina Revisited," 36. Another text we will explore below is Ištar's descent and is quite earlier. The importance of divine clothing is consistent and demonstrated throughout Mesopotamian history from the early texts of the Sumerian version or Ur Text of Istar's descent, Inanna's descent to the underworld (and its early Sumerian Vorlage) until the reign of Darius I.

15. We even know the weight of this, 1.5 kgs/3.3 lbs. Foster, "Clothing in Sargonic Mesopotamia," 126–27.

16. The god Baal also wearing the kilt is known in some iconography and is suitable for his status as a younger warrior god. Limestone stele.Ugarit. Louvre AO15775 ANEP 490.

17. Foster, "Clothing in Sargonic Mesopotamia," 126–27.

18. For example, forms of this can be seen in the Black Obelisk of Shalmaneser III where the Judahite king Omri and the Neo-Assyrian emissaries are wearing different cultural forms of this longer wrap. The Assyrian forms are slightly more stylized. For discussion and figures, see David Ussishkin, "Symbols of Conquest in Sennacherib's Reliefs of Lachish-Impaled Prisoners and Booty," pages 207–17 in *Culture through Objects; Ancient Near Eastern Studies in Honour of P.R.S. Moorey*, ed. T.F. Potts et al. (New York: Oxford University Press, 2003).

decorated version of the longer cloak could indicate status. These other garments are distinct from the flounced *pala* with its highly stylized features, use in religious and cultic contexts, use for deities, and greater length than other forms of clothing.

A brief overview of Hebrew lexemes for clothing shows a similar distinction between generic and specific types but also opens an important connection between a specific type of garment and its communicative power. The שמלה (*simla*) is likely a generic term that can have a variety of meanings. Such range makes connecting any specific garment to the lexeme difficult.[19] It may be the outer/overgarment, but its wide range suggests the most appropriate translation would be "clothes."[20] For example, שמלה (*simla*) occurs in the well-known event where Shem and Japheth walk backwards and cover their father's nakedness (Gen 9:23) and could, thus, refer to any garment, an overshirt, an undershirt, a kilt, or a robe. The lexeme's wide range is also evident as the garment changed after mourning, anointing, and washing oneself (2 Sam 12:20; Ruth 3:3) and at the same time is considered a most basic need (Isa 3:7). It may have been the outer most noticeable garment since it was given to Benjamin as a reward along with 300 shekels (Gen 45:22) and in other texts it is associated with wealth (Exod 12:35). This may imply that it is a form of the toga (*šaqītu*). While it seems to be a generic catchall term, in the HB it is not used to imply the undershirt (*šakattu*) or the kilt. It is clear there is something else underneath and that a person is not left naked without it. A helpful example is Amos 2:8 that echoes a law from Exod 22:25–26, both of which use בגד and שמלה. This legal case involves not taking another's garment as a pledge (perhaps for an outstanding debt owing) and allowing them to retain their *outer* garment since "if you take your neighbor's cloak as a pledge, you shall return it to him before sunset; for this cloak of his is the only covering he has for his body. What else has he to sleep in? If he cries out to me, I will hear him; for I am compassionate." (Exod 22:25–26). This is confirmed in a letter from Yavneh Yam, a legal case similar to the legal background of the Amos text. In the inscription, an

---

19. This is used around 30 times in the HB. One can see its very basic and generic use in passages that are meant to refer to women's clothes, but are clearly generic and not specific: "Seven women will take hold of one man on that day, saying: 'We will eat our own food and wear our own clothing; Only let your name be given us, put an end to our disgrace!'" (Isa 4:1) or consider: "Rising from the ground, David washed and anointed himself, and changed his clothes" (2 Sam 12:20). The other generic term is *bgd* and is the most used in the HB. It is used for a wide variety of textiles. For example, it is used of regular garments that are rent (2 Sam 1:11) in times of mourning and at the same time as a blanket used to cover the teraphim (1 Sam 19:13).

20. This could be made of "wool" perhaps in a common way or in a special way such as "white wool" (Ezek 27:18). Perhaps in very special cases it was made of "linen," which was less common and more expensive; for example it was used by the priests (Lev 6:3). See the discussion in Phillip J. King and Lawrence E. Stager, *Life in Biblical Israel* (Louisville: Westminster John Knox, 2001), 146–62.

appeal is made to the שר (governor) because the outer garment was taken.[21] The person may not have a cloak to sleep in, but they are not naked.

Compared to generic lexemes, the most significant term for this study—YHWH's garment in Isaiah 6:1 (שול; *shul*: the train or hem)—has a more specific use throughout its eleven occurrences in the HB.[22] For example, in Exod 28:33-34 (repeated in Exod 39:24-26) this is an elaborate decoration for the priests' garments. It may, thus, correspond to similar cultic functions as the flounced *pala* in Mesopotamia. Remembering that the garments of royalty are restrictive and longer, the שול associated with kingship or priesthood in a cultic context is understandable.

But there is a more communicative function for this garment than occurs with the more generic garments. שול is consistently connected to shame and honor. Hebrew texts primarily use שול to capture loss of honor related to divestiture. For example in Jer 13:22–26, it refers to the stripping of a garment to expose shame. It also occurs in Lamentations 1:9, another text that links the garment as a metaphor for what holds sin and in this case the sin of Jerusalem. In Nah 3:5 the sin is less pronounced, but as in Jeremiah, the שול is stripped to expose shame. Now it is entirely possible that the use of שול in Jeremiah and similar texts is meant to be a generic garment. Yet something different is occurring. Why select this specific term and not what seems like the more generic שמלה? We will see later how garments associated with the elite/royalty are connected to ideas of power. For now we will observe that in all these texts with שול, there is some association with power or the stripping of the garment resulting in shame or a sinful state and thus a loss of power. It is as if the shameful/sinful person does not deserve to have the שול. The same cannot be claimed of [23] שמלה. As communicative tools, specific types of garments with a higher status may be connected to communicating something about those who have and do not have the garment.

---

21. Yavneh Yam (639–609 BCE) also known as the Mesad Hashavyahu inscription; Sandra Gogel, *A Grammar of Epigraphic Hebrew* (Society of Biblical Literature, Resources for Biblical Study, no. 23) (Atlanta: Scholars Press, 1998), 425–26.

22. Since in the Targum it is later interpreted, as in Jer 6:9, as the lower part of the vine, we may assume that the hem is the lowest part of the garment. This implies a longer garment, likely more reminiscent of the folded or ruffled garment.

23. There are two more possibilities for garments related to how YHWH was imagined. One is a hapax and the other is more well known. The hapax occurs in Isa 3:24. This perhaps references a gown of a wealthy person and is typically criticized by First Isaiah. The next word is "mantle." Again this is an overgarment. We even have in the HB a Mesopotamian connection in which a Babylonian mantle is referenced among the spoils of war (Josh 7:21). It is also the same term for the mantle of the prophet Elijah and what he covers Elisha with (1 Kgs 19:19) to pass on the authority of the prophetic ministry. In this context it is the bearer of some power, like splitting the waters (2 Kgs 2:8, 14). It is also associated with the Mesopotamian king in Jonah 3:6.

This cursory linguistic survey provides a simple set of conclusions helpful for this discussion. Both in ancient Mesopotamia and in Israel there is a clear distinction between generic versus specific garments, even if some of the lexemes overlap and the correspondence between lexeme and textile is at times obscure. In particular, the royal/cultic garment of deities is a very specific and a stylized flounced garment distinct from generic uses. Finally, the lexeme for YHWH's garment in Isaiah 6, which we can envision, thanks to the Mesopotamian images, is used elsewhere in the HB to communicate power or a loss of power. Therefore, שׁוּל has a consistent connection between clothing, power, and the symbolic/communicative (perhaps constitutive) meaning of the garment. The lexeme is used in Isaiah 6 as representative of divine kingship, it is used for the priestly garments in Exodus, and its removal in Jeremiah exposes shame. These features are particularly helpful as we explore similar connections between clothing and power in Mesopotamia and ask how a broad cultural background can help clarify the rarely referenced divine clothing in ancient Israel.

Power and clothing in Mesopotamian deities

The connection between clothing and power for Mesopotamian deities is evident in both the cultic and the mythological literatures.[24] Divine clothing was not peripheral to Mesopotamian deities but essential to the identity of the god and connected to his/her kingship by manifesting that kingship in particular ways. Below we focus on two textual traditions from Mesopotamia that are particularly helpful for contextualizing the divine power–clothing relationship. The first group are the mīs pî and pit pī rituals that link divine clothing to the status of a god as king. The second, the Descent of Ištar, corroborates that power as essential to the divine expression and moves beyond the symbolic function of the deity's garment. These connections then establish some expectation of how YHWH's clothing relates to power and kingship and offers a foundation for how the Israelite tradition uses these connections and moves beyond them.

---

24. The same connections can be claimed in the human sphere. For example, the connection between the divine garments and activities of the human king is often done in conversation with the same activities and paraphernalia of the divine king. For the relationship between the expressions of divine and human kingships, see Ekart Frahm, "Rising Sun and Falling Starts: Assyrian Kings and the Cosmos," in *Experiencing Power, Generating Authority: Cosmos, Politics, and the Ideology of Kingship in Ancient Egypt and Mesopotamia*, ed. J.A. Hill et al. (Philadelphia, 2013), 97–120. Likewise, a son in an Ugaritic context, if he misbehaved, must place his clothes on the bolt of the door and go outside exposed; see Karl van der Toorn, *Family Religion in Babylon, Ugarit and Israel: Continuity and Changes in the Form of Religious Life* (Leiden: Brill, 1996), 43–46.

The mīs pî and pit pī rituals

The mīs pî and pit pī rituals (better known as the mouth washing and mouth opening) contain a whole complex of prayers and rituals detailing the creation or recreation of the cult statue.[25] These rituals were widely used in Mesopotamia and in Egypt as well. The ceremony could take place after a cult statue was kidnapped in times of war and then reinstalled (a HB analogue would be 1 Samuel 5 when the ark of YHWH is stolen and placed before Dagon) or when a king found an older temple in disarray and in need of renovation. These ceremonies reinforce the process of making the statue in heaven and purifying the statue so the divine presence could indwell in it.[26] Some forms of the rite also outline the divine clothing placed on the statues during the ceremony.[27] These were important since an incorrect dressing of the statue (or some other part of the ritual) would inhibit the divine presence in the statue.[28] In the ANE, divine statues were commonly made of wood, plated with precious metals, and then covered in jewels and a garment (Jer 10:1-6). In such a ritualized/cultic context where a specific garment is used for a divine king, the possibilities of communicative power for the garment are enhanced.

In the mīs pî ritual, a specific garment is widely used in texts like the Nineveh ritual text, the Babylonian ritual text, Incantation Tablet 5, as well as various Neo-Assyrian letters that refer to this ceremony. We even have a form of it in a biblical text like Isaiah 6.[29] In the Nineveh ritual tablet we read, line 192 the incantation, "exalted garment, lamahuššu-garment of white linen."[30] This occurs on the second day of the ritual where this specific garment is first in the list of divine paraphernalia, along with the crown in the next line. Thus, the garment is not merely a covering but is part of the divine paraphernalia that demonstrates the role of the god as king. Specifically, this is the *lamahuššu* garment: a precious garment made of wool or linen that was used in almost all periods of Mesopotamian literature, as evidenced in its use in multiple dialects (Old Babylonian, Middle

---

25. Thanks to Michael Dick for providing guidance on the key passages regarding divine clothing in the miš pī ritual.

26. One of the most recent studies, on the biblical side, is Gregory Yuri Glazov, *The Opening of the Tongue and the Bridling of the Mouth and the Opening of the Mouth in Biblical Prophecy* (JSOTSup 311; Sheffield: Sheffield Academic Press, 2001).

27. Also see, Neumann, "Gods among Men," 11-13.

28. Neumann, "Gods among Men," 12.

29. For a discussion of the various texts and the general breadth of this ritual across Mesopotamia, see Christopher Walker and Michael Dick, *The Induction of the Cult Image in Ancient Mesopotamia: The Mesopotamian Miš Pī Ritual* (SAALT 1; Helsinki: Neo-Assyrian Text Corpus Project, 2001), 8-13. For a discussion of Isaiah 6 in relation to this ritual, see the classic study by Victor Hurowitz, "Isaiah's Impure Lips and Their Purification in Light of Akkadian Sources," *Hebrew Union College Annual* 60 (1989): 39-89.

30. Walker and Dick, *The Induction of the Cult Image in Ancient Mesopotamia*, 51.

Babylonian, Standard Babylonian, Neo-Babylonian)[31] and also at el-Amarna.[32] This is clearly the flounced garment identified earlier in this study and the one seen on the statue of Shamash in the Nabu-apla-iddina text. Therefore, like YHWH's garment in Isaiah 6, in this Mesopotamian ritual we have a specific rather than a generic garment in both cultic and ritual settings that is associated with divinity and widely known both geographically and chronologically across the ANE.

An almost identical formula of the garment placement is repeated in the Babylonian ritual text[33] and Tablet 5 of the Incantations that connect the garment with the power of divine kingship.[34] In the latter text the garment stands alone in the context of establishing the throne and kingship of the god. The placement of the lamaḫuššu garment in line 42 follows immediately after the incantation of the throne in line 41. Not only does the garment stabilize the throne but the lead-up to the throne in lines 29–32 reinforce the type of divine rule expressed:

> May the foundation of his throne be firm, let them place it in security,
> May the foundation of its throne be stable like a mountain
> At the command of the great Lord Marduk, Prince of the Apsu, King of the entire heavens and the Earth. (lines 29a–32)[35]

The garment, thus, manifests and makes tangible the security and stability of that kingship by being the action after the claim to kingship, effectively making the garment a tangible manifestation of this power. The *lamaḫuššu* garment is not merely peripheral dress but integral to divine kingship since it is placed on the deity after this incantation, as part of the divine paraphernalia. Specifically, Marduk, as supreme king, utters the stability of a god's kingship because of the garment (lines 29–32).

Therefore, in the mīs pî ritual the garment (along with the throne) makes apparent the kingship that is described and manifests the essential features of kingship like power, rule, and stability. Since security and stability are also features of YHWH's kingship, we should be cognizant of the comparative potential between YHWH's kingship and the Mesopotamian ones, and ask whether or not YHWH's claims to kingship at times leverage divine clothing for similar purposes.[36]

---

31. CAD, L.
32. See Jeremy Black, Andrew George, and J. Nicholas Postgate, eds., *A Concise Dictionary of Akkadian* (Harrassowitz: Wiesbaden, 2000), 176.
33. Walker and Dick, *The Induction of the Cult Image in Ancient Mesopotamia*, 76.
34. Ibid., 198. This is based on a reconstruction.
35. Ibid., 198, 205.
36. For the various passages of YHWH's throne, consider any reference to the ark. But for passages that link the ark to YHWH's kingship and power, consider texts like Psalm 132:8; Ps 78:61; Ps 96:6, etc. For a discussion, see John Day, "The Ark and the Cherubim in the Psalms," in *Psalms and Prayers*, ed. B. Becking and E. Peels; Old Testament Studies (Leiden: Brill, 2007), 65–77.

One more consideration is to whom such divine clothing would have been accessible or noticeable. In this case Neuman, referencing the Neo-Assyrian forms, brings up the theoretical frame of Wobst who "differentiates the target groups of stylistic messages within sociocultural settings with respect to their distance from and levels of reception and understanding of an artifact ('emitter') in the process of information exchange."[37] It is important to ask whether the average public may not have much connection to encounter the nuances of these messages. That said, whatever form mythology had in the culture (perhaps by oral account) could have disseminated the messages about divine clothing. Likewise, iconography may have been more available to a wider segment of the population. Furthermore, we must also consider that the act of procession in multiple cultures across the ANE would have introduced the concept of divine clothing to wider populations echoed in biblical texts such as 2 Samuel 6, 1 Kings 8, and Psalm 132.[38] While it is true that the specific of ritualized garments for the deity may have been accessed by a small group, the concepts of the divine clothing and their importance likely had broad communicative power, thanks to their presence in ritual (both public and private), myth, and iconography.[39] We will at least explore one such myth below that communicates the essential role of divine clothing. In particular, the visual nature of textiles allows them to be represented without written forms. Textiles, like buildings, thus lend themselves well to broad communicative power as encoded objects.[40]

Descent of Ištar

The mīs pî example helps establish a tangible expression of kingship, but the constitutive power of divine garments is even more marked in one mythical text. In the Desent of Ištar, the use and expression of divine clothing is not merely symbolic of divine kingship but had a real connection to the specific power of the goddess. In the Desent of Ištar into the nether world, the connection between garment and power is so marked that the threat of removing the garments has immediate implications for the goddess' divine sphere of her authority. Thus, the

---

37. Neumann, "Gods among Men," 13.

38. Daniel E. Fleming, "David and the Ark: A Jerusalem Festival Reflected in Royal Narrative," pages 75–95 in *Literature as Politics, Politics as Literature: Essays on the Ancient Near East in Honor of Peter Machinist*, ed. D. Vanderhooft and A. Winitzer (Winona Lake, IN: Eisenbrauns, 2013).

39. The tangible and striking imagery in the upcoming mythological text is referred to by some as "dans l'imaginaire 'filmographique' des Assyriologues." Corinne Bonnet and Iwo Slobodzianek, "Les Enjeux Multiples du Déshabillage D'Inanna/Ishtar dans L'au-Dela," pages 135–44 in *Vêtements antiques: S'habiller, se déshabiller dans les mondes anciens*, ed. F. Gherchanoc and V. Huet (Arles: Éditions Errance, 2012).

40. For some discussion of theory related to how textiles communicate ideas, see the discussion in Neumann, "Gods among Men," 13–16.

power connected to divine garments in the cult is brought to its logical conclusion in myth.

Found in Assurbanipal's library but known to have an earlier Sumerian form, this 139-line Akkadian poem narrates an account of Ištar (Inanna).[41] She was easily the most important female deity throughout Mesopotamian history and found expression in 'Athtar and Astarte in the Levant.' One of her primary roles is as a goddess of sexuality and procreation.[42] Another feature is her role as a warrior goddess.[43] These two features and the domains her royalty commands are important for understanding the connection between clothing and power in the expression of the deity.[44] Losing that power is connected to losing her garments.

In this poem Ištar descends to the underworld to meet her sister Ereshkigel. In order to enter, her sister commands that Ištar be stripped of her garments and adornments. This occurs at a series of gates as the gatekeeper gradually strips Ištar of single pieces of divine dress at each gate. This allows Ereshkigel to then attack Ištar with diseases and demons because she is completely naked and vulnerable. For example at the first gate[45]:

He brought her to the first gate and removed the great tiara of her head
Why gatekeeper did you take the great tiara of my head?
Enter my lady, thus are the customs of the lady of the underworld?

Each gate follows this similar formula as another item of her kingship and clothing is stripped from her. As soon as Ištar enters the underworld and is stripped of her divine garments, her sister lets loose sixty diseases (line 75). The garments of Ištar do not only represent her power, but they are her power and, thus, protect her. As Bonnet and Slobodzianek observe: "En dépouillant Inanna de sept vêtements et attributs, de la tête aux mains, puis en terminant par l'habit souverain et ne laissant que la perruque et le mascara, Ereshkigal anéantit les me et la puissance de la déesse, donc son être."[46] The removal of garments is not only symbolic but a real

---

41. While the date is unknown, it was a widely available text. See Bonnet and Slobodzianek, "Les Enjeuex Multiples du Déshabillage D'Inanna/Ishtar dans L'au-Dela," 135–36.

42. See the Gilgamesh Epic, Tablet 6, for an example.

43. For a brief description of her role, see Jeremy Black and Anthony Green, *Gods, Demons and Symbols of Ancient Mesopotamia: An Illustrated Dictionary* (Austin: University of Texas Press, 1992), 108–09.

44. Thus as also concluded elsewhere, power is an important part of this text: "L'intrigue autour du voyage d'Inanna, en effet, se noue autour de sa possession de prerogatives ou de pouvoirs." Bonnet and Slobodzianek, "Les Enjeuex Multiples du Déshabillage D'Inanna/Ishtar dans L'au-Dela," 135–36.

45. Translations for the Desent of Ištar are my own; the text is based on the cuneiform line drawings of the Akkadian version, represented in CT XV; K.162 plate 45 and plate 46.

46. Bonnet and Slobodzianek, "Les Enjeuex Multiples du Déshabillage D'Inanna/Ishtar dans L'au-Dela," 141.

removal of power and, as suggested, the being of the goddess. With those garments removed, she is vulnerable.

Such vulnerability has real effects.[47] Most importantly because the garments are removed Ištar can die. In this context the death of the goddess impacts the real world in the form of chaos over everything Ištar controls. For the goddess to not have the garments of her kingship, and by extension to not have her kingship, invites chaos into the real world. Since every god/goddess is king over his/her own sphere of authority the clothing of the deity is, thus, linked to their power and that power is related to a particular sphere of life.[48] The results are immediate and clear:

> After Istar went down to the netherworld
> The oxen would not mount the cow, the donkey would not impregnate the she ass
> The young man did not impregnate the girl in
> The young man laid in his chamber
> The young woman laid on her side (76–80)

This formula occurs just after Ištar is stripped of her final piece of divine dress (60–65) and as a result the diseases are set upon her (68–75). The formula appears again when the head god Ea laments her death. Through his flowing tears (84), he reflects on Ištar's death and on its effects (84–90). To be stripped of one's divine garments is to become vulnerable and lose power over the realm that god/goddess commands. The stages of divestiture thus create an increasingly uncertain situation that threatens the divine life and its sphere. In this particular case, infertility infects the world and creation cannot continue, neither with animals nor with humans.

The Descent of Ištar makes a clearer connection than the ritual texts between the power of the deity as monarch over her realm and the function of divine dress in relation to that power. Like the Descent of Ištar, in the mīs pî ritual, divine dress is connected to kingship by solidifying and representing the security and stability of the throne. Albeit this connection is depicted inversely. The mythical text explores the negative implications of divestiture of the divine garment by reversing the advantages presented in the cultic text where the garment was placed on the deity in the ritual. The function of these garments for divine royalty is not merely symbolic of that kingship but is constitutive and thus directly connected to their power and has real-life consequences for the deity and by extension for humanity.

---

47. At the same time, Ištar is transgressive in these acts, going beyond the agreed boundaries of one deity to another deity's realm. See Bonnet and Slobodzianek, "Les Enjeuex Multiples du Déshabillage D'Inanna/Ishtar dans L'au-Dela," 138. They go on to discuss reflections of mourning rites in the myth.

48. For a discussion of the spheres of authority in relation to gods and goddesses, especially in the Levant and Ugaritic literature, see Lowell K. Handy, *Among the Host of Heaven* (Winona Lake, IN: Eisenbrauns, 1994), 114.

With this wider context in mind, how does one interpret the rare references to YHWH's clothing in the HB?

Echoes of YHWH's clothing in the Hebrew Bible

For YHWH, divestiture was not an option. Combined with the lack of focus on YHWH's clothing and that no discernible cult statue was functioning in Israel, there was no threat that the other gods could remove YHWH's divine garments. Ehud Ben Zvi's contribution in this volume discusses this in more detail. That said, informed by its broader cultural context, the connection between power and dress remains a rarely used analogue to articulate the stability and effect of YHWH's kingship. YHWH's clothing echoes Mesopotamia's connection of clothing to power, and this backdrop is essential to understand how YHWHism moves beyond divine clothing while retaining the power and stability of kingship. By studying the function of YHWH's clothing in Isaiah 6 and select Psalms in comparison with Marduk's power, we see YHWHism retain expressions of clothing with power. But in those texts we also see a development in Israelite expression away from its cultural context that maintains the power of YHWH's throne yet intentionally lacks references to dress. Dress would certainly be expected in any other ancient texts with similar features. However, the Israelite tradition does echo the ANE custom according to which dress signifies the divine king's power.

Isaiah 6:1 is a helpful text for exploring the use of YHWH's clothing:

> I saw the Lord sitting upon a throne high and lofty
> and his שׁול filled the temple.

Most scholars do not know what to do with the garment in this text.[49] As such, little interpretive attention is given to the function of divine clothing in the text. Kaiser maintains that YHWH's power is evident because of his throne and his dignity because of the cloak.[50] But these are arbitrary associations without specific linguistic connection. Others like Watts and Oswalt play with the similarity between the robe and the presence of YHWH although they do not fully explicate what that means. For them, the description is too mysterious to be captured or too nebulous to have a meaningful historical explanation.[51] While Oswalt and

---

49. For some discussion of YHWH's garment, see Greenfield, "Ba'al's Throne and Isa. 6:1," in *Festschrift Delcor*, AOAT 215 (Neukirchen-Vluyn, 1985), 193–98, and in particular G.R. Driver, "Isaiah 6:1: his train filled the temple," in *Near Eastern Studies in Honor of W.F. Albright*, ed. H. Goedicke (Baltimore: The Johns Hopkins, 1971), 87–90.

50. Otto Kaiser, *Isaiah 1–12: A Commentary* (OTL Philadelphia: Westminster, 1972), 74.

51. Watts says: "his glorious presence dominates the scene as his robes fill the room," John D. Watts, *Isaiah 1–33* (Word Biblical Commentary; Nashville: Thomas Nelson, 2005), 74. For Oswalt: "It is as though words break down when one attempts to depict God himself ... Did his robe fill the temple? No, God did! The import is clear. The experience is

Watts avoid the ANE background of this text, as do the LXX translators,[52] the lack of a cultic statue in Israel need not imply that Israelite descriptions of YHWH's clothing do not have a context.

The wider Mesopotamian linguistic, cultic, and mythological texts provide a cultural frame for the rare biblical references to YHWH's clothing and help contextualize the function of שׁול in Isaiah 6. We know that some form of the flounced *pala* is intended. It restricts movement and is reserved for cultic and royal contexts, precisely the context described in Isaiah 6. Unlike past scholarly discussion on divine clothing in Isaiah 6, we can also observe that there is nothing mysterious or unknown about the reference since it reflects accurately the attitude toward the clothing of the god in a cultic and ritual context. The reference to this garment specifically establishes and manifests the power and stability of YHWH's throne. From the above linguistic discussion, we also know that שׁול is a specific term consistently connected to divestiture and loss of power. This should also not be a surprise, since the flounced *pala* of the deity in the temple not only establishes the god's kinship (mīs pî) but is a tangible force of their power (Desent of Ištar). The choice of שׁול reflects the openness and connection between clothing and communicative power of YHWH's kingship through the garment. Therefore, YHWH's garment here is not simply descriptive but solidifies authority and kingship in the scene even if the cultic statue is not implied.

Studying select Psalms in comparison with Mesopotamian clothing can further clarify the Israelite perspective, motivated by the reference to divine clothing, but no longer limited by it in expressing YHWH. For both Marduk in the Enūma eliš and YHWH in select Psalms, the tangible manifestations of divine radiance intentionally recall divine dress. We know that Marduk, like other Mesopotamian gods, is comfortably expressed in divine clothing recalling the relevant cult statue and the ritual. Specifically, Marduk as supreme king is the deity that utters the stability of a god's kingship after the divine garment is placed on the statue (lines 29a–32) in some mīs pî rituals.[53] Likewise, from the Descent of Ištar the function of that divine clothing is more than symbolic of kingship but is proof and manifestation of that kingship. Therefore, when speaking about the god's "wearing" something in relation to kingship and in enthronement scenes, like

---

too personal, too awesome, too all encompassing for mere reportage. Each one of us must aspire to our own experience of his presence." John N. Oswalt, *The Book of Isaiah: Chapters 1–39* (NICOT; Grand Rapids MI.: Wm D. Eerdmans, 1986), 178. This seems to fill gaps when the historical context is not familiar to the commentator.

52. As is sometimes typical, the LXX reduces possible anthropomorphisms, rather than "robe" or "hem," in this case it translates "And his glory filled the house." Likewise *Tg. Ps.-J* uses "glory"/יקר. For another example where the LXX, Targum, and Peshitta correspond in their avoidance of anthropomorphism of the deity, see Shawn W. Flynn, "Where Is YHWH in Isaiah 57, 14–15?" *Biblica* 87.3 (2006): 358–70.

53. Walker and Dick, *The Induction of the Cult Image in Ancient Mesopotamia*, 198, 205.

Isaiah 6 and select Psalms, the text echoes the connection between divine dress and power, whether or not it references dress in any detail.

The connection between what YHWH and Marduk both wear provides a clue to the vestiges of divine clothing in the Israelite tradition. Both Marduk and YHWH "wear" aspects of their kingship. In the Enūma eliš *melammu* (divine radiance) is an important aspect of Marduk's kingship.[54] Thus the Enūma eliš describes the son of UTU/Šamaš during Marduk's birth in Tablet 1: *la-biš me̓-lam-mi eš-ret* DINGER.MEŠ "he wore the divine radiance of ten gods" (I. 103). Similarly, Marduk is *ma-ri-u̓-tu ma-ri-u̓-tu ma-ri* ᵈUTU-*ši* ᵈUTU-*ši ša'*DINGIR.DINGIR *la-biš me̓-lam-mi eš-ret* DINGER. MEŠ *ša̓-qiš et-pur pu-ul-ḫa-a-tu ḫa-šat-si-na e-li-šu̓'ka̓m-ra*, "The son UTU, the son UTU, the son, the sun, the sunlight of the gods. He wears (*la-biš*) the radiance (*me̓-lam-mi*) of ten [gods], he is decked with[55] highness (*ša̓-qiš*), the terror of fifty [gods] are piled (*ka̓m-ra*) on him" (I 100–104).[56] In a Mesopotamian context, the wearing of divine radiance clearly echoes and references the divine cultic garment in enthronement scenes.

Like Marduk, YHWH's radiance is also essential to his kingship. YHWH's divine nature in the Psalms of YHWH's kingship is similarly expressed.[57] YHWH's radiance is repeated in Pss 93:1; 96:6; 97:4; and 97:11. For example, in Ps 96:6 "splendor and majesty are before him, might and beauty are in his holy place." Both deities are dressed or wrapped in the elements of their divine kingship and this recalls the god's flounced garment in enthronement scenes.[58] Marduk "wears" (*la-biš*) divine radiance: *la-biš me̓-lam-mi eš-ret* DINGER.MEŠ, "he wore the

---

54. For a further discussion on this term in Mesopotamian religion, and especially its Sumerian origins, see Vladimir V. Emelianov, "On the Early History of melammu" (Proceedings of the RAI 53; Winona Lk, Ind: Eisenbrauns), 1109–19. Also see the single monograph on the phrase by Elena Cassin, *La splendeur divine: Introduction á l'étude de la mentalité mésopotamienne* (Sorbonne: Paris Mouton & Co., 1968). This study connects the *melammu* with features of terror or fear as in the term *pulḫu* with some discussion in paralleling *melammu* with the "glory" of YHWH. Cassin, *La splendeur divine*, 133.

55. Reading *et-pur* as a Gt stative of *aparum*.

56. Any god or goddess, due to their royal character within their divinity, can possess this divine radiance. Tiamat and her monsters also have it: *me-lam-mu uš-taš-ša-a i-li-iš um-taš-ši-il*, "she loaded them with melammu and made them equal to gods" (II 24; III 28; 86).

57. Despite the lack of a cognate, the relationship between *melammu* and biblical expressions of divine radiance do overlap. For example, it is typical to think of Moses' radiance after coming down from Mt. Sinai as a type of melammu known in the ANE in Exod 34:35. The improper understanding of קרן as "horn" has led to the Vulgate rendition *quod cornuta esset facies sua* "for horned was his face." A statue by Michelangelo informed by the Vulgate thus represented a horned Moses. More likely, in Exod 34:35, the term means "shone." See also, Hab 3:4. In Mesopotamia, it was often the king who displayed the divine *melammu*. At times, the god could remove his divine radiance from the king.

58. As we can see, it is clear that the clothing in which the deity is wrapped is intimately tied to the concepts and aspects of the type of deity being promoted. It is clear above that the deities wear their divine natures. Podella has provided a useful discussion and defense

divine radiance of ten gods" (I 103). So too YHWH "wears (לבש) majesty and girds on strength" (Ps 93:1). YHWH and Marduk לבש/*la-biš* aspects of their divine kingship and wearing that kingship implies and secures the power over that sphere of authority, similar to the function of divine clothing in the mīs pî ritual and the Descent of Ištar. YHWH's divine power is thus rooted in the divine garment even though it is only an echo of that earlier tradition.

That the origins of YHWH's divine authority is rooted in the divine garment is especially obvious in the shared order in both textual traditions, since the wearing is followed by the power connected to the garment. In the ritual in Tablet 5 of the incantations, after the crown is placed on the head of the statue, but just before the incantation of the throne, the lamaḫuššu garment is placed on the statue, the stability of that kingship is secured and proclaimed. "May the foundation of his throne be firm, let them place it in security, May the foundation of its throne be stable like a mountain" (lines 29–32). [59] Likewise, a similar order is found in the YHWH kingship Psalms. YHWH secures his kingship by *wearing* divine attributes: "YHWH is king, robed with majesty, YHWH is robed with might" (Ps 93:1a). Immediately after YHWH *wears* this aspect of kingship, "the world is established and will not be shaken" (Ps 93:1b).[60] Specifically after YHWH wears radiance, his divine kingship is described as: "Your throne stands firm from before, you are for eternity" (Ps 93:2). The Psalms share the order of wearing the garment followed by establishing kingship in the mīs pî ritual. What YHWH wears, thus, secures and demonstrates the effectiveness of kingship; through the connection between clothing and power the same is accomplished with the lamaḫuššu garment in a Mesopotamian context.

In these ways YHWH retains the power of divine clothing without reference to the tangible cultic statue and with only an echo to divine clothing. This provides the possible intention behind the use of YHWH's clothing in Isaiah 6. With a similar cultic setting as the mīs pî ritual, Isaiah 6 links YHWH's clothing to the power of divine kingship, echoing this common way of expressing divinity and its associated authority, but gives the reference little emphasis and does not risk association with the cultic statue.[61] Similarly the Psalms, read in a wider cultural

---

of this concept in describing the kingship of YHWH. Podella goes on to discuss how dress alters the form of the wearer and their sociopolitical standing. Thomas Podella, *Das Lichtkleid JHWHs: Untersuchungen zur Gestalthaftigkeit Gottes im Alten Testament und seiner altorientalischen Umwelt* (FAT 15; Tübingen: J.C.B. Mohr, 1996), 265. For a broader discussion of YHWH's glory, see the discussion in Michael B. Hundley, *Keeping Heaven on Earth* (FAT 50; Tübingen: Mohr Siebeck, 2011), 44–47.

59. Walker and Dick, *The Induction of the Cult Image*, 198, 205.

60. The stability of YHWH's throne is a common feature: Ps 89:5; 14; 97:2; Ps 11:4; 45:7; 93:2; 103:19.

61. This may reinforce elements of Mowinckel's akitu festival context for these Psalms. For a discussion of the importance of genre when making parallels between ANE text and the HB, see Kenton L. Sparks, *Ancient Texts for the Study of the Hebrew Bible: A Guide to the Background Literature* (Peabody: Hendrickson, 2005), 7–21.

context, have all the features to imply the divine garment but avoid a direct reference to it. This move could explain the eventual connection of divine garments to a trait like righteousness, as discussed by Scott Starbuck in this volume. In the Israelite expression, all the powers of the divine garment are adopted and even *worn*, and the results of stability and authority are even made manifest as a result of that wearing but without requiring reference to the garment itself. This is the method by which the Israelite tradition both retains its cultural matrix and moves beyond it for its own purposes.

Conclusions

Three considerations contextualize the function and purpose of YHWH's dress in the HB. First, the linguistic considerations across Akkadian and Hebrew caution that connecting lexemes to specific garments is difficult. That said, the Hebrew שׁול emerges as some form of the flounced or ruffled *pala* known in Mesopotamia, with cultic and royal functions, where its presence on the individual demonstrates honor, or more commonly, its removal communicates shame. Second, Mesopotamian ritual and mythological texts, specifically the mīs pî ritual and the Descent of Ištar, demonstrate that divine garments are not only representative of power but tangibly establish divine power and security of the deity's throne. The Mesopotamian material proves that reference to divine dress in that context is not simply descriptive. Dress is essential to articulating the impact of the deity's power and stability over their sphere of authority. Third, Isaiah 6 and select YHWH kingship Psalms, illumined by the wider context of Marduk's radiance connected to his garments, also suggest that the garment in Isaiah 6 is more than descriptive. Selected Psalms in comparison with what Marduk wears show that the connection between divine garment and divine power is known and is utilized by the YHWH traditions in the HB. In particular, the HB uses YHWH's clothing to communicate establishing and confirming kingship, while avoiding negative consequences of the clothed cultic statue in the ANE. This move in Israelite tradition, in dialogue with its context while moving from it, opens up significant space for the deity to now order creation through the clothing of others as discussed in Ehud Ben Zvi's study in this volume. Entities, like the human king, can now adopt what was once the deity's. As always, when the Israelite expression makes a unique move within its cultural matrix, this both leverages that matrix and moves beyond it, opening space for new expressions in the human sphere. This study provides the background behind the meaning, origins, and logic of YHWH's clothing from its context to a unique Israelite expression, while Ben Zvi picks up on this discussion to explore more of the reasons that sustained this change.

2

BETWEEN TWO WORLDS: THE FUNCTIONAL AND SYMBOLIC SIGNIFICANCE OF THE HIGH PRIESTLY REGALIA

Carmen Joy Imes

With few exceptions, descriptions of dress in the HB are terse or absent altogether. This is not to suggest that dress is inconsequential to the biblical writers. Where mentioned, articles of clothing may carry enormous significance in the narrative. For example, consider the skins covering Adam and Eve (Gen 3:21); Tamar's veil (Gen 38:13–14); Joseph's ornate tunic (Gen 37:3); Achan's stolen robe from Shinar (Josh 7:22); Jonathan's robe, tunic, and belt given to David (1 Sam 18:4); the hem of Saul's robe (1 Sam 24:4); and Elijah's cloak (2 Kgs 2:10–15), all of which figure prominently in their respective stories. However, none of these passages describes an article of clothing in detail.[1] This makes the lengthy and detailed description of the priestly and high priestly garments in Exodus and Leviticus all the more striking. In Exodus 28, YHWH dictates the full wardrobe of the priest, complete with the types and colors of fabric, added adornments (embroidery, gold, and precious stones), and the design of each garment. The garments are redescribed in Exodus 39 when they are sewn. This detailed treatment already distinguishes the priestly garments from any other apparel in the HB. Furthermore, Exodus 29 prescribes and Leviticus 8 describes the ordination ritual by which Aaron and his four sons were cleansed and dressed so that they could assume their roles as priests in the completed tabernacle. These rich descriptions stand out in the HB and deserve exploration.[2]

This chapter will proceed from a close reading of the instructions and their fulfillment in Exodus 28 and 39 to a consideration of similar garments in other ANE

This chapter is dedicated to my creative mother, Verna Camfferman, talented seamstress, artist, and fashion designer. This research gave me a window into your world, as this chapter will give you a window into mine.

1. No more than two words describe any of these garments.
2. For a recent exploration of the significance of the high priestly pectoral, see Christophe Nihan, "Le pectoral d'Aaron et la figure du grand prêtre dans les traditions sacerdotales du Pentateuque," forthcoming. Nihan and I did not discuss our projects until both essays were heading to press. Nevertheless, we agree on many points. For basic overviews of clothing in the Hebrew Bible, including some discussion of priestly clothing, see Alban Cras, *La*

cultures.³ It will also examine Aaron's ordination ritual to highlight the functional and symbolic significance of his regalia. Aaron's official garments authorized him to act as YHWH's representative to the people and the people's representative to YHWH. He was the bridge between two worlds. The high priestly garments were not merely symbolic of the role he played, but they were constitutive of that role.

A man of the cloth: Fashioning Aaron's garments

Aaron's high priestly garments distinguished him from every other Israelite, including his sons, the priests. While ordinary priests wore fine white linen breeches, caps, and tunics tied with an embroidered sash (Exod 28:39–43), Aaron's regalia also included a decorated blue robe, a golden ephod, and a breastpiece studded with gold and jewels. On his head he wore a fine turban with an engraved gold diadem (see Figure 2.1). Leviticus prescribed that once annually, on the Day of Atonement, Aaron wear only the plain linen garments of the common priesthood (Lev 16:4).⁴ Otherwise Aaron donned his full, splendid wardrobe, a signal of his status and responsibility. The instructions at Sinai identify these as "sacred vestments" (בגדי־קדש; Exod 28:2), crafted "for dignity and for splendor"

Symbolique Du Vêtement Dans La Bible: Pour Une Théologie Du Vêtement, Lire La Bible (Paris: Cerf, 2011); Alicia J. Batten, "Clothing and Adornment," *BTB* 40.3 (2010): 148–59; Philip J. King and Lawrence E. Stager, *Life in Biblical Israel*, LAI (Louisville: Westminster John Knox, 2001), 259–318; Douglas Edwards, "Dress and Ornamentation," *Anchor Bible Dictionary* 2 (1992): 232–38; Edgar Haulotte, *Symbolique du Vêtement Selon la Bible*, Collection Théologie 65 (Paris: Aubier, 1966).

3. I have intentionally set aside questions of textual origins and development. Given the state of fluctuation in the discipline regarding the dating of sources, I do not want my contribution tethered to a single approach. I sought instead to offer on the one hand a close, synchronic reading of the text and on the other hand (quite separately) a broad exposure to possible historical analogues. Flexibility is thereby maintained for readers to consider the contribution the chapter makes to their own schema. Comparative material was chosen based on similarity of form. For an argument that Exodus 28 dates to the Persian period, see Nihan, "Le pectoral d'Aaron."

4. The linen material of the priestly garments is variously denoted with בד (*bād*) or שש (*šēš*). While שש signifies an especially fine linen, בד does not necessarily connote a fabric of lesser quality. It may simply mean linen in general. The terms appear in apposition in 1QM7₁₀ and are used both together and interchangeably to describe the priestly attire (cp. the undergarments in Exod 28:42 [מכנסי־בד] and Exod 39:28 [מכנסי הבד שש משזר] or the tunic in Exod 28:39 [שש הכתנת] and Lev 16:4 [כתנת־בד]). See also *DCH* 8:572. Contra Gordon J. Wenham, *The Book of Leviticus*, NICOT (Grand Rapids: Eerdmans, 1979), 230. Curiously, Haran (*Temples and Temple-Service in Ancient Israel: An Inquiry into Biblical Cult Phenomena and the Historical Setting of the Priestly School* [Winona Lake, IN: Eisenbrauns, 1985], 174) speculates that Aaron's Day of Atonement uniform was of higher quality than his regular linen vestments.

(לכבוד ולתפארת; Exod 28:2, 40), appropriate for the splendid tabernacle where God's glory was manifest.[5]

Several passages describe these articles of clothing. Variations in the order of garments depend on the purpose of the list (see Table 2.2, 36). Exodus 28:4 lists six garments in summary, roughly in the order in which they would have been perceived, with the outermost eye-catching items first. Exodus 28:6–43 offers detailed instructions for fashioning all nine items, proceeding from the costliest to the most common.[6] Exodus 39:1–31 describes the crafting of the nine garments in the order they were produced.[7] Leviticus 8:7–9 lists eight items in the order in which Aaron would have been clothed (Figure 2.1).[8]

Haran notes three levels of quality in the artisanship of these articles of clothing: חשב (ḥōšēb), רקם (rōqēm), and ארג (ʾōrēg; Table 2.1). The first two involved a combination of dyed wool and linen. Haran suggests that חשב fabric contained

Figure 2.1 Priestly garments.

5. NRSV takes this as a hendiadys: "for glorious adornment." According to Deut 26:19, the whole nation would be exalted in splendor (תפארת). In Isaiah this term was applied to the remnant of Israel (Isa 4:2; 46:13; 62:3) and to the temple (64:10).

6. The first two items (breastpiece and ephod) from Exod 28:4 are reversed in the instructions that follow, perhaps because the breastpiece depends on the ephod to "hang" it in place. The rest of the list in Exod 28:6–43 proceeds from the most expensive high priestly items to those worn by all the priests.

7. Why this order differs from Exodus 28 is not clear.

8. Drawing from Carmen Joy Imes, *Bearing YHWH's Name at Sinai: A Reexamination of the Name Command of the Decalogue* (University Park, PA: Eisenbrauns, 2018), 154. Used by permission. Numbers correspond to the order given in Lev 8:7–9, plus the cap (for ordinary priests) and breeches. 1. Tunic, 2. Sash, 3. Robe, 4. Ephod, 5. Band, 6. Breastpiece, 7. Turban, 8. Medallion. Many questions remain unanswered: *Was the tunic short or long? Did the robe have sleeves? Was the ephod open in front or back? What shape were the turban and medallion? How were the breeches wrapped?* These drawings represent one possibility.

Table 2.1 Haran's levels of fabric styles[11]

Hebrew	Type of Fabric	Design	Priestly Garments	Tabernacle
חשב	Mixed, dyed wool and linen	Includes figures	Ephod and band Breastpiece and straps	Inner curtains Inner veil
רקם		No design	Sash	Entrance curtain Outer gate
ארג	Single color, unmixed wool or linen		Robe (blue wool) Tunic (white linen) Undergarments Caps and turban	Loops (Outer curtains)

figures, especially cherubim, while רקם was a fine mixed fabric without design.[9] ארג, on the other hand, was a single-color unmixed fabric of either wool or linen.[10] Descriptions of each item follow:

Ephod (אפד; ēpōd) and band (חשב)

Over time the Hebrew term אפד may have had more than one referent,[12] but in these instructions the word applies to a type of apron made of fine linen material (שש) woven with wool dyed bluish-purple (תכלת), reddish-purple (ארגמן), and crimson (תולעת שני) in the חשב style.[13] In addition, craftsmen hammered out gold

---

9. Most English translations assume the opposite, translating רקם as "embroidered" (NRSV, NIV, ESV, NLT, TNK, NET).

10. Haran, *Temples and Temple Service*, 160–61.

11. The style of items in brackets is not specified in the text, but they fit the ארג style.

12. E.g., Samuel wears a linen ephod, though he is not the high priest (1 Sam 2:18; cf. 22:18). Haulotte (*Symbolique du Vêtement*, 47, 50–51) suggests that the ephod itself evolved: a simple linen loincloth later became a long band wound above the waist and finally in the post-exilic period a type of chest apron with twelve engraved stones. Alternatively, these items may have coexisted while the semantic range for the term אפד fluctuated. Jenson suggests that "ephods were found in a variety of different forms, the more practical garments of a simple design and the more ceremonial types made of costly materials and heavily ornamented." P. Jenson, "#680 אֵפוֹד," in *New International Dictionary of Old Testament Theology and Exegesis*, ed. Willem VanGemeren (Grand Rapids: Zondervan, 1997), 476–77. All biblical ephods are associated with the priesthood. See Wilson's chapter for discussion of a text in which an ephod is a priestly undergarment, in this volume, 125.

13. While precisely identifying the colors mentioned in ancient texts is difficult, both bluish-purple and reddish-purple dye (known by these names) were produced along the Mediterranean coast in the biblical period by processing the contents of two types of

leaf and cut it into threads to work into the design, yielding an ornate and costly garment, perhaps similar to those worn by divine images in other ANE cultures.[14] The Hebrew אפד is etymologically related to the Old Assyrian *epattu*, a "costly garment," as well as the Hittite *ipantu*, which was worn by a divine image and either adorned with or made of silver.[15] Between the value of the gold and the exorbitant price of these dyes, the resulting fabric was a fitting choice for both the tapestries of the inner tabernacle and the high priestly garments.

Two shoulder straps and a decorated band (also חשב) crafted from the same materials secured the ephod around Aaron's shoulders and waist. Two engraved onyx stones mounted in gold rested on the shoulder straps, attached with gold corded chains to the breastpiece. Each stone bore the names of six of the Israelite tribes.

Breastpiece (חשן)

This decorated square pouch worn on the chest of the high priest contained the Urim and Thummim, which facilitated decision-making.[16] In style it matched the ephod, woven (חשב) with gold, bluish-purple, reddish-purple, and crimson thread and fine white linen. The square measured a hand-breadth wide and was adorned with four rows of precious stones in gold settings. It is possible that each row featured a single color of stones that varied in intensity.[17] Each stone bore the name of one of the Israelite tribes, engraved like a signet ring.[18] Gold corded chains

---

murex shells, on which see King and Stager, *Life in Biblical Israel*, 160–61. These discoveries improve upon Lutz's earlier suggestion that blue dye was derived from various plants, while purple-red came from henna leaves. See Henry F. Lutz, *Textiles and Costume among People of the Ancient Near East* (Leipzig: Hinrichs, 1923), 77–80.

14. This technology is also attested in royal Assyrian embroidery. Lutz, *Textiles and Costume*, 97. See also *HALOT* 1:77.

15. Harold A. Hoffner, "Hittite Equivalents of Old Assyrian Kumrum and Epattum," *WZKM* 86 (1996): 154–56. Other possible analogues include the Ugaritic *ipd* and an apron-like garment associated with royalty/divinity in New Kingdom Egypt. See Bruce Wells, "Exodus," in *Zondervan Illustrated Bible Backgrounds Commentary: Old Testament*, 5 vols., ed. John H. Walton (Grand Rapids: Zondervan, 2009), 1: 253–56.

16. Nihan suggests that the משפט signifies more than decision-making but could symbolize a sense of cosmic order, like the Egyptian *ma'at*. He explains, "la présence de l'Urim et du Tummim dans le pectoral souligne le rôle central d'Aaron à la fois dans la transmission des oracles divins et dans le maintien d'un ordre social acceptable par la divinité" ("Le pectoral d'Aaron," *37).

17. For discussion, see J. S. Harris, "The Stones of the High Priest's Breastplate," ed. John MacDonald, *ALUOS* 5 (1963): 40–62. For a comparison of this list of stones with that in Ezekiel 28, see Nihan, "Le pectoral d'Aaron."

18. Harris posits that these gemstones would have been cut flat or in rounded hemispheres rather than faceted as modern gems. Harris, "The Stones of the High Priest's

attached to gold rings at the top corners of the breastpiece and to the shoulder straps of the אפד, while a blue cord joined the breastpiece and אפד at the bottom corners. Of all the priestly garments, this one received the most attention in these instructions.

Robe (מְעִיל)

Under the breastpiece, Aaron wore a sleeveless, ankle-length robe, woven of blue (wool) thread,[19] with a woven binding around the head opening to prevent tearing.[20] The robe may have been open on both sides, poncho-style (see Figure 2.8, below).[21] Perhaps because it was woven of only one type of material, the workmanship was designated as ארג, rather than the more elaborate חשב or רקם style. However, the lower hem was richly ornamented with alternating bluish-purple, reddish-purple, and crimson pomegranates with gold bells between them, making it more precious.[22] The robe was sonorous, meant to announce Aaron's whereabouts as he moved in and out of the holy place of the tabernacle, "that he may not die" (Exod 28:35).[23] The sound of the bells signaled to all within earshot that the high priest was authorized to approach YHWH.

Breastplate," 43. The passage does not specify whether the engraving was intaglio (reversed) or was to be read on the stone itself.

19. Given the difficulty of dying linen, the blue robe was probably wool. See Victor P. Hamilton, *Exodus: An Exegetical Commentary* (Grand Rapids: Baker Academic, 2011), 491; Nahum Sarna, *Exodus [Shemot]*, 1st edn., The JPS Torah Commentary (Philadelphia: Jewish Publication Society, 1991), 182. Josephus describes the robe as ankle-length, sleeveless, and free-flowing (*Ant* 3.7.4). See also *HALOT* 1:612.

20. In addition to the high priestly "robe," מעיל identified garments worn by Samuel (1 Sam 2:19; 15:27), Jonathan (1 Sam 18:4), Saul (1 Sam 24:5, 12), the king's virgin daughters (2 Sam 13:18), David (1 Chr 15:27), Ezra (Ezra 9:3, 5), Job and his friends (Job 1:20; 2:12), and princes (Ezek 26:16). This garment appears to have been a status symbol. Cf. Robert L. Alden, "מְעִיל," VanGemeren, *NIDOTTE*, 2:1018. Saul was able to recognize the apparition of the prophet Samuel because he was wrapped in his characteristic מעיל (28:14). For a fuller discussion of the מעיל in the HB, see Starbuck's chapter in this volume, 143–59.

21. This could account for the dual form of שול (שׁוּלָיו), indicating the hem (Exod 28:33). So Cornelis Houtman, *Exodus*, trans. Sierd Woudstra, HCOT (Leuven, Belgium: Peeters, 2000), 508–09.

22. So Haran, *Temples and Temple Service*, 169; Gerald A. Klingbeil, *A Comparative Study of the Ritual of Ordination as Found in Leviticus 8 and Emar 369* (Lewiston, NY: Mellen, 1998), 188.

23. Haulotte (*Symbolique du Vêtement*, 50) suggests the bells were for the benefit of gathered crowds.

Tunic (כתנת)

Underneath the robe, Aaron wore a long-sleeved, linen, shirt-like garment with an opening for the neck.[24] Tunics were typically worn by either sex during the Late Bronze and Iron Ages and were usually ankle length.[25] The high priestly tunic is described as woven, or maybe checkered or fringed (תשבץ), possibly indicating a finer quality than the ordinary priestly tunics.[26] Still, the tunics of both were described as fine linen, ארג style (Exod 39:27). Because of the difficulty of dyeing linen, it is safe to assume they were white. Aaron's sons wore tunics without a robe, ephod, or breastpiece.

Turban (מצנפת) and Diadem (ציץ)

Around his head, Aaron wound a linen turban, ornamented with a gold medallion in front, engraved with the words "Holy to YHWH" (קדש ליהוה; *qōdeš lyhwh*) as a signal that the high priest was set apart as belonging to YHWH.[27] This medallion was fastened with a blue cord (Exod 28:36–37) to his turban, which was superior to the caps (מגבעה) of the ordinary priests.[28] These instructions do not specify the shape of the gold medallion, but the term ציץ can indicate a "blossom" or "flower."[29] It is described epexegetically as a "sacred crown" or "holy diadem" (נזר הקדש; Exod 29:6; cf. 39:30; Lev 8:9).

---

24. Though some tunics were sleeveless, Josephus describes this one as long-sleeved. Josephus, *Ant.* 3.7, 2. See Gillian Vogelsang-Eastwood, *Pharaonic Egyptian Clothing*, Studies in Textile and Costume History 2 (Leiden: Brill, 1993), 136.

25. Sarna, *Exodus*, 184. Contra William H. C. Propp, *Exodus 19–40*, 1st edn., AB 2A (New York: Doubleday, 2006), 523. Inhabitants of Middle Kingdom Egypt first wore tunics (either short or long), but the garments were uncommon until the New Kingdom. Vogelsang-Eastwood, *Pharaonic Egyptian Clothing*, 149.

26. Umberto Cassuto, *A Commentary on the Book of Exodus*, trans. Israel Abrahams (Jerusalem: Magnes, 1967), 385. So also Haran, *Temples and Temple Service*, 169–70. Contra Houtman, who says the garments are not woven from raw materials but rather "from the materials at hand." He prefers to read תשבץ as an indication that the tunic was "shaped by sewing ... [with] folds or creases" (*Exodus*, 3:475). Sarna suggests "fringed" (*Exodus*, 184).

27. Ancient sources differ regarding the exact content and placement of the engraving. Josephus (*Ant.* 3.7, 6) says only the divine name was written in paleo-Hebrew.

28. Given the difficulty of dying linen, the turban was likely white. Contra Wenham, *The Book of Leviticus*, 140. Turbans were associated with royalty (see Ezek 21:31; Isa 62:3), whereas a cap was worn by a bridegroom (Isa 61:10). So Haran, *Temples and Temple Service*, 170.

29. See Num 17:23. In 1 Kgs 6:18–29, ציץ refers to carved cedar blossoms plated with gold, decorating the interior of Solomon's temple alongside cherubim, gourds, and palm trees. Spoelstra defends the "floral" interpretation, in this volume, 63–86.

Sash (אבנט)

All the priests wore a sash either made of fine linen embroidered with colored needlework or woven of mixed colored threads (רקם), tied at the waist over their tunics.[30] The sash was the only colored garment worn by Aaron's sons. His own sash would have been covered by his blue-purple robe and bejeweled ephod.[31] The colors of the sash are not mentioned in Exod 28:39, but 39:29 specifies that they included linen, bluish-purple, reddish-purple, and crimson. The mention of linen before dyed wool may indicate the greater proportion of the former in its construction.[32]

In addition to the high priestly garments, Exodus 28 includes instructions for making fine white linen caps (מגבעה) and undergarments (מכנסי־בד) for Aaron's sons. The undergarments covered the priests' nakedness from hips to thighs. Failure to wear them brought guilt deserving death upon the priests (Exod 28:43).[33]

Table 2.2 A comparison of lists of priestly garments

(High*) Priestly Garments בגדי־קדש	Exod 28:4 Order of Observation	Exod 28:6–43 Instructions for Crafting	Failure to wear them brought guilt deserving death upon the priests	Exodus 39 Order of Crafting	Lev 8:7–9 Order of Dressing
*Breastpiece חשן	1	2	4	2	6
*Ephod אפד	2	1	3	1	4
*Band חשב		5			5
*Robe מעיל	3	3	2	3	3
Tunic כתנת	4	5	1 [1]	4	1
*Turban מצנפת	5	6	6	5	7
*Diadem ציץ		4	7	9	8
Sash אבנט	6	7	[2]	8	2
[Headgear] מגבעה	–	8	[3]	6	–
[Breeches] מכנסי־בד	–	9	–	7	–

The asterisk (*) indicates garments worn only by the high priest. Brackets [] indicate garments worn by ordinary priests. Table from Imes, *Bearing YHWH's Name at Sinai*, 152. Used by permission.

---

30. Haran conjectures that the high priestly sash was of finer quality than the others.

31. Though uncommon, a few examples of embroidery have survived from ancient Egypt. Lutz, *Textiles and Costume*, 91. Canaanite chiefs wore dyed and elaborately embroidered robes (cf. Judges 5:30). Lutz, *Textiles and Costume*, 96.

32. So Haran, *Temples and Temple Service*, 170. Alternatively, linen may have come first because the previous four items in the list were made of linen (Exod 39:27–28).

33. Undergarments were rare in the ancient world, but King Tut's tomb preserved a few. Wells, "Exodus," 253–56. Haulotte speculates that these undergarments constituted the sole garment of Israelite priests in earlier times, basing this view on the altar instructions in Exod 20:26. *Symbolique du Vêtement*, 47. However, Exod 20:26 is directed to laypeople, who would not normally have worn undergarments. See Sarna, *Exodus*, 117.

The white priestly garments symbolized the purity of the sanctuary that each priest dedicated himself to maintain, while Aaron's vibrant vestments illustrated the majesty of YHWH.[34] Notably, all priests served barefoot in the tabernacle. Like Moses' burning bush, the tabernacle was holy ground; footwear was inappropriate (Exod 3:5; cf. Josh 5:15).[35]

The material similarities between Aaron's attire and the tabernacle furnishings are significant.[36] The inner curtains of the tabernacle were woven of fine twisted linen and bluish-purple, reddish-purple, and crimson wool, with two cherubim woven into them (חשׁב-style; Exod 26:1). Similarly, the veil separating the holy place from the most holy place was woven of fine twisted linen and bluish-purple, reddish-purple, and crimson wool (again, חשׁב-style; Exod 26:31–33). These corresponded in material to Aaron's outer garments, his ephod, breastpiece, and band. The loops to hang the curtains were made of bluish-purple wool and clasped with gold (Exod 26:4–6), corresponding to Aaron's robe and the cords securing his breastpiece and diadem. Bluish-purple was the most expensive of the dyes. Only Aaron's gemstones have no corresponding entity in the tabernacle.[37]

The outer curtains were made of fine twisted linen (Exod 27:9–15),[38] comparable to the fine linen tunic under Aaron's robe. The screens for the entrance to the tent of meeting and the outer gate were made of bluish-purple, reddish-purple, and crimson with fine twisted linen (רקם-style; Exod 27:16), corresponding to Aaron's embroidered sash. The finest and most colorful fabrics decorated the inner sanctum of the tabernacle, with simpler fabric reserved for the outer courts. The screens were an exception. Entrances to the courtyard and tabernacle exhibited a higher quality than the rest of the perimeter, creating a richly ornamented east–west axis across sacred space.[39] While ordinary priestly garments corresponded in quality to the outer curtains of the courtyard, the workmanship of the high priestly vestments spanned the whole range from outer to inner furnishings. Haran observes that the high priestly garments inversely corresponded to the gradations of holiness of the tabernacle, with the most precious garments worn on the outside and the most common garments underneath.[40]

---

34. See Cras, *La Symbolique Du Vêtement Dans La Bible*, 37, 40.

35. Sarna notes this as well. Sarna, *Exodus*, 177. Contra Ziony Zevit ("Preamble to a Temple Tour," in *Sacred Time, Sacred Place: Archaeology and the Religion of Israel*, ed. Barry M. Gittlen [Winona Lake, IN: Eisenbrauns, 2002], 75), who assumes priests were shod.

36. Sarna notes this as well. *Exodus*, 184.

37. Noted by Nihan, "Le pectoral d'Aaron," *14.

38. The style of these curtains is unspecified, but a single-source fabric was normally designated as ארג.

39. Haran, *Temples and Temple Service*, 164–65.

40. Ibid., 164–65. These gradations of workmanship also correspond to the value of the furniture at each level and the materials used to wrap them during transport. See Haran, *Temples and Temple Service*, 158–59. Propp (*Exodus 19–40*, 528) calls the high priest an "inside-out Tabernacle."

Exodus 25:8 unveils the purpose for the construction of the tabernacle, its furnishings, and the priestly vestments: "And let them construct a sanctuary for me, so that I may dwell among them."[41] The tabernacle facilitated the presence of YHWH among his people. The magnificence of its furnishings was appropriate to the glory of the divine resident. Accordingly, Aaron was dressed to reflect his status as the prime functionary in the tabernacle. All the priestly garments were designed "for dignity and for splendor" (לכבוד ולתפארת; Exod 28:2, 40), and while the garments specifically set apart the men who wore them as priests (v. 3), Aaron's garments far exceeded the rest. For the tabernacle to function properly as the locus of YHWH's presence, the purity of priestly clothing had to be maintained.[42] Separation between the high priest and other priests and laypeople was maintained in part by the prohibition of wool and linen blends in common clothing, as well as the ban on personal use of the sanctuary recipes for anointing oil or incense (Exod 30:22–38). However, the text of Exodus authorized the high priest, in his consecrated state, to represent the entire nation and serve a mediatorial role between them and the deity. He bore their tribal names and approached YHWH on their behalf.

Cut from the same cloth?: Aaron's garments in their ANE context

The magnificence of Aaron's priestly garments was appropriate for their ANE environment. High priestly and royal figures in other ANE cultures dressed in elaborate clothing as befit their status.[43] As Guralnik demonstrates, "garment

---

41. The first verb (ועשו) retains the volitional force of the command in v. 2 (ויקחו), which results in a sense of purpose for the second *weqatal* verb (ושכנתי): "so that." See Bruce Waltke and M. O'Connor, *An Introduction to Biblical Hebrew Syntax* (Winona Lake, IN: Eisenbrauns, 1990), 39.2.2.

42. See M.E. Vogelzang, "Meaning and Symbolism of Clothing in Ancient Near Eastern Texts," in *Script Signa Vocis: Studies about Scripts, Scriptures, Scribes, and Languages in the Near East, Presented to J. H. Hospers by His Pupils, Colleagues and Friends*, ed. L. J. Vanstiphout et al. (Groningen, The Netherlands: Forsten, 1986), 269. The seriousness of the role was underscored by the instructions to wash hands and feet each time the priests entered the tent of meeting "that they may not die" (Exod 30:19–21).

43. On clothing in the ANE, see James Laver, *Costume in Antiquity* (London: Thames and Hudson, 1964); Eleanor Guralnick, "Fabric Patterns as Symbols of Status in the Near East and Early Greece," in *Reading a Dynamic Canvas: Adornment in the Ancient Mediterranean World*, ed. Cynthia S. Colburn and Maura K. Heyn (Newcastle, UK: Cambridge Scholars, 2008), 84–114; Eleanor Guralnick, "Neo-Assyrian Patterned Fabrics," *Iraq* 66 (2004): 221–32; Marie-Louise Nosch and C. Michel Nosch, eds., *Textile Terminologies in the Ancient Near East and the Mediterranean Area from the 3rd to the 1st Millennium BC*, Ancient Textiles 8 (Oxford: Oxbow, 2010); Cynthia S. Colburn, *Reading a Dynamic Canvas: Adornment in the Ancient Mediterranean World* (Newcastle, UK: Cambridge Scholars, 2008); Vogelsang-Eastwood, *Pharaonic Egyptian Clothing*; A. Leo Oppenheim, "The Golden Garments of

decorations incorporate a systematic symbolism of status in the material world."[44] When garments spanning several millennia across the ANE are examined, several analogues regarding status stand out. Garments of similar quality and style to Aaron's were typically associated with royal, priestly, or divine figures. I will begin with a comparison of royal garments, followed by the garments of divine images. The examples below are among the most similar in terms of construction. Differences exist in embroidered patterns or designs because these culturally mediated status symbols are specific to each civilization. First the Egyptian and then the Mesopotamian royal garments will be considered. In each case, the clothing that most resembles Aaron's garments dates between the sixteenth and eighth centuries BCE.

Egyptian royal garments

In Egypt, the clothing of royalty (priest-kings) and deities depicted in the New Kingdom period (1550–1069 BCE) is most like Israel's high priest. Pharaoh Rameses III (c. 1186–1155 BCE) wore an ankle-length wraparound with a wide ornate collar, a highly decorated belt and sash, an elaborately designed apron, and a fancy headdress (Figure 2.2).[45] In another portrait of Pharaoh Rameses III, he is seen wearing an ornamented royal war helmet, a wide collar and armbands with no shirt, and the characteristically stiff, pleated kilt with sash and elaborate apron. He stands barefoot, presenting the deity with an offering (Figure 2.3).[46] Occasionally the Pharaoh wears a long transparent skirt under his kilt and apron (see Figure 2.4). Though these examples lack chest ornaments, several royal Egyptian pectorals are attested elsewhere. These contain gemstones and precious metals in various designs, making them suitable for comparison with Aaron's breastpiece.[47]

---

the Gods," *JNES* 8.3 (1949): 172–93; Elizabeth Riefstahl, *Patterned Textiles in Pharaonic Egypt* (Brooklyn: Brooklyn Institute of Arts and Sciences, 1944); Lutz, *Textiles and Costume*; Megan Cifarelli and Laura Gawlinski, eds., *What Shall I Say of Clothes?: Theoretical and Methodological Approaches to the Study of Dress in Antiquity* (Boston: Archaeological Institute of America, 2017). On the dating of the Sinai instructions, see n. 4.

44. Guralnick, "Fabric Patterns as Symbols of Status," 100.

45. Drawing from Mary G. Houston, *Ancient Egyptian, Mesopotamian & Persian Costume* (Mineola, NY: Dover, 2002), 30, fig. 34. Public domain. An unabridged replication of the 1954 second edition of the work originally published in 1920 by A. and C. Black Ltd., London, under the title *Ancient Egyptian, Mesopotamian, & Persian Costume and Decoration*. See also Laver, *Costume in Antiquity*, 30–31. A portrait of Pharaoh Merneptah (c. 1213–1203) shows him similarly dressed. Unlike the Israelite high priest, he wore wrist bands and sandals. King Tutankhamun's tunic had also a woven "collar" mostly in blue. Sarna, *Exodus*, 141. Spoeltra also compares the Israelite high priest's headdress with Egyptian pharaohs, in this volume, 74–76.

46. Original drawing for this book by Abigail Guthrie from a photograph of the stone relief. Pharaoh Rameses III, Medinet Habu, Thebes.

47. For example, Riefstahl includes a photograph of King Tutankhamun's (c. 1332–1323) jeweled corselet, complete with a wide jeweled collar, shoulder straps, and a breastpiece. Riefstahl, *Patterned Textiles in Pharaonic Egypt*, 32.

Earlier royal examples from the Eighteenth Dynasty (c. 1543–1292 BCE) are similar, with a barefoot pharaoh at Thebes (Qurna) wearing a pleated tunic reaching the elbows and ankles with a patterned apron, a wide collar, and a large headdress with an ornamented forehead.[48] Similarities between Egyptian royal garments and Israelite high priestly vestments include an ornamented headdress, several layers of clothing, often including a long tunic and a decorative apron with a belt or sash, a wide collar, and (sometimes) bare feet.

Figure 2.2 Pharaoh Rameses III (Necropolis, Thebes).

48. Laver, *Costume in Antiquity*, 25. Cf. Houston, *Ancient Egyptian, Mesopotamian & Persian Costume*, 42.

Figure 2.3 Pharaoh Rameses III (Medinet Habu, Thebes).

The clothing of Egyptian gods and goddesses was simpler but shared a few basic characteristics with the Israelite high priest. The temple relief of Pharaoh Seti (c. 1290–1279) at Thebes depicts the king making an offering of oil to the goddess Maat, who is barefoot, wearing a tall, feathered headdress and a fitted, ankle-length tunic with a wide collar-like necklace (Figure 2.4).[49]

Aaron dressed more ornately than these Egyptian divinities, though similarities include bare feet, white tunics, headdresses (for some), and a collar. He most resembled the pharaohs, who shouldered the primary responsibility for cultic worship. As such the Israelite high priestly garments were an appropriate portrayal of Aaron's indispensable cultic role.

49. Original drawing for this book by Abigail Guthrie from a photograph of the stone relief. Pharaoh Seti I and the goddess Maat, Temple of Seti I, Abydos, Egypt.

Figure 2.4 Pharaoh Seti I with the goddess Maat (Abydos).

Mesopotamian royal garments

Egyptian royalty were not the only impressively dressed ancient Near Easterners. A rich array of other Mesopotamian examples can be proffered as well. Their departure from Egyptian styles is self-evident; not only are the figures stockier, but the Mesopotamian exemplars below lack pleats, transparent fabric, and wide collars. Late Assyrian kings preferred stripes, grid patterns, concentric circles, concentric squares, and rosettes, often with dots in the center of each repeated item.[50] Kings often wore aprons in the back, ribbons hanging from their crowns, and shirts and skirts rather than the tunic of earlier times. In two periods,

---

50. Assyrian patterns were reserved for the king or crown prince. Early Greeks adapted oriental patterns for use by commoners. See Guralnick, "Fabric Patterns as Symbols of Status," 110–11.

embroidered scenes are attested.[51] However, late Babylonian and early Assyrian royal garments share certain elementary and decorative features in common with the Israelite high priestly garments.[52]

The late Babylonian king Marduk-Nadin-Akhe (c. 1050 BCE) is depicted wearing a short-sleeved, ankle-length tunic (or shirt and long skirt) with a fringed apron and elaborate belt and headdress (Figure 2.5).[53] The drawing of the early Assyrian king Ashur-nasir-pal (ninth century BCE) depicts a short-sleeved, ankle-length tunic with a fringed hem, a fringed apron, wide belt, and a soft headpiece (Figure 2.6).[54] Note, too, the wide belt, tassels, and patterned hem on the short-sleeved, ankle-length tunic of the court musician from Ashur-nasir-pal's palace (Figure 2.7).[55]

From the following century (eighth century BCE) is a depiction of what is perhaps a chief of the Medes presenting model cities to the Assyrian king Sargon II (Figure 2.8).[56] This man wears a long, possibly fringed tunic with a poncho-style cloak open at the sides. Both are decorated with intricate hemlines. His simple wrapped headdress and soft shoes complete his outfit. True, the geometric patterns of Babylonian and Assyrian fabrics differ from the Israelite designs. In the Mesopotamian world, these shapes held culturally mediated symbolic value,

---

51. Guralnick, "Fabric Patterns as Symbols of Status," 98.

52. Cornelis Van Dam, *The Urim and Thummim: A Means of Revelation in Ancient Israel* (Winona Lake, IN: Eisenbrauns, 1997), 60.

53. Drawing from Houston, *Ancient Egyptian, Mesopotamian & Persian Costume*, 129 (fig 128a). Public domain. An unabridged replication of the 1954 second edition of the work originally published in 1920 by A. and C. Black Ltd., London, under the title *Ancient Egyptian, Mesopotamian, & Persian Costume and Decoration*.

54. Drawing from Houston, *Ancient Egyptian, Mesopotamian & Persian Costume*, 133 (fig 129). Public domain. An unabridged replication of the 1954 second edition of the work originally published in 1920 by A. and C. Black Ltd., London, under the title *Ancient Egyptian, Mesopotamian, & Persian Costume and Decoration*. He is shown elsewhere with a more elaborate full-length shawl with long fringes, draped similarly to a toga over his tunic. See Houston, *Ancient Egyptian, Mesopotamian & Persian Costume*, 135. For a three-dimensional color rendition, see http://www.agesofsail.com/ecommerce/figures/ashurnasirpal-ii-assyrian-king.html (accessed May 22, 2015). In keeping with convention, these royal images almost always include beard, muscles, and elaborate dress. See Kiersten Neumann, "Gods among Men: Fashioning the Divine Image in Assyria," in *What Shall I Say of Clothes?: Theoretical and Methodological Approaches to the Study of Dress in Antiquity*, ed. Megan Cifarelli and Laura Gawlinski (Boston: Archaeological Institute of America, 2017), 15.

55. Also ninth century BCE. Drawing from Houston, *Ancient Egyptian, Mesopotamian & Persian Costume*, 143 (fig 135). Public domain. An unabridged replication of the 1954 second edition of the work originally published in 1920 by A. and C. Black Ltd., London, under the title *Ancient Egyptian, Mesopotamian, & Persian Costume and Decoration*.

56. Late 700s BCE. Drawing from Houston, *Ancient Egyptian, Mesopotamian & Persian Costume*, 149 (fig 146). Public domain. An unabridged replication of the 1954 second edition of the work originally published in 1920 by A. and C. Black Ltd., London, under the title *Ancient Egyptian, Mesopotamian, & Persian Costume and Decoration*.

Figure 2.5 Babylonian king Marduk-Nadin-Akhe.

Figure 2.6 Assyrian king Ashur-nasir-pal.

Figure 2.7 Court musician for Ashur-nasir-pal.

Figure 2.8 Unknown nationality before Assyrian King Sargon II.

signifying the status of the wearer. However, the basic construction of this regalia shows enough resemblance to conclude that Aaron's garments would have been "at home" in this wider context.[57]

Priestly garments in Egypt and Mesopotamia

In contrast to the costumes of Egyptian, Babylonian, and Assyrian royalty, priests in these cultures typically wore plain white clothes (linen in Egypt and wool in Mesopotamia). This compares to the white linen tunic of Aaron's sons. In style, Aaron looked more like royalty. However, royal figures in other ANE cultures were often the chief functionaries in the temple. Even when kings did not regularly perform temple rituals, the priests functioned as their designated representatives. Rosalie David explains that the stone reliefs decorating Egyptian temples "perpetuate the fiction" that the king himself performed the rituals when in fact those duties were usually delegated to priests.[58] The maintenance of the cult was a matter of national security; therefore, the king was naturally responsible.

The instructions at Sinai include no official role for a king in the worship of YHWH and nowhere is the clothing for an Israelite king prescribed. YHWH alone is king (cf. Exod 15:18). It is fitting, then, that the regalia of the high priest, who represents YHWH, would communicate the prestige and power normally reserved for royalty.[59]

Garments of the gods in Egypt and Mesopotamia

In addition to these royal Egyptian and Mesopotamian analogues, it is worth considering whether Aaron's clothes compare favorably to the "golden garments" worn by cult statues in both civilizations during roughly the same periods. Egyptian cult statues were well dressed and the process of clothing them was

---

57. A much older counterpart to the Israelite high priestly breastpiece was found in the Phoenician ruins of Byblos, dating around 1700 BCE. This object contained gemstones, a frontpiece, and cords. Wells, "Exodus," 253–56. See also Van Dam, *The Urim and Thummim*, 76.

58. A. Rosalie David, *Religious Ritual at Abydos (c. 1300 BC)* (Warminster, England: Aris & Phillips, 1973), 4; A. Rosalie David, *The Ancient Egyptians: Religious Beliefs and Practices*, Library of Religious Beliefs and Practices (London: Routledge & Kegan Paul, 1982), 134. An exception was Herihor, high priest of Amun and head of the Theban theocracy in the late New Kingdom period. Herihor was sometimes depicted in sandals and sometimes barefoot. He is usually shown wearing a knee-length, angular kilt with an apron and a leopard skin draped around his shoulders. See *Scenes of King Herihor in the Court with Translations of Texts*. The Temple of Khonsu, Vol 1. University of Chicago Oriental Institute Publications, Vol 100. Chicago: The Oriental Institute, 1979.

59. Danny Mathews argues that Moses is portrayed as "an authoritative surrogate king." Danny Mathews, *Royal Motifs in the Pentateuchal Portrayal of Moses*, LHBOTS (New York: Bloomsbury T&T Clark, 2014), 150, n. 57. However, Moses' "temporal sovereignty" (147–48) provides little precedent for future kings (apart from Deut 17:14–20). Since we are told nothing about Moses' garments, any prestige signaled by fashion is reserved for Aaron.

ritually significant. A royal official from Middle Kingdom Egypt (c. 1878–1843 BCE) described his restoration of one cult statue, saying, "I adorned the breast of the Lord of Abydos [i.e., Osiris] with lapis-lazuli, along with turquoise, electrum, and all kinds of precious minerals that are adornments of the limbs of a god, and provided the god with his regalia."[60]

Likewise, Neo-Babylonian cult statues wore a mix of linen and dyed wool, adorned with precious stones, gold threads, and golden ornaments.[61] In at least some temples, large inventories of gaudy jewelry were set apart to adorn cult statues.[62] At Sippar in Akkad, statues wore garments of sheep's wool or occasionally linen. The former was white or dyed bluish-purple or red.[63] Most goddesses at Sippar wore a *kusitu*, or long, sequined mantle.[64] The garments belonging to Shamash indicated his status as chief god of the pantheon at Sippar. His regalia was "most elaborate," with better quality and heavier weight.[65]

Given the elaborate nature of the Israelite high priestly regalia and the Priestly text designating humankind as God's "image" (Gen 1:26–27), it is tempting to hypothesize that Aaron dressed in such elaborate regalia because he functioned as a living cult statue of YHWH. Unlike other ANE temples, the most holy place in Israel's tabernacle contained no image. Since the high priest was the one figure permitted to enter that sacred space, perhaps he mediated or even embodied the presence of YHWH in his person.[66] At least two factors work against divine

---

60. David Lorton, "The Theology of Cult Statues in Ancient Egypt," in *Born in Heaven, Made on Earth: The Making of the Cult Image in the Ancient Near East*, ed. Michael B. Dick (Winona Lake, IN: Eisenbrauns, 1999), 126. For an alternate translation, see "Stela of Ikhernofret" in *Ancient Egyptian Literature: A Book of Readings*, ed. M. Lichtheim (Berkeley: University of California Press, 1973), 1: The Old and Middle Kingdoms:124.

61. See Oppenheim, "The Golden Garments of the Gods." Oppenheim insists that gold thread was not used in the textile industry until "very late," apparently referring to the "last centuries of the first millennium and later." However, he also notes that the gold rosette bracteates so characteristic of these garments date "as far back as the third millennium" and are attested in multiple cultures of the ANE. Oppenheim, "The Golden Garments of the Gods," 188–89. See also Neumann, "Gods among Men"; and Flynn, in this volume, 21, 28–29.

62. For a Syrian example, see J. Bottero, "Les Inventaires de Qatna," *RA* 43 (1949): 1–40, 137–215. On the ritual act of clothing cult images, see David, *Religious Ritual at Abydos*, 289. David, *The Ancient Egyptians*, 132–33.

63. Stefan Zawadzki, *Garments of the Gods: Studies on the Textile Industry and the Pantheon of Sippar according to the Texts from the Ebabbar Archive*, OBO 218 (Göttingen: Vandenhoeck & Ruprecht, 2006), 22–23.

64. Ibid., 196.

65. Ibid., 194. For more on divine clothing, see Ben Zvi's chapter in this volume, 161–81.

66. As suggested by Samuel Terrien, *The Elusive Presence: Toward a New Biblical Theology*, ed. Ruth Nanda Anshen, Religious Perspectives 26 (New York: Harper & Row, 1978), 399–400. See also Catherine L. McDowell, *The Image of God in the Garden of Eden: The Creation of Humankind in Genesis 2:5—3:24 in Light of Mīs Pî Pīt Pî and Wpt-r Rituals of Mesopotamia and Ancient Egypt*, Siphrut 15 (Winona Lake, IN: Eisenbrauns, 2015), 211.

embodiment as a possibility: (1) Aaron did *not* wear his elaborate regalia on the annual occasion on which he entered the most holy place (see Lev 16:4). If Aaron was the living image of YHWH, he naturally would have dressed the part when entering the space in which YHWH was thought to be "present." (2) The Mesopotamian *mīs pî* ritual, which transformed a statue so that it manifested the living presence of a deity, bore little to no resemblance to the high priestly ordination ritual, whereby Aaron was made priest. The *mīs pî* is far more complex than the Israelite ceremony, including a multiplicity of symbols, including a throne, that do not seem to correspond.[67] However, it remains a possibility that although the Israelite high priest was not the image per se, he provided a visual lexicon that partly explains the absence of an image in the Israelite cult. As a representative Israelite, separated from them in order to singly represent them to the deity, he prompted recognition that humanity functions as YHWH's image.

The Egyptian ritual often called "birth of the gods" corresponds to the Mesopotamian *mīs pî* and provides a closer equivalent. Noting profound differences from its Mesopotamian counterpart, Lorton describes the Egyptian cultic ceremony whereby the cult statue was adorned with gold, ornaments, jewelry, and a headdress.[68] Not only was the statue decorated, but it was also "branded" or inscribed with the name and/or the features of the one being honored.[69] The climax of cultic ceremonies was the "lifting up of the beauty" of the statue or its formal presentation to the people.[70] Aaron's garments were "for dignity and for beauty/splendor," branded with the names of YHWH and the twelve tribes. At the conclusion of his ordination, he appeared before the people in his splendid regalia, where he "lifted up" his hands to pronounce the blessing. Thus, he mediated the presence of YHWH among the Israelites like an Egyptian cult statue while reminding the Israelites that they were the true image.

Royal statuary vestments of Mesopotamia constitute another possible analogue. Winter describes "a process of ritual transformation" whereby a statue of a living ruler was "animated" so that it could "actually manifest" the ruler's presence in a particular place.[71] These royal statues were inscribed with the name of the deity to

---

67. See, for example, Michael B. Dick and Christopher Walker, "The Induction of the Cult Image in Ancient Mesopotamia: The Mesopotamian Mīs Pî Ritual," in *Born in Heaven, Made on Earth: The Making of the Cult Image in the Ancient Near East* (Winona Lake, IN: Eisenbrauns, 1999), 55–122; Sidney Smith, "The Babylonian Ritual for the Consecration and Induction of a Divine Statue," *JRAS* 1 (1925): 37–60. But see Flynn, who speaks of the investiture of power activated by clothing the statue with a specific linen garment (*lamaḫuššu*) in the *mīs pî* ritual, in this volume, 19–21.

68. Lorton, "Theology of Cult Statues in Ancient Egypt," 66, 128, 166.

69. Ibid., 154.

70. Ibid., 126.

71. Irene J. Winter, "'Idols of the King': Royal Images as Recipients of Ritual Action in Ancient Mesopotamia," *JRitSt* 6 (1992): 13.

whom they belonged and were placed in temples or funerary chapels.[72] There they were provided with food and were authorized to "speak" to the deity. Similarly, Aaron's diadem was inscribed with the name of YHWH, he served in the temple, and his food rations were taken from sacrifices offered there.

While no comparable *purpose* has been identified pertaining to the elaborate regalia of ANE kings, priests, or divine images vis-à-vis the Israelite high priest, the garments explored here share cultural affinities,[73] each participating in the visual rhetoric of sacred privilege and responsibility. Given the expense of dyed cloth in the ancient world, commoners wore "entirely plain clothing" in contrast to those with political or religious status.[74] As the most elaborately dressed Israelite, Aaron's status was unmistakable. Neumann points out that in Assyria royal dress provided a "cue for appropriate behavior," signaling the hierarchy of the court and the role of the "king as intermediary between gods and humans."[75] In ancient society, which was on the whole less literate than modern Western society, cultic garments communicated powerfully to the populace, engendering honor and deference and reinforcing the authorized role of the bearer. The well-being of the entire nation rested on Aaron's shoulders, a fact made explicit by his bearing of the onyx stones inscribed with the names of all twelve tribes.

The clothes make the man: Aaron's ordination ritual

Having considered the design and fabrication of the priestly garments as expressed in Exodus 28 and 39, and having compared them with Egyptian and Mesopotamian garments, I will now consider the donning of these garments by Israel's priests, prescribed in Exodus 29 and carried out in Leviticus 8. More exhaustive studies of these texts are available elsewhere.[76] My purpose here is to situate Aaron's garments in their ritual context and to shed light on their significance.[77] Aaron and his sons could not simply put on their new uniforms; first they had to be ritually

---

72. Ibid., 25–26. See also Neumann, "Gods among Men."

73. Van Dam, *The Urim and Thummim*, 78. After exploring Egyptian, Ugaritic, and other Mesopotamian sources for parallels, Van Dam concludes that the colors, shapes, patterns, and jewels of the breastpiece were "not at all out of place in the ancient Near East." Ibid., 63.

74. Guralnick, "Fabric Patterns as Symbols of Status," 100.

75. Neumann, "Gods among Men," 16.

76. See, for example, Klingbeil, *A Comparative Study of the Ritual of Ordination*; Jacob Milgrom, *Leviticus 1–16*, AB 3 (New York: Doubleday, 1991). Both authors argue that Leviticus 8 is dependent upon Exodus 29. See Milgrom, *Leviticus 1–16*, 545; Klingbeil, *A Comparative Study of the Ritual of Ordination*, 105–7.

77. By "ritual" I refer to the "'conventional' action" prescribed by YHWH and undertaken by Moses to designate and ordain Aaron as high priest and his sons as priests. On the general problems associated with defining ritual, see Jack Goody, "Religion and Ritual: The Definitional Problem," *British Journal of Sociology* 12.2 (1961): 142–64.

qualified. The detailed procedure for their ordination lends further weight to the significance of their garments.

Victor Turner helpfully identifies three principal phases by which a rite of passage works: separation, liminality, and reintegration. The desired effect of this particular ritual is to change, usually elevate, someone's status in the community.[78] Passage through a liminal state, where the subject experiences loss, nakedness, or anonymity for a time, makes it possible for the initiate to leave behind the former life and undergo transformation. These stages are evident in the Hittite high priestess' installation ceremony. She was chosen and anointed, thereby separating her from commoners. Then she was shaved, inducing a liminal state lasting up to nine days. After daily sacrifices, adornment, seven days of feasting, and a final procession from her father's house, she arrived at the temple to take up residence, an indication that the ritual was complete and she had begun her new role commensurate with her new status.[79]

Although the Israelite high priestly ordination ceremony is dissimilar to this in many ways, it includes all three defining marks of a rite of passage, sharing several features with the Hittite ritual: separation, anointing, sacrifices, adornment, and the use of sacred temple space.[80] First, Aaron and his four sons were set apart from the people, selected to serve YHWH as priests (Lev 8:1–4). They spent seven days and nights at the entrance, or threshold (Latin: *limen*), of the tabernacle, separated from the community but not yet allowed to enter sacred space.[81] Noting their vulnerability to impurity during this period of liminality, Milgrom explains, "Each day's rites will

---

78. On this, see Victor Turner, "Liminality and *communitas*," pages 74–84 in *Foundations in Ritual Studies: A Reader for Students of Christian Worship*, ed. Paul Bradshaw and John Melloh (Grand Rapids: Baker Academic, 2007). The ritual itself had no magical qualities. Rather, its efficacy depended upon obedience to YHWH. See John Witvliet, "For Our Own Purposes: The Appropriation of the Social Sciences in Liturgical Studies," pages 17–42 in Bradshaw and Melloh, *Foundations in Ritual Studies*.

79. Daniel E. Fleming, *The Installation of Baal's High Priestess at Emar*, Harvard Semitic Studies 42 (Atlanta: Scholar's Press, 1992), 63–65; 173–98. Also "The Installation of the Storm God's High Priestess (1.222)," trans. Daniel Fleming, in William Hallo and K. Lawson Younger, eds., *Context of Scripture* (Leiden: Brill, 2003), 427–31. On a smaller scale, daily temple rituals in Egypt in the fourteenth century BCE included removal of robes from the cult image, purification, and reclothing, followed by provision of food and "insignia." See David, *Religious Ritual at Abydos*, 289. Cf. *COS* 1.34. Even daily rituals like these involved a liminal period. On cultic parallels between Israel, Mari, Emar, and the Horite-Hittite kingdom, see Israel Knohl, "P and the Traditions of Northern Syria and Southern Anatolia," in *Text, Time, and Temple: Literary, Historical and Ritual Studies in Leviticus*, ed. Francis Landy, Leigh M. Trevaskis, and Bryan D. Bibb (Sheffield: Sheffield Phoenix, 2015), 63–69.

80. Unlike the Hittite high priestess, who eventually proceeded from her father's house to the temple, Aaron occupied the temple doorway for the duration of the ritual. His prescribed clothing was more complete (hers included only jewelry and a headdress).

81. Leviticus 1:5 describes the altar as being "at the entrance of the tent of meeting." From this I conclude that Aaron and his sons were ordained somewhere in the courtyard, where

remove them farther from their former profane state and advance them to the ranks of the sacred, until they emerge as full-fledged priests."[82] As a transitional place between the sacred and the common, the entrance or courtyard of the tabernacle was the most appropriate venue for the seven-day vigil (Lev 8:33–35).[83]

During this liminal phase, Moses publically washed and reclothed the priests in their sacred garments (Lev 8:6–9, 13), anointed them and the tabernacle (Lev 8:10–12), offered sacrifices, and sprinkled and smeared blood on them to consecrate them to YHWH (Exod 29:21; Lev 8:23–24, 30). It may seem shocking that Moses would deliberately pour oil and sprinkle blood on such carefully crafted and expensive garments. However, blood was an essential symbol, indicating that priest and tabernacle were set apart for YHWH's use and effectively cleansed by the sacrificial rites (Lev 4:5–7; 16:15).[84] Very little was required of initiates, except to wait and allow Moses to carry out YHWH's instructions.[85] Aaron and his sons merely laid their hands on the head of each sacrifice, identifying with their need for cleansing (Lev 8:14, 18, 22), and elevated an offering to dedicate it to YHWH (Lev 8:27).[86] Then they cooked and ate the meat with the bread (Lev 8:31–32). The sacrifices Moses offered on their behalf were transitional, including some features of well-being offerings and others of holy offerings.[87] Moses ate some, but not all, of the meat usually designated for the priests, in keeping with his own transitional role (Lev 8:26).[88] The purpose of the sevenfold offerings was

---

laypeople were permitted. They laid hands on the heads of the animals to be slaughtered, just as laypeople did (Lev 4:13–18).

82. Milgrom, *Leviticus 1–16*, 538.

83. For a discussion of liminal or transitional space, see Klingbeil, *A Comparative Study of the Ritual of Ordination*, 147, 319, 572.

84. On the cleansing properties of blood, see the helpful comparative study by Yitzhaq Feder, *Blood Expiation in Hittite and Biblical Ritual: Origins, Context, and Meaning*, SBLWAWSup 2 (Atlanta: SBL, 2011). On the significance of the dual anointing, see Michael Hundley, *Keeping Heaven on Earth: Safeguarding the Divine Presence in the Priestly Tabernacle*, FAT 2/50 (Tübingen: Mohr Siebeck, 2011), 78–80.

85. Statistical analysis shows that Moses was responsible for 45.45 percent of the ritual action and Aaron only 29.09 percent. Gerald A. Klingbeil, *Bridging the Gap: Ritual and Ritual Texts in the Bible*, BBRSup 1 (Winona Lake, IN: Eisenbrauns, 2007), 192–93.

86. On תנופה as an "elevation" rather than a "wave" offering, see Milgrom, *Leviticus 1–16*, 464–65, 469–73. The idiom מלא יד ("ordain"; Exod 29:9) only appears in the context of priestly ordination and may derive from this practice of placing certain ritual elements "upon the palms" of the priests (על כפי אהרן ועל כפי בניו; Lev 8:27). "Ordination" is explicitly linked with these sacrificial elements in Lev 8:28; cf. Exod 29:26–29. Propp (*Exodus 19–40*, 452) notes a lexical parallel from Mari, *mullû qātam*, which means "fill the hand(s), hand over, entrust" [CAD 10.1.187] and connotes "a divine commissioning, a transfer of authority from a god to a sacred human."

87. Milgrom, *Leviticus 1–16*, 527.

88. Ibid., 531.

purification and consecration of the initiates (Exod 29:14, 21) as well as to please YHWH (Exod 29:18, 25).

After carefully following YHWH's ritual instructions for the liminal state, Aaron and his sons could approach the sanctuary to begin their duties לפני יהוה (*lipnê yhwh*; "before YHWH").[89] On the eighth day, the priests performed the first set of sacrificial rites on behalf of the community (Lev 9:1–21). After this important work, Aaron approached the congregation to pronounce the blessing, an act confirming his mediatorial role and elevated status as well as the efficacy of the sacrifices (Lev 9:22–23). With this third phase, reintegration, the ritual was complete. YHWH's response confirms this.[90] Only after the blessing did YHWH's glory appear and fire consume the offerings (Lev 9:23–24a). The people's visceral response included shouts of joy and falling facedown (9:24b).

Exod 29:44–46 prescribes this ordination ritual and identifies its overall purpose: "So I will consecrate the tent of meeting and the altar and will consecrate Aaron and his sons to serve me as priests. Then I will dwell among the Israelites and be their God. They will know that I am YHWH their God, who brought them out of Egypt so that I might dwell among them. I am YHWH their God." For YHWH to dwell among the people rescued from Egypt, the cultic furniture, tabernacle furnishings, and most notably Aaron and his sons had to be clothed and consecrated, set apart for the task of mediating YHWH's presence among the Israelites.

Dressed for success: The functional and symbolic significance of Aaron's regalia

Now that the function of Aaron's regalia has been thoroughly examined in terms of its materials, design, execution, and ritual purpose, I will address their practical function and significance, drawing on the biblical text as well as comparative studies. The prominence afforded Aaron's garments in the Sinai instructions makes clear that they were not mere decoration. They were considered essential. Without his vestments, Aaron could not rightly perform the rituals assigned to him as high priest. Alongside the furniture and curtains of the tabernacle, Moses ritually anointed Aaron and his regalia to set each apart for cultic service. Aaron's garments were his means of consecration (Exod 28:3). The splendor of his attire not only qualified him for service by separating him from the community but also

---

89. The phrase "before YHWH" (לפני יהוה) usually refers to acts that occur in and around the tabernacle. Exod 27:21 specifies an act done "*outside* the curtain that is before the covenant tablets" as "before YHWH" (cf. Exod 40:23). In addition to rituals enacted in the holy place, those done in the courtyard or entrance to the tabernacle were "before YHWH" (Exod 29:11, 23–25, 42). However, because God's presence was not limited to the tabernacle, on occasion events outside sacred space were "before YHWH" (Gen 27:7; Exod 16:9; Lev 23:40; Num 10:9; Deut 6:25; 29:9).

90. For discussion, see Hundley, *Keeping Heaven on Earth*, 90.

signified his indispensability to the tabernacle. Aaron's clothing qualified him to cross the boundary between sacred and common.[91]

Form begets function. Haran notes that the "functional character [of Aaron's clothing] is quite conspicuous."[92] Aaron was not permitted to dishevel his hair or tear his clothes in mourning because that would constitute a defilement or disruption of the cultic apparatus itself (Lev 10:6; 21:10).[93] Stated positively, Aaron's regalia signaled his role as one authorized to atone for iniquity and uncleanness in the sanctuary. As such he bore several weighty responsibilities, each of them related to his mediatorial role. Exodus 28 makes explicit the purpose for several of his garments, usually signaled by the Hebrew prefixed preposition ל or the prefixed conjunction ו.[94] Four times in Exodus 28, a *weqatal* form identifies an active purpose for Aaron's regalia.[95] In each case, the verb נשא (*nāśāʾ*; "to bear" or "to carry") identifies what Aaron will carry on his person as he goes about his duties (Table 2.3).

Table 2.3 Stated purposes for the high priestly garments in Exodus 28

Reference	Signal	Article of Clothing	Purpose
Exod 28:12	ונשא	Inscribed shoulder stones	"so that Aaron may **bear their names** before YHWH on his two shoulders *as a memorial*"
Exod 28:29	ונשא	Inscribed chest stones	"so that Aaron may **bear the names of the Israelites** on the breastpiece of decision over his heart when he enters the holy place *as a memorial* before YHWH regularly"
Exod 28:30	ונשא	Urim and Thummim	"so that Aaron may **bear the decision of the Israelites** over his heart before YHWH regularly"
Exod 28:38	ונשא	Inscribed gold medallion	"so that Aaron may **bear the iniquity of the holy [offerings]** that the Israelites consecrate, for all their holy gifts, *that they may be acceptable* before YHWH"

Table from Imes, *Bearing YHWH's Name at Sinai*, 162. Used by permission.

---

91. On the constitutive nature of divine clothing in Mesopotamia, see Flynn's chapter in this volume, 13, 33, and 36.

92. Haran, *Temples and Temple Service*, 212.

93. See also Houtman, *Exodus*, 467.

94. Eleven purpose clauses in Exodus 28 are introduced by a ל, ten by ו, and two without a grammatical signal (vv. 12 and 32). Purpose statements in Exodus 29 and 39 are less relevant for this study because they mostly concern sacrifices rather than garments.

95. Each carries the force of an imperative, instructing the Israelites in the proper design and wearing of priestly clothing. For a discussion of the prefix-conjugation verb as a statement of purpose or result, see Waltke and O'Connor, *Hebrew Syntax*, 34.6. The three other purposive *weqatals* in Exodus 28 relate to the blue cords on the breastpiece ("so that the breastpiece will not swing out from the ephod"; v. 28), the placement of the Urim and the Thummim ("and it shall be over Aaron's heart"; v. 30), and to the bells on the hem of his robe ("so that he may not die"; v. 35). None of these denotes an active duty for Aaron.

First, on his breastpiece and shoulders Aaron bore the names of each tribe "for a memorial" (לזכרן) to YHWH when entering the holy place (Exod 28:12, 29). The grammatical construction in verse 12, אבני זכרן לבני ישראל, could indicate that the shoulder stones are either a reminder *for* the Israelites or a memorial *pertaining to* the Israelites, that is, a reminder for YHWH. Since the stones are also said to be worn לפני יהוה (28:12b), this suggests that YHWH is the primary one who "remembers."[96] Verse 29 confirms this by specifying the location of the "memorial," namely, the holy place, which was off-limits for laypeople.[97]

The inclusion of all twelve tribal names ensured that members of each tribe would continue to have access to YHWH via the high priest's ministry. Aaron bore all twelve names as "representative of the entire community."[98] YHWH remembered them collectively on the shoulder stones and as individual tribes on the chest stones.[99]

It is also significant that these names were engraved on gemstones rather than embroidered or affixed in some other way. While the text does not indicate the reason for the use of gemstones, their inherent value, unmatched by any other tabernacle furnishing, would have signaled the importance of the tribes to YHWH. The stones were also engraved like a seal (חותם פתוחי; Exod 28:21), perhaps underscoring Aaron's representative function with the virtual "signature" of each tribe.[100] This is reinforced by the fact that the tribal leaders

---

96. Cassuto suggests that the shoulder stones faced upward so YHWH could read them. (*Exodus*, 377). However, both sets of stones were designated לפני יהוה. Houtman helpfully suggests that the shoulder stones "focus the attention (of YHWH) on the Israelites." Houtman (*Exodus*, 476). Nihan connects this "memorial" with votive gemstones in other ANE temples, suggesting that the stones recall the Israelites' donations to the tabernacle construction project. "Le pectoral d'Aaron," *19.

97. On the other hand, Joshua instructed the Israelites to make a heap of stones in the middle of the Jordan River to commemorate their crossing into Canaan, with one stone representing each of the twelve tribes. These stones were also called "stones of remembrance" (האבנים האלה לזכרון לבני ישראל, Josh 4:7; cf. אבני זכרן לבני ישראל, Exod 28:12), signaling that all twelve had a share in the land—a symbol of national unity. The shoulder stones of the high priest may have carried a dual connotation—reminding the tribes of their brotherhood and reminding YHWH of YHWH's commitment to them.

98. Sarna, *Exodus*, 179–80.

99. For a discussion of other possible reasons for two sets of gemstones, see Propp, *Exodus 19–40*, 524.

100. So also Propp, *Exodus 19–40*, 438. The practice of inscribing seals with one's personal name was widespread in ancient Israel. Most names are preceded with a possessive *lamed* (="belonging to"). See Ruth Hestrin and Michal Dayagi-Mendeles, *Inscribed Seals: First Temple Period Hebrew, Ammonite, Moabite, Phoenician and Aramaic from the Collections of the Israel Museum and the Israel Department of Antiquities and Museums* (Jerusalem: Israel Museum, 1979), 9–10. A primary function of these seals was to indicate ownership,

provided the gemstones (Exod 35:27; cf. 16:22; Num 1:44).[101] Each had a share in his ministry.

Second, Aaron carried the (means of) decision for the Israelites inside the pouch of his breastpiece, or חשן המשפט ("breastpiece of decision," v. 30). These stones, called the Urim and Thummim, enabled him to discern the will of YHWH.[102] Mystery shrouds these stones; no one is certain exactly how they functioned, and a full exploration is outside the scope of this chapter. However, the high priest was responsible to seek guidance from YHWH, a role authorized by his wearing of the ephod and breastpiece לפני יהוה. Significantly, the means for decision-making hung "over his heart" (על־לב, v. 30). In Hebrew, the לב was the seat of understanding and decision-making.[103] Aaron's decision "before YHWH," that is, the decision submitted to YHWH's guidance, was then binding for the whole community.[104] This further underscores Aaron's representative role.

Third, because of the gold medallion on Aaron's turban, inscribed with YHWH's name, he bore the iniquity arising from any failure to follow YHWH's instructions regarding the sanctuary—that is "the iniquity of the consecrated things" (את־עון הקדשים; Exod 28:38; Num 18:1).[105] The inscription on his medallion

---

especially between 1000 and 500 BCE, but they could also authenticate trade goods, letters, or other documents. See Alan Millard, "Owners and Users of Hebrew Seals," *Eretz Israel* 26 (1999): 129. Hestrin and Dayagi-Mendeles, *Inscribed Seals*, 7. One Hebrew seal reads *lḥnn bn ḥlqyhw hkhn*, or "Belonging to Ḥanan son of Ḥilqiyāhu, the priest." "ʿAśayāhū," trans. Michael Heltzer, *COS* 2.79:204. Seals such as this were used to stamp physical property or important documents, functioning as a signature. See also Spoelstra's chapter, in this volume, 63–86.

101. See also ibid., 438. In Num 7:2 the "leaders of Israel" (ישראל נשיאי) are further defined as "heads of their fathers' household" (אבתם בית ראשי) and listed by name in vv. 11–34, one נשיא per tribe. Cf. Houtman, *Exodus*, 2:346, 3:353; Sarna, *Exodus*, 224.

102. Most scholars assume the stones were cast like lots to achieve binary results. That the Israelites were already familiar with these stones prior to these instructions is evident from the direct article attached to "Urim and Thummim" (את־האורים ואת־התמים). See Van Dam, *The Urim and Thummim*. The words אורים (ʾûrîm) and תמים (tummîm) appear to be related to "light" (אור) and "perfection" (תמים), which may offer a clue for how they operated. Van Dam ("אורים," in VanGemeren, *NIDOTTE* 1:330) suggests the presence of "a confirmatory sign of a special or miraculous light" and argues that a prophetic component was also likely (see, e.g., 1 Sam 10:22). So also Houtman, *Exodus*, 495.

103. See Gen 6:5, for example. Alex Luc, "לב," in VanGemeren, *NIDOTTE*, 2:749–54.

104. For a comparison of divination and magic in Israel and in other ANE cultures, see John H. Walton, *Ancient Near Eastern Thought and the Old Testament: Introducing the Conceptual World of the Hebrew Bible* (Grand Rapids: Baker Academic, 2009), 239–74.

105. See Baruch J. Schwartz, "The Bearing of Sin in Priestly Literature," in *Pomegranates & Golden Bells*, ed. D. Wright, D.N. Freedman, and A. Hurwitz (Winona Lake, IN: Eisenbrauns, 1995), 16. Contra Houtman, *Exodus*, 516, who posits that the gold medallion enabled the high priest to *avoid* bearing iniquity. Propp (*Exodus 19–40*, 448–49) agrees that Aaron bore Israel's sin only until Yom Kippur.

set Aaron apart as "holy, belonging to YHWH," using the *lamed inscriptionis* common to seals.[106] The high priestly medallion indicated that he belonged to YHWH and was authorized to bear sanctuary-related sin and thereby erase the communal effects of individual defiance.[107] It appears, then, that the sin Aaron was authorized to bear related primarily to maintenance of the cult.[108] Leviticus 22:2 reconfirms this conceptual link between YHWH's name (written on the gold medallion) and the holy offerings. YHWH warned the high priest[109] to "treat with awe" the holy offerings lest the holy name be "profaned." Priestly responsibilities inside the sanctuary included a charge to keep the lamps burning in the tabernacle and keep everything in order (Exod 27:21), to burn perpetual incense on the altar in the holy place (Exod 30:7–8), and to perform sacrifices and offerings on behalf of the people (Leviticus 1–7). Should the priests fail to carry out these instructions, sin would accrue on the holy diadem, thus "profaning" the name (Exod 28:38; cf. Ezek 20:39). Careful maintenance of the cult would ensure the honor of YHWH's name.

The instructions in Leviticus 16 imply that iniquity gradually accumulated at the sanctuary, requiring an annual purgation ceremony known in Hebrew as Yom Kippur, or the Day of Atonement.[110] On that day, Aaron made atonement by offering sacrifices, smearing blood on the altar of incense just outside the Most Holy Place, and sprinkling blood over the ark (Exod 30:10; Lev 16:18). Curiously, Aaron was *not* to wear the most elaborate of his official vestments (breastpiece and ephod) while entering the Most Holy Place, when it would seem most appropriate to do so. He wore them only when performing regular sacrifices and maintaining service in the Holy Place, implying that his representation of Israel to God pertained especially to the sacrificial system and the ongoing maintenance

---

106. The form of the inscription was a *lamed inscriptionis*, or *lamed* plus a personal name, indicating ownership. See discussion above, note 102. See also Propp, *Exodus 19–40*, 524–25.

107. Joseph Lam (*Patterns of Sin in the Hebrew Bible: Metaphor, Culture, and the Making of a Religious Concept* [New York: Oxford University Press, 2016], 22) also notes the theological link between Aaron's headdress and his role. He explains, "The mediating role of Aaron on behalf of the sins of the people, which is expressed by a symbol on the forehead, is metaphorically described as the persistent carrying of a load."

108. According to Milgrom (*Leviticus 1–16*, 1033–34), the sin of the community defiled the sanctuary incrementally, and the Day of Atonement (or "Purgation") was needed to cleanse the sanctuary of the effects of those sins annually. Therefore, the Day of Atonement relates more directly to community sin. Cf. Schwartz, "Bearing of Sin," 21. Here the sins are specifically connected to "the sacred offerings that the Israelites consecrate as any of their sacred gifts" (הקדשים אשר יקדישו בני ישראל לכל־מתנת קדשיהם; Exod 28:38; cf. Num 18:1).

109. "Aaron and his sons" need not mean "all the priests." It can designate Aaron and any of his descendants who serve as high priest, as in Exod 28:4, where the phrase appears in relation to the high priestly garments.

110. Milgrom, *Leviticus 1–16*, 1033–34.

of the cult; he did not "bear the names" of the Israelites into the Most Holy Place. When he entered, he had to come humbly, without status or pretense, and in so doing symbolize Israel's undeserved access to YHWH's presence.[111]

Most importantly, Aaron's diadem signified what was true of the entire nation, namely, that they were set apart—"holy, belonging to YHWH" (see Deut 7:6; 14:2). On that basis, he appealed to YHWH for forgiveness of their sin. To wear only ארג-style garments (cf. Exod 39:27), which corresponded to the outer curtains of the tabernacle courtyard, concretized Aaron's mediatory role. He brought the outer courtyard into the inner sanctum, representing every Israelite as he approached YHWH. This is the converse of his usual stance; on regular days Aaron in effect wore the elaborate furnishings of the Most Holy Place as he moved about the Holy Place and the courtyard, representing the glory of YHWH to ordinary priests and laypeople via richly colored and ornamented fabrics, gold, and gemstones. This interpenetration of spheres was an essential component of Aaron's ministry.

However, in addition to his plain linen garments, on the Day of Atonement Aaron also wore his turban (מצנפת; Lev 16:4).[112] Without his other splendid garments to distract, Aaron's turban would have been more noticeable. It is fitting that the day designed to purge the sanctuary of accumulated sin is the day on which Aaron's costume featured the turban—the article of clothing that uniquely designated Aaron as sin-bearer for the tabernacle. During the ritual, Aaron placed his hands on the head of a goat, confessing the sins of the community and thereby transferring the iniquity from himself to the goat. While Aaron had "borne iniquity" (נשא עון; *nāśā' 'āwōn*) all year within the tabernacle, the goat then "bore iniquity" (נשא עון) into the wilderness, signifying the permanent physical removal of those sins and their effects from the sanctuary.[113] No other sacrificial offering accomplished the cleansing of the tabernacle itself. The Day of Atonement was the unique occasion annually where such cleansing occurred. Naturally, the responsibility for this ritual rested on the high priest alone. Aaron's careful enactment of the rite benefited the entire nation, but by wearing YHWH's name

---

111. Cras suggests that wool garments (i.e., dyed cloth) were prohibited on that day because the high priest should not carry death when approaching the living God. See Cras, *La Symbolique Du Vêtement Dans La Bible*, 34. However, sheep are normally sheared without killing them. Furthermore, a prohibition of animal fibers would be strange, since the curtains of the Most Holy Place were woven of dyed wool and the outside was covered with ram and fine goatskin leather (ערת תחשים). On תחש as dyed leather, see N. Kiuchi, "תַּחַשׁ," in *NIDOTTE*, 4:287.

112. Although the gold medallion is not mentioned in Leviticus 16, the only turban (מצנפת) named among the holy garments of Exodus 28 is that worn by the high priest, which was decorated with the gold medallion. Regular priests wore a simple cap, or מגבעה.

113. Joseph Lam (*Patterns of Sin*, 38–39, 58–65) concludes that נשא עון refers to bearing punishment when used in P but is lexicalized in later texts as "forgiving sin." By lexicalization, he means that it has lost the underlying metaphorical association of sin as a burden.

on his forehead, he especially represented YHWH, dealing definitively with the defiling effects of human sins.¹¹⁴

Within the cluster of passages about the high priest's clothing and official duties, one more significant task remains to be mentioned—the blessing.¹¹⁵ The blessing relates to Aaron's regalia in two ways: (1) He first pronounced the blessing

Numbers 6:23–27	
דבר אל־אהרן ואל־בניו לאמר	"Speak to Aaron and to his sons, saying,
כה תברכו את־בני ישראל	'In this way you shall bless the Israelites,
אמור להם:	saying to them,
יברכך יהוה וישמרך:	"May YHWH bless you and guard you.
יאר יהוה פניו אליך ויחנך:	May YHWH smile upon you and be gracious to you.
ישא יהוה פניו אליך וישם לך שלום:	May YHWH show you favor and grant you peace."'
ושמו את־שמי על־בני ישראל	**So they shall set my name upon the Israelites**
ואני אברכם:	and I myself will bless them."

114. Haran identifies a unified complex of six rites inside the sanctuary (לפני יהוה) for which Aaron was responsible: trimming the lamp, offering incense, setting out the Sabbath bread, sounding the bells, evoking memory by wearing the gemstones, and prompting grace by wearing the diadem. Haran, *Temples and Temple Service*, 212–15. Like the other passages in Table 2.3, the bells are marked grammatically with a *weqatal*, indicating their purpose: to prevent Aaron's untimely death in the sanctuary. I did not include this in Table 2.3 because it identifies what Aaron will *not* do: "that he may not die" (Exod 28:35). Aaron actively performed the first three tasks. According to Haran, the final three tasks were passively accomplished by wearing the holy vestments. Aaron's garments did not merely qualify him to do certain things, but became ritually efficacious. Haran, *Temples and Temple Service*, 212. This interpretation highlights the basic nature of each rite (sight, smell, taste, sound, memory, and grace) as well as their interconnectedness. However, Haran falters in his explanation of the diadem. Haran, *Temples and Temple Service*, 214. He also neglects the grammatical signals in Exodus 28 that identify the Urim and Thummim alongside these other "rites," bringing the total to seven. Like the other rites, Aaron carried the Urim and Thummim תמיד לפני יהוה, suggesting that they belong on this list and were restricted to one wearing the official vestments. Haran excludes sacrificial rites from his list, insisting that Aaron could not possibly have worn his elaborate regalia while slaughtering animals, because it was heavy, awkward, and precious. Haran, *Temples and Temple Service*, 212. However, although this ritual text carefully prescribes each step of the process, including his clothing, the text does not say Aaron was to remove his vestments before sacrificing. Moreover, Aaron did not work alone; he had help performing the sacrifices and he may not have done much of the messy labor (Lev 9:9, 12–13, 18–20). We need not assume he was unadorned.

115. Deuteronomy 10:8 and 21:5 either reflect the extension of this privilege to all the Levites or could be read as a summary of Levitical (including Aaronide) duties. Since Aaron was a son of Levi, his duties could also be considered "Levitical."

as the culmination of his first day in uniform (Lev 9:22–23).[116] Aaron's vestments authorized him to give the blessing as YHWH's representative. (2) In the act of blessing the people, Aaron conferred YHWH's name upon them, as Num 6:27 explicitly states. While Aaron literally bore YHWH's name on his forehead, the people, having been blessed, bore an invisible brand that marked them as belonging to YHWH.[117]

This prescription appears immediately before the description of the dedication of the tabernacle (see Num 7:1; cf. 2 Chr 30:27), suggesting that this blessing was integral to proper tabernacle service. The blessing itself proclaimed the name of YHWH three times and linked it with YHWH's commitment to them—expressed as protection, grace, favor, and peace.[118] Just as the gold medallion indicated that the high priest belonged to YHWH and was set apart for divine service, so the blessing functioned as an act of verbal branding, affixing the divine name to the people belonging to YHWH.[119]

The overarching purpose of the tabernacle, including the priestly garments, was to facilitate YHWH's glorious presence among YHWH's chosen people: "And I will dwell among the Israelites and I will be their God" (Exod 29:45; cf. 42–43). When the construction was complete and the priests clothed, this goal was realized as Aaron blessed the people and God's glory appeared to them (Lev 9:23–24; cf. 40:33–35).

---

116. Given the cultic context and the divine theophany that follows the blessing, this was most likely the so-called "Aaronic blessing" prescribed in Num 6:24–26. See Christopher Wright Mitchell, *The Meaning of BRK "To Bless" in the Old Testament*, SBLDS 95 (Atlanta: Scholars Press, 1987), 97. According to Milgrom (*Leviticus 1–16*, 587), the following Jewish texts assume this as well: *Sipra*, Millu'im Shemini 30; *b. Sota* 38a; *y. Ta'an.* 4:1.

117. For a much fuller defense of this interpretation, see Imes, *Bearing YHWH's Name at Sinai*. See also Spoelstra in this volume, 82.

118. On the structure and significance of the blessing, see Jacob Milgrom, *Numbers [Ba-Midbar]*, The JPS Torah Commentary (Philadelphia: JPS, 1990), 50–52, 360–62. The Masoretes set apart each line of the blessing as a distinct utterance with a *setuma* and framed the whole blessing with *setuma* and *petuha*. This indicates the ongoing ritual significance of the text. On the antiquity of this blessing, see David Noel Freedman, "The Aaronic Benediction (Numbers 6:24–26)," in *No Famine in the Land: Studies in Honor of John L. McKenzie*, ed. James W. Flanagan and Anita Weisbrod Robinson (Missoula, MT: Scholars Press, 1975), 35–48. The Ketef Hinnom amulets also attest to the antiquity of the Aaronic blessing. For discussion, see G. Barkay et al., "The Amulets from Ketef Hinnom: A New Edition and Evaluation," *BASOR* 334 (2004): 41–71.

119. Milgrom (*Numbers*, 52.) suggests that Num 6:27 may indicate a physical prophylactic, but acknowledges that most think it refers to a figurative wearing of the name or its invocation through the blessing. For a concrete interpretation, see Meir Bar-Ilan, "They shall put my name upon the people of Israel," *HUCA* 60 (1989): 19–31.

Conclusion

To those involved in the production and preservation of the biblical text, Aaron's official garments authorized him to act as YHWH's representative to the people and the people's representative to YHWH. He was the bridge between two worlds. Not only were the high priestly garments symbolic of the role he played, but they were constitutive of that role. As such, their importance can hardly be overstated. His vestments enabled him to perform his appointed tasks—taking responsibility for sacrifices, maintaining daily and weekly rites in the holy place, seeking the will of YHWH via the Urim and Thummim, and pronouncing the blessing over the people. These responsibilities began when he donned the clothing and ended at death, when his garments were transferred to his son, Eleazar (Num 20:28). On the annual Day of Atonement, Aaron removed his elaborate outer garments—all but his turban—to appear as a common priest in the holy of holies, but with special authorization to address the problem of accumulated sin.[120]

One final analogy may shed light on Aaron's cultic vocation. Lorton notes a complicated system of mutual representation in the Egyptian cult, involving an interpenetration of personality. The officiant in the cult was identified by name as the god being served, resulting in a seemingly redundant cultic practice whereby the god served and sustained himself so that he would live to sustain the people. In his example, the priest to the god Horus was himself renamed Horus, in hopes that Horus would favor the people, who were also represented by the priest.[121]

This Egyptian example may be analogous to Aaron's role in the Israelite cult. Inscribed with YHWH's name on his forehead, Aaron represented YHWH to the people, blessing them in YHWH's name. Yet he also represented the people to YHWH, causing YHWH to remember them by wearing their names on his breastpiece and shoulders. As YHWH's representative, did Aaron also represent YHWH to YHWH (especially on the Day of Atonement) and the people to themselves, reminding them of their identity? If so, this interpenetration of roles and identities secured his mediatorial position. Both high priest and people were said to be "holy to YHWH" (Exod 28:29; Deut 26:18–19). Aaron embodied his ministry at the sacred juncture between two worlds, facilitating their interaction by maintaining the cultic apparatus. Dressed in the splendor of the Most Holy Place before the people and in plain linen before YHWH, Aaron's wardrobe exemplified his mediatorial role.

---

120. Some commentators suggest Aaron wears other linen garments, more common than the ordinary priestly garments. This view can be traced to a misunderstanding of the Hebrew בד (Lev 16:4). See note 4, above.

121. Lorton, "Theology of Cult Statues in Ancient Egypt," 135.

3

APOTROPAIC ACCESSORIES: THE PEOPLE'S TASSELS AND THE HIGH PRIEST'S ROSETTE

Joshua Joel Spoelstra

Introduction

When examining dress in the HB, attention ought to be paid to accoutrements and titivations to clothing in addition to the vestments they adorn. The ornamentation of garments, in the HB, is not merely for reasons of beautification and style, as significant as that is. They also have mnemonic and didactic purposes and possess attracting and repelling affects.[1]

The clothing adornments and accessories examined herein are the people's tassels (Num 15:37–41) and, correspondingly, the high priest's rosette (Exod 28:36; 39:30; Lev 8:9). Ancillary accoutrements, such as fringes (Deut 22:12) and phylacteries (Exod 13:16; Deut 6:4–9; 11:18–21), shall also be addressed to argue aggregate issues raised by the function and placement of the tassels and rosette. Further, I will explore the correlating features that such items have in Levantine culture and religion. I am particularly interested in exploring cases in which the decorative accoutrements, such as tassels and rosette, had apotropaic functions.

The issue of magic in the ANE as well as in Hellenistic times is a complex one. Indeed, this matter is one of relativity, for "one group's holy man [or woman] is another group's magician."[2] Of the Israelites, Joseph Naveh and Shaul Shaked explicate:

I wish to express thanks to Antonios Finitsis for organizing the Clothing in the Hebrew Bible research group and serving as the editor of this volume. Also, thanks to Shawn W. Flynn and Antonios Finitsis for their invaluable critique of earlier drafts of this chapter and to all the contributors for a rigorous and stimulating discussion.

1. Cf. Alicia J. Batten, Carly Daniel-Hughes, and Kristi Upson-Saia, "What Then Shall We Wear?" in *Dressing Judeans and Christians in Antiquity*, eds. Alicia J. Batten, Carly Daniel-Hughes and Kristi Upson-Saia (Burlington, VT: Ashgate, 2014), 1–20.

2. Jacob Neusner, "Introduction," in *Religion, Science, and Magic: In Concert and In Conflict*, eds. Jacob Neusner, Ernest S. Frerichs, and Paul Virgil McCracken Flesher (Oxford: Oxford University Press, 1989), 4. I cite Neusner for his pithy phrase; however,

Magic is officially condemned, but many people who practised what we call "magic" would deny that they indulged in a practice which was against Jewish law. They would say that they practised healing, protection, etc., and that they relied not on magical powers, but on the power of God and His angels.[3]

Consequently, I will avoid the term *magic*, since it is contested and vague. Instead, I will use the adjective *apotropaic*;[4] I understand this term, within religious praxis, to qualify objects (e.g., clothing accoutrements, talisman, or amulets) possessing the capacity or imbued with the quality to protect the wearer from evil, thus warding off the presence, inclination, or allure of evil from the wearer.[5] It does not make a difference whether or not the aforementioned capacity or quality is real or perceived. Thus, I will argue that the people's tassels, as an extension of the high priest's rosette, are apotropaic in that their donning and "using" purport to guard a person from any menacing spiritual force or sinister existential phenomenon. Such threats should be successfully averted through said articles of adornment.

In advancing my thesis I submit two qualifications to the research, and both concern the postexilic milieu of the Jews. To argue that the tassels and rosette functioned apotropaically, it must be established that these clothing apparatuses served as amulets or had amuletic purposes—which are also apotropaic in nature.[6] If they can be so demonstrated, then their apotropaism can legitimately be defended.[7] While the HB does restrain apotropaism, its presence is discernible

---

for an authority on magic, see Fitz Graf, *Magic in the Ancient World*, trans. Franklin Philip (Cambridge: Harvard University Press, 1997). Cf. Robert K. Ritner, "Magic," *OEAE* 2:321–36; J.A. Scurlock, "Magic (ANE)," *ABD* 4:464–68; Joanne K. Kuemmerlin-McLean, "Magic (OT)," *ABD* 4:468–71; Ludwig Blau, "Magic," *JE* 6:255–57.

3. Joseph Naveh and Shaul Shaked, *Amulets and Magic Bowls: Aramaic Incantations of Late Antiquity* (Jerusalem: Magnes; Leiden: Brill, 1985), 36. See, e.g., Num 5:11–31.

4. *Prophylactic*, a near synonym of *apotropaic*, will not be used either for the sake of cogency; for, it is difficult and inadvisable to distinguish some accoutrements and talisman as *prophylactic* with others *apotropaic*.

5. Ezekiel 16:21 LXX utilizes the verb ἀποτροπιάζεσθαί, *apotropiazesthai*, to avert evil. While it is not speaking of articles of clothing or titivations thereto, the express intention of immolating children is to appease, thus ward off, the ire of the gods.

6. Lawrence H. Schiffman and Michael D. Swartz (*Hebrew and Aramaic Incantation Texts from the Cairo Genizah: Selected Texts from Taylor-Schechter Box K1*, Semitic Texts and Studies 1 [London: Bloomsbury T&T Clark, 1992], 22–23) note: "The authors and practitioners of these amulets were, by all appearances, devout Jews who integrated the traditions of Scripture, midrash and classical Jewish theology into their conception of magical piety." See also Ludwig Blau, "Amulets," *JE* 1:546–50.

7. That amulets (are purported to) have apotropaic properties, see Jeremy D. Smoak, "Amuletic Inscriptions and the Background of Yahweh as Guardian and Protector in Psalm 12*," *VT* 60 (2010): 421–32; Jeremy D. Smoak, "'Prayers of Petition' in the Psalms and West Semitic Inscribed Amulets: Efficacious Words in Metal and Prayers for Protection in

nonetheless.⁸ Later, during Hellenistic times or Late Antiquity, apotropaism is clearly exhibited in religious practices.⁹ This period is, moreover, not too far removed from the Persian period, wherein the Pentateuch received its final form.¹⁰ Thus, it can be expected that the world of the Pentateuch is, to an extent, a literary retrojection of the milieu (or ideal milieu) contemporaneous with the redactors.

Lastly, there are three methodological remarks I must tender. I work with the assumption that the primary texts in focus herein are written by P (P^G/P^S) and H, and that their theological outlook is colored by "priestly" ideology;¹¹ accordingly, I will appropriate "priestly" ideology in order to critically examine the primary

---

Biblical Literature," *JSOT* 36 (2011): 75–92; Bernd Ulrich Schipper, "Die 'eherne Schlange': Zur Religionsgeschichte und Theologie von Num 21, 4–9," *ZAW* 121 (2009): 369–87; Michael D. Swartz, "The Aesthetics of Blessing and Cursing: Literary and Iconographic Dimensions of Hebrew and Aramaic Blessing and Curse Texts," *JANER* 5 (2005): 187–211; Michael D. Swartz, "Scribal Magic and Its Rhetoric: Formal Patterns in Medieval Hebrew and Aramaic Incantation Texts from the Cairo Genizah," *HTR* 83 (1990): 163–80; Eli Davis, "The Psalms in Hebrew Medical Amulets," *VT* 42 (1992): 173–78; L.Y. Rahmani, "A Magic Amulet from Nahariyya," *HTR* 74 (1981): 387–90.

8. Many scholars perceive the TR of the HB has been sterilized almost entirely of apotropaic reverberations for the sake of orthodoxy; see, e.g., Rolf P. Knierim and George W. Coats, *Numbers*, FOTL 4 (Grand Rapids: Eerdmans, 2005), 203, 214; Martin Noth, *Numbers: A Commentary*, trans. James D. Martin, OTL (Philadelphia: Westminster, 1968), 117–18; Norman H. Snaith, *Leviticus and Numbers*, NCB (Greenwood, SC: Attic, 1977), 156. Some scholars stop shy of assenting apotropaic properties of the tassel and similar paraphernalia, proffering instead a superstitious observance; see, e.g., George Buchanan Gray, *Numbers*, ICC (New York: Scribner's Sons, 1903), 184–85; Jeffery H. Tigay, "On the Meaning of *T(W)ṬPT*," *JBL* 101 (1982): 326. Still other scholars reject the notion of any adornment of or accessory to clothing having the capacity to ward off evil by any means; see, e.g., Dale A. Brueggemann, "Numbers," in *Cornerstone Biblical Commentary*, ed. Philip W. Comfort (Carol Stream, IL: Tyndale House, 2008), 320–21.

9. See, e.g., Naveh and Shaked, *Amulets and Magic Bowls*; Schiffman and Swartz, *Hebrew and Aramaic Incantation Texts*, 18. See also Erin Darby, *Interpreting Judean Pillar Figurines: Gender and Empire in Judean Apotropaic Ritual*, FAT 2/69 (Tübingen: Mohr Siebeck, 2014), 5–14.

10. See, e.g., Jan C. Gertz et al., eds., *The Formation of the Pentateuch: Bridging the Academic Cultures of Europe, Israel, and North America*, FAT 111 (Tübingen: Mohr Siebeck, 2016); Jean-Louis Ska, *Introduction to Reading the Pentateuch*, trans. Pascale Dominique (Winona Lake, IN: Eisenbrauns, 2006), 217–34; James W. Watts, ed., *Persia and Torah: The Theory of Imperial Authorization of the Pentateuch*, SymS 17 (Atlanta: SBL Press, 2001).

11. See Erhard Blum, *Studien zur Komposition des Pentateuch*, BZAW 189 (Berlin: de Gruyter, 1990), 318–28; cf. also Christophe Nihan, *From Priestly Torah to Pentateuch: A Study in the Composition of the Book of Leviticus*, FAT 2/25 (Tübingen: Mohr Siebeck, 2007).

sources.¹² Additionally, I will employ literary and linguistic analysis in order to examine relevant ANE texts. Finally, I will explore iconography (of bas-reliefs and ostraca) from the Levant to analyze constellations of symbol systems.¹³ By *constellations* I mean a cluster of related elements which form a recognizable pattern (of symbols).¹⁴ Thus, ANE iconographic evidence will be juxtaposed with the material design of Israel's tassels and rosette.

Tassels (Num 15:37–41) and Rosette (Exod 28:36; 39:30; Lev 8:9)

Initially the forms of *ציץ, ṣîṣ* shall be examined,¹⁵ with special attention given to the HB occurrences with decorative import. The purpose of my examination will be twofold, first to establish a connection of this term to flowers and second to explore the implications of such a connection.

Tassels

The pericope regarding tassels in Num 15, a unit of H legislation,¹⁶ reads as follows:

---

12. For selective scholarship regarding the methodology of theological and ideological criticism, see, e.g., Eryl W. Davies, *Biblical Criticism: A Guide for the Perplexed* (London: Bloomsbury T&T Clark, 2013), 64–82; David Jobling and Tina Pippin, eds., *Ideological Criticism of Biblical Texts*, SemeiaSup 59 (Atlanta: Scholars Press, 1992); Konrad Schmid, *Is There Theology in the Hebrew Bible?*, trans. Peter Altmann (Winona Lake, IN: Eisenbrauns, 2015); Rolf Rendtorff, *Canonical Hebrew Bible: A Theology of the Old Testament*, trans. David E. Orton (Leiden: Deo, 2005).

13. See Othmar Keel and Christoph Uehlinger, *Gods, Goddesses, and Images of God in Ancient Israel*, trans. Thomas H. Trapp (Minneapolis: Augsburg Fortress, 1998), 12–13.

14. For this terminology in discourse analysis, see, e.g., Roy L. Heller, *Narrative Structure and Discourse Constellations: An Analysis of Clause Function in Biblical Hebrew Prose*, HSS 55 (Winona Lake, IN: Eisenbrauns, 2004). Here I am using the same terminology in respect to the linguistics of iconography.

15. *HALOT* 2:1023–24; BDB, 847, 851.

16. So H, see, e.g., Jacob Milgrom, "H$_R$ in Leviticus and Elsewhere in the Torah," in *The Book of Leviticus: Composition and Reception*, eds. Rolf Rendtorff and Robert A. Kugler, VTSup 93 (Leiden: Brill, 2003), 31–32; Snaith, *Leviticus and Numbers*, 156; Jeffrey Stackert, *Rewriting the Torah: Literary Revision in Deuteronomy and the Holiness*, FAT 52 (Tübingen: Mohr Siebeck, 2007), 7–8; Alexander Rofé, *Introduction to the Composition of the Pentateuch*, BibSem 58 (Sheffield: Sheffield Academic, 1999), 81; Joel S. Baden, "The Structure and Substance of Numbers 15," *VT* 63 (2013): 351–67.

That Num 15:37–41 is P, see, e.g., Jason M.H. Gaines, *The Poetic Priestly Source* (Minneapolis: Fortress, 2015), 11; Philip J. Budd, *Numbers*, WBC 5 (Nashville: Thomas Nelson, 1984), 175; cf. S.R. Driver, *Deuteronomy*, ICC (New York: Scribner's Sons, 1895), 253.

The LORD said to Moses, "Speak to the people of Israel, and bid them to make tassels on the corners of their garments throughout their generations, and to put upon the tassel of each corner a cord of blue; and it shall be to you a tassel to look upon and remember all the commandments of the LORD, to do them, not to follow after your own heart and your own eyes, which you are inclined to go after wantonly. So you shall remember and do all my commandments, and be holy to your God. I am the LORD your God, who brought you out of the land of Egypt, to be your God: I am the LORD your God." (Num 15:37–41 RSV)

צִיצִת, *ṣîṣit*, as *tassels* only appears here (Num 15:38ˣ², 39); in its solitary other occurrence צִיצִת refers to the *locks* of the prophet Ezekiel's hair (Ezek 8:3). A cognate of this lexeme (צִיצַת, *ṣîṣat*) means *flowers* (Isa 28:4). The *wilting flowers* (צִיצַת נֹבֵל, *ṣîṣat nōbēl*) of Isa 28:4 find varied construct in a few verses preceding: וְצִיץ נֹבֵל, *wəṣîṣ nōbēl* (Isa 28:1); and this alternate form of *flower* (צִיץ I), or *blossom*, is more ubiquitous in scripture. Of these (צִיץ I) occurrences, they refer to a piece of natural (Job 14:2; Isa 28:1; 40:6–8)[17] or miraculous (Num 17:23; cf. Ezek 7:10) flora, and *open flowers* engravings in the temple (צִצִּים, *ṣiṣṣîm*: 1 Kgs 6:18, 29, 32, 35)[18] or a flower-patterned piece of priestly apparel, i.e., a *rosette* (צִיץ, *ṣîṣ*: Exod 28:36; 39:30; Lev 8:9).[19] Thus, open blooms or blossoms (צִיץ/צִיצַת) are a part of the semantic range of צִיצִת.[20] Consequently, it is worthwhile to inquire whether the tassel was fashioned as an embroidered flower. Indeed, certain iconography demonstrates a vague likeness between an individual's tassels and the flowers held in hand.[21] This correlation shall be delineated in the Tetrateuchal usages, most of which detail the high priest's headdress.

---

17. Cf. also Isa 27:6; Pss 72:16; 90:6; 92:8; 103:15.

18. The germane fringe law (גְּדִלִים, *gədilîm*, *fringes*) of Deut 22:12 also finds decorative counterpart in the temple (1 Kgs 7:17a). See Mordechai Cogan, *1 Kings*, AB 10 (New York: Doubleday, 2001), 262; Martin G. Abegg, Jr., "גְּדִל," *NIDOTTE* 1:827–28.

19. Many translations have *plate*; e.g., ESV, RSV, NIV, KJV, NKJV, NASB, ASV, CEB has *ornament*, and HCSB and NLT *medallion*; TNK renders it *frontlet*. Thomas B. Dozeman (*Exodus*, ECC [Grand Rapids: Eerdmans, 2009], 647) explicates: "The translation 'plate' derives from the LXX *petalon*, meaning 'leaf.'"

20. *HALOT* 2:1023–24; BDB, 847, 851. Also, 2 Chr 20:16 refers to a location called *Ziz* (cf. *HALOT* 2:1023); and Jer 48:9 appears to speak either of *wings* (ESV, RSV, etc.) or *salt* (Stanley Gevirtz, "Jericho and Shechem: A Religio-Literary Aspect of City Destruction," *VT* 13 [1963]: 62 n.2) of Moab.

21. See Austen Henry Layard, *The Monuments of Nineveh* (London: John Murray, 1853), pls. 34, 38(a-b); Henri Frankfort, *The Art and Architecture of the Ancient Orient*, ed. Nikolaus Pevsner, PHA 27 (Harmondsworth: Penguin, 1954), pl. 97; William H. Goodyear, *The Grammar of the Lotus: A New History of Classic Ornament as a Development of Sun Worship* (London: Sampson Low, Marston & Co., 1891), 392–93, 400–01.
For tassels, see *ANEP*, 1, 2, 5–8, 11, 18, 23, 43, 45, 52, 64, 196, 200, 281, 351–55, 441, 445, 460, 476, 530, 549, 646, 772; see also Layard, *Monuments*, 4–5, 8 (pls. 34, 47, 48, 87).

Rosette

The rosette of the high priest's headdress is described as follows (cf. also Sir 45:12):[22]

> You shall make a rosette [ציץ] of pure gold, and engrave on it, like the engraving of a signet, "Holy to the LORD." You shall fasten it on the turban with a blue cord; it shall be on the front of the turban. It shall be on Aaron's forehead, and Aaron shall take on himself any guilt incurred in the holy offering that the Israelites consecrate as their sacred donations; it shall always be on his forehead, in order that they may find favor before the LORD. (Exod 28:36–38 NRSV)
>
> They made the rosette [ציץ] of the holy diadem of pure gold, and wrote on it an inscription, like the engraving of a signet, "Holy to the LORD." They tied to it a blue cord, to fasten it on the turban above; as the LORD had commanded Moses. (Exod 39:30–31 NRSV)
>
> And he set the turban on his head, and on the turban, in front, he set the golden ornament [ציץ], the holy crown, as the LORD commanded Moses. (Lev 8:9 NRSV)

The rosette is, actually, one piece of the high priest's complex headdress; it is affixed to the מצנפת, *mišnepet*, turban, and is appositionally referred to as a נזר, *nēzer*, diadem or *crown* (Exod 39:30–31; Lev 8:9; cf. Exod 29:6). Both the turban and crown are, in the HB, exclusively reserved for the king and high priest.[23] For the high priest, the golden-rosette *crown* of holiness is a physical sign of his *consecration*—the typical meaning of נזר.[24] Regarding its design, Josephus writes the high priest's "golden plate" was in the image of a "calyx" (*Ant.* 3:178; cf. *Ant.* 11:331), thus strengthening its floral association.[25]

Rosettes as prominent fixtures to royal headdresses are not unprecedented in ANE cultures. In the Ugarit Epic of Baal and Anat (*'nt* V), Baal wears a head

---

22. While I focus on high priest's rosette, in this volume Carmen Joy Imes analyzes each piece of the high priest's regalia. See also Christophe Nihan, "Le pectoral d'Aaron et la figure du grand prêtre dans les traditions sacerdotales du Pentateuque," in *Congress Volume Stellenbosch 2016*, eds. Louis Jonker, Gideon Kotzé, and Christl M. Maier, VTSup 177 (Leiden: Brill, 2017), 23–55.

23. Turban (מצנפת): high priest (Exod 28:4, 37, 39; 29:6, 28; 39:31; Lev 8:9; 16:4) and king (Ezek 21:31). Crown (נזר): high priest (Exod 29:6; 39:30; Lev 8:9) and king (2 Sam 1:10; 2 Kgs 11:12 / 2 Chr 23:11; Pss 89:[20?]40; 132:18; Zech 9:16).

24. *HALOT* 1:684; BDB, 634. Cf. Martin Noth, *Exodus: A Commentary*, trans. J.S. Bowden, OTL (Philadelphia: Westminster, 1962), 226; G. Steins, "ציץ," *TDOT* 12:366.

25. *Calyx(es)* is a botanical design of the tabernacle's lampstand (Exod 25:31, 33–36; 37:17, 19–22 NRSV). See Jack Goody, *The Culture of Flowers* (Cambridge: Cambridge University Press, 1993), 48.

ornament called ṣṣ (≈ Heb. ṣîṣ) which may also be of gold composition;²⁶ Marvin Pope and Jeffrey Tigay evaluate Baal's accessory as "an apotropaic ornament" which "appears to be a sign of his kingship."²⁷ *CAD* likewise defines Assyr. *ṣiṣṣtu*, the equivalent of ציץ, as "denoting [a] golden floral ornamentation."²⁸ Rosettes feature on Mesopotamian headdresses²⁹ and headbands;³⁰ rosettes also prefigure on Egyptian crowns³¹ and circlets.³² Those donned in rosette ornamentation, moreover, are routinely gods/deities and kings/royalty.³³

Significant terminological mirroring exists between the biblical texts above regarding the rosette and the tassel legislation. First, the tassel must have a פתיל תכלת, *pətîl təkēlet*, *blue cord* (Num 15:38),³⁴ and so also must the rosette be

---

26. See *ANET*, 137. See also Charles Virolleaud, "La déesse 'Anat: Poème de Ras Shamra (Deuxième article, ou V AB, B)," *Syr* 18 (1937): 85–102. Cf. Gregorio Del Omo Lete and Joaquín SanMartín, *A Dictionary of the Ugaritic Language in the Alphabetic Tradition, Part One: [ʻ(a/i/u-k]*, trans. Wilfred G.E. Watson (Leiden: Brill, 2003), 771. In a similar description (RŠ 24.245), Baal wears a *tply*, which is equivalent to Heb. *tplh*: (head) phylactery; see Marvin H. Pope and Jeffrey Tigay, "A Description of Baal," *UF* 3 (1971): 126.

27. Pope and Tigay, "A Description of Baal," 126. They aver (ibid.), "the biblical analogue to this type of rosette is the *ṣîṣ* (also apotropaic) worn on the high priest's forehead."

28. *CAD* 16:214. See also J. Bottéro, "Les Inventaires de Qanta," *RA* 43 (1949): 15. For the golden quality, see A. Leo Oppenheim, "The Golden Garments of the Gods," *JNES* 8 (1949): 172–93; cf. also Goodyear, *Lotus*, 19.

29. See Austen Henry Layard, *Discoveries among the ruins of Nineveh and Babylon* (New York: Harper & Brothers, 1853), 433; Oppenheim, "Golden Garments," 183; *ANEP*, pl. 72 (p. 258); Frankfort, *Art and Architecture*, pl. 30.

30. Layard, *Monuments*, 92 (ibid., pls. 34, 35, 37); Georges Perrot and Charles Chipiez, *A History of Art in Chaldæa & Assyria*, trans. and ed. Walter Armstrong (London: Chapman and Hall, 1884), 1:105,109, 2:354.

31. Jane M. Cahill, "Royal Rosettes: Fit for a King," *BAR* 23 (1997): 54. Renate Germer, "Flowers," *OEAE* 2:543 notes, "a few mummies have been found with wreath-shaped arrangements [of lotus flowers] on their heads."

32. H.E. Winlock, "An Egyptian Headdress," *BMMA* 32 (1937): 173–75; see also H.E. Winlock, "Three Egyptian Gold Circlets," *BMMA* 28 (1933): 156–60.

For natural flora surmounted on (fore)heads, see Carol Andrews, ed., *The Ancient Egyptian Book of the Dead*, trans. Raymond O. Faulkner (Austin: University of Texas Press, 1990), 182(–83); see also Goodyear, *Lotus*, 103–04, 391; Goody, *Flowers*, 41, 66–70; Thomas Schneider, "Das Schriftzeichen 'Rosette' und die Göttin Seschat," *SAK* 24 (1997): 241–67. Cf. Naomi F. Miller, "Symbols of Fertility and Abundance in the Royal Cemetery at Ur, Iraq," *AJA* 117 (2013): 127–33.

33. See, e.g., Oppenheim, "Golden Garments," 172–93.

34. תכלת is variously defined and translated: *blue, purple, violet*, etc.; see *HALOT* 2:1732–33. Herein, *blue* shall be used. For explanation of the dyeing process, see Jacob Milgrom, *Numbers*, The JPS Torah Commentary (Philadelphia: Jewish Publication Society of America, 1990), 411–12; cf. John Sturdy, *Numbers*, CBC (Cambridge: Cambridge University Press, 1976), 113.

affixed to the turban with a blue cord (פְּתִיל תְּכֵלֶת: Exod 28:37; 39:31).³⁵ Second, the inscription on the golden rosette is קדש ליהוה, *qōdeš layhwah*, holy to YHWH (Exod 28:36; 39:30)³⁶; and the ultimate purpose of the tassels observance is to be/live קדשים לאלהיכם, *qədōšîm lēʾlōhêkem*, holy unto God (Num 15:40b). Third, again, tassels (ציצת) may well resemble the visual likeness of a rosette (ציץ I)—a paronomasia at least or at most a design pattern.³⁷

Communalization

If the people's tassels may be seen as the equivalent of the high priest's rosette, due to its common design, color, and purpose (see above and below), then one implication is that the communalization of the high priest's holiness and priestly role in general is thence extended to the populous. Scott R.A. Starbuck, in this volume, likewise develops how communalization—the governing ideology which "attempts to reorganize the post-exilic community"—resonates with the populous, vis-à-vis clothing, in terms of both the royal office and the priesthood.³⁸ The communalization aim, as it concerns the priesthood, is palpable in the very materiality of the tassel as *shaʿatnez*, as Milgrom notes,³⁹ that is, a mixture of wool (blue cord) and linen (white threads).⁴⁰

Mixing different materials is otherwise prohibited in the Law (Lev 19:19; Deut 22:11); and the leading explanation as to why the germane fringe law (Deut 22:12) is placed where it is in Deut is because of an alleged thematic connection of separateness and distinction.⁴¹ However, there are exceptions

---

35. Another blue cord, in the priests' garments, attaches the breastpiece to the ephod; see Exod 28:28; 39:21.

36. Menahem Haran ("The Priestly Image of the Tabernacle" *HUCA* 36 [1965]: 211) notes: "The Rabbis assumed that the diadem was engraved with the two words קֹדֶשׁ לַיה' (Shabbath, 63b *et al.*). But according to the Hellenistic sources it was only the tetragrammaton which was inscribed. Cf. Josephus, *Antiquities* iii, 7,4; Josephus, *Wars* v, 5,7; Aristeas, 98; Philo, *De Vita Mosis* ii, 114, 132." Cf. also A. de Buck, "La Fleur au Front du Grand-Prêtre" in *OTS* 9, ed. P.A.H. De Boer (Leiden: Brill, 1951), 29.

37. So Stephen Bertman, "Tasseled Garments in the Ancient East Mediterranean," *BA* 4 (1961): 119–28.

38. Scott R.A. Starbuck, "Disrobing an Isaianic Metaphor," in this volume, 145 and 152–5; cf. also Ehud Ben Zvi, "Were YHWH's Clothes Worth Remembering," in this volume 175, and 179–81.

39. Milgrom, *Numbers*, 413; also Noth, *Exodus*, 225.

40. White, in many cultures, represents goodness, purity, life, and health, yet it also at times portents remembrance (cf. tassels), power, and apotropaism. See Victor Witter Turner, *The Forest of Symbols: Aspects of Ndembu Ritual* (Ithaca, NY: Cornell University Press, 1967), 69–70.

41. E.g., Peter Craigie, *The Book of Deuteronomy*, NICOT (Grand Rapids: Eerdmans, 1976), 291. Cf. further Calum M. Carmichael, "Forbidden Mixtures," *VT* 32 (1982): 394–415; Cornelis Houtman, "Another Look at Forbidden Mixtures," *VT* 34 (1984): 226–28.

to this injunction only for the high priest's regalia (Exod 28:6; 39:29; cf. Yoma 12b) and the people's tassel. This discordance may be explained by H (Num 15:37–41) writing later than D's legislation (Deut 22:11) and even intentionally revising D.[42]

Ultimately, the intention of the tassels is to stimulate covenantal faithfulness, thereby impelling the people of Israel to truly be "a kingdom of priests and a holy nation" (Exod 19:6 RSV).[43] Along this line of thought, a cognate of the Assyr. ṣiṣṣtu is ṣiṣṣu, which means *manacles* or *handcuffs* and has the conceptual imagery of tying, that is, manacles fastened or tied onto a person.[44] The import for the HB may indicate the method of fabricating the tassels, namely by ties of twisted cord (cf. גדלים, *gədilîm*, *fringes*, in Deut 22:12) perhaps with a loom.[45] More probable, though, is the likelihood of ṣiṣṣu circuitously and figuratively evoking the binding (Assyr. *kašāru[m]* || קשר, *qāšar*, *bind*)[46] of oneself to covenantal (Assyr. *bir[ī]tu* ≈ ברית, *bərît*, *covenant*)[47] obligations (cf. Num 15:37–41).[48] The theological implication is crucial: life and blessing are secured and guarded, while death and curses are warded off and averted—all through adhering to covenantal obligations (cf. Deut 30:15–20).

Mnemonic

A second implication is that tassels served as a mnemonic device for covenantal obedience.[49] According to Jewish tradition, the tassel consisted of five double knots of eight threads, making 13, plus the numerical value of the word 600 (ציצת) which equals 613—the traditional number of the total commandments comprising the Mosaic/Sinaitic Law.[50] Thus, to look upon the tassels was to remember the commandments of YHWH (Num 15:39).

---

42. See Stackert, *Rewriting the Torah*. Cf. also Rofé, *Introduction*, 81; Budd, *Numbers*, 178; Knierim and Coats, *Numbers*, 215.

43. See David L. Stubbs, *Numbers* (Brazos Theological Commentary; Grand Rapids: Brazos, 2009), 141; Milgrom, *Numbers*, 127, 413–14; see also Keel and Uehlinger, *Gods, Goddesses, and Images of God*, 350.

44. *CAD* 16:214–15.

45. *CAD* 16:214: ṣiṣītu is a "part of a loom."

46. *CAD* 8:284; *HALOT* 2:1153–54.

47. *CAD* 2:250–51; *HALOT* 1:157–59.

48. Cf. also phylacteries (Exod 13:16; Deut 6:8; 11:18) and amulets below.

49. Cf. Dennis T. Olson, *Numbers*, IBC (Louisville: John Knox, 1996), 96; Bertman, "Tasseled Garments," 128.

50. Milgrom, *Numbers*, 127; Jeffrey H. Tigay, *Deuteronomy*, The JPS Torah Commentary (Philadelphia: Jewish Publication Society of America, 1996), 203; Snaith, *Leviticus and Numbers*, 156; Driver, *Deuteronomy*, 253.

Certainly, of the three occurrences of ציצת in Num 15:38 and 39 the final usage is abstruse: "... make tassels ... and it shall be to you a tassel to look upon ... " (RSV). Even for H (or P) it seems too pedantic to say that item A is, in fact, an A-item.[51] It is feasible, then, that an alternate usage of a cognate is meant, for example, צוץ II, *ṣûṣ, look, gaze* (as in Song 2:9).[52] To *gaze*, or have a contemplative *look*, implies mental activity beyond mere ocular recognition. If this is the intended meaning, as I contend it is, the verse would read: "Thus it [the tassel] shall be for you an observance, so that when you look at it you will remember all the commandments of YHWH—and do them." What is being looked upon and observed (צוץ II) is, via circumlocution, the tassels (ציצת).[53]

Similar etymological cognates and semantic interrelationships are present among the major Levantine languages. Among Northwest and Eastern Semitic languages, the Aram. verb צוץ means *gaze*, which is identical to Heb. (H); and, again, the Assyr. noun *ṣiṣṣatu* is the loanword for Heb. צִיצָה, *ṣîṣâ, flower*.[54] In Eg. there is even etymological parallel between the verb and the noun in question. The equivalent of *flower* is *dd*, vocalized *dí-dí*.[55] Its cognate verb *dd*, while commonly rendered *to say, speak*, etc.,[56] is given the additional translational value *to think* by Alan Gardiner.[57] The act of thinking (*dd*) is analogous to the observance-like (צוץ II) intention of the tassel legislation, especially if the tassels (ציצת) are flower-like (ציץ || *dd*). Thus, the mnemonic purpose of the tassels is reinforced by the rumination upon the commandments of YHWH, via sight, thought, and, most likely, oral recitation.

---

51. Gray (*Numbers*, 185) states: "possibly there is a play here on two senses of the word ציצת (cp. 127f.)."

52. *HALOT* 2:1013–14; BDB, 847. Cf. also Jackie A. Naudé, "צוץ," *NIDOTTE* 3:786; Steins, *TDOT* 12:366.

53. Cf. Josua Blau, "Über Homonyme und angeblich Homonyme Wurzeln," *VT* 6 (1956): 247–48. Of a future Davidic king, the psalmist states: "His enemies I will clothe with shame, but on him his crown will shine" (Ps 132:18 ESV; cf. Zech 9:16). Here, the shining (צוץ I) of the crown and the crown (נזר) itself are apparently interfused semantically; further, this shining crown is poetically antithetical to the enemy's advances—apotropaism.

54. *CAD* 16:214. Cf. *HALOT* 2:1024.

55. *HALOT* 2:1023; Edwin C. Hostetter, "צוץ," *NIDOTTE* 3:784–86. "H. Grinne invoked Egyptian *ddf.t* which means 'snake', including the uraeus snake often worn on the headdress" (Tigay, "*T(W)TPT*," 323 [cf. n.13]).

56. James P. Allen, *Middle Egyptian: An Introduction to the Language and Culture of Hieroglyphs* (Cambridge: Cambridge University Press, 2000), 472.

57. Alan H. Gardiner, *Egyptian Grammar: An Introduction to the Study of Hieroglyphs* (Oxford: Oxford University Press, 1973), 604. Cf. William F. Albright, "Notes on Egypto-Semitic Etymology. II," *AJSL* 34 (1918): 224 (§24); Cf. also de Buck, "La Fleur," 26 n.35.

Comparative analysis of the sacred flower/tree and its cultic rituals

The outstanding Tetrateuchal reference to *ציץ (Num 17:23 MT), as a flowering phenomenon, shall now be considered. The nature of this occurrence thence introduces germane attestations among ANE cultures of the sacred flower or tree, along with their cultic rituals. In the context of neighboring nations, Israel's sacred flower/tree (*ציץ) will be juxtaposed with that of Egypt and Assyria. It is worth noting that this term appears as part of an ideological-theological constellation. This cluster of related elements that form a recognizable pattern is comprised of the following three components: (1) the aforementioned sacred flower or tree, as well as floral patterned representations, (2) celestial bodies and/or divine winged creatures, and (3) clothing apparel and décor with the foregoing imaged patterns.

Within each element in the constellation of symbols/icons, there is often an entire spectrum of variation; nevertheless, the pictorial cluster is still identifiable. (1) The botanical imagery among Levantine cultures may be represented on a continuum with both poles having literal flora and in the middle a stylized, artificial botany: lotus (Egypt)–rosette (Israel)–palm(ette) (Assyria).[58] Regarding the evolving intermediate stages, the yellow lotus nimbus (ovary stigma) is visually akin to the stylized rosette; and half a stylized rosette, with modification, is the likeness of a palmette.[59] Concurrently, (2) a continuum of celestial imagery exists among Levantine cultures too; again, on both ends of the spectrum is a literal heavenly body: sun (Egypt)–star and lunar crescent (Assyria).[60] All across the spectrum are assorted winged orbs and discs, and the like, all representing stylized gods and goddesses. (3) The concurrent existence of the two image continua sometimes makes the identification of decorative imagery difficult, for example differentiating between a (eight-petalled) rosette and a (seven-pointed) star.[61] Below, I will map this ideological-theological constellation in order to delineate the broader context of the potential significance of the tassels and rosette.

---

58. This continuum is a general representation; nearly every Levantine culture at some time utilized rosettes.

59. Goodyear, *Lotus*, 99–110 (ibid. 28–33, 149–53, 175–85). Cf. Keel and Uehlinger, *Gods, Goddesses, and Images of God*, 352–53. Cf. also Goody, *Flowers*, 48; Edward B. Tylor, "The Winged Figures of the Assyrian and Other Ancient Monuments," *PSBA* 12 (1890): 392; Germer, *OEAE* 2:541.

60. See Goodyear, *Lotus*, 19, 104; Frankfort, *Art and Architecture*, 19; Tylor, "Winged Figures," 383–84, 389–90; Keel and Uehlinger, *Gods, Goddesses, and Images of God*, 74–76, 354; William Hayes Ward, "The Asherah," *AJSL* 19 (1902): 33–44.

61. See Perrot and Chipiez, *Chaldæa & Assyria*, 2:328, 331; Layard, *Discoveries*, 152; *ANEP*, pls. 74–75 j (p. 259).

Egyptian

In Egypt, the most "common and nearly indispensable feature of all royal headdresses was the uraeus (i.e., cobra) attached to the front."[62] Set on the pharaonic plumed *atef*-crown, and in reflection of the gods who wore it (primarily Osiris),[63] its composition is of "brilliant blue and white with the *uraeus* (protective serpent) probably covered by [a] gold leaf."[64] The uraeus functioned in an apotropaic manner for the wearer,[65] protecting the pharaoh,[66] for the golden coiled cobra was considered a representation of Ra's fiery eye, the sun.[67] Consequently, the headdress was conceived to have the high god mounted upon it, poised to hurl fire at the pharaoh's enemies; conversely, Ra may cause the pharaoh's benefactors to prosper—and this is represented, as in the Stela of Tanetperet (*c.* 850 BCE), by lotus blooms emitting from the sun/Ra, atop the king's head, upon the supplicant.

Inversely, to appease the royalty/deity and safeguard favor, subjects are represented, in Egyptian iconography, extending the (bouquets of) lotus(es) before the king/god[68] or setting them on an offering table before the same.[69]

---

62. Pascal Vernus and Jean Yoyotte, *The Book of the Pharaohs*, trans. David Lorton (Ithaca, NY: Cornell University Press, 2003), 56. Vernus and Yoyotte continue: "To the extent that the theological equivalence of the crowns seems obvious, it is difficult to make out the mythologies and practices that were specific to each of them." Yet, they date back to the Sixth Dynasty, *c.* 2325–2150 BCE (ibid., 154). For 24th–25th Dynasty (*c.* 732–653 BCE) discussion, cf. Jack A. Josephson, "A Variant Type of the Uraeus in the Late Period," *JARCE* 29 (1992): 123–30; Jack A. Josephson, "Egyptian Sculpture of the Late Period Revisited," *JARCE* 34 (1997): 1–20.

63. Geraldine Pinch, *Handbook of Egyptian Mythology* (Santa Barbara, CA: ABC-CLIO, 2002), 178 (cf. ibid., 58, 200).

64. Sherman E. Lee, "A Royal Portrait of Amenhotep III," *BCMA* 40 (1953): 181 (emphasis original). The statue examined is the wooden Amenhotep III (New Kingdom, 1550–1069 BCE) in the Brooklyn Museum. See also Goodyear, *Lotus*, 22–23, for plates of the same.

65. Miriam Lichtheim, *Ancient Egyptian Literature* (Berkeley: University of California Press, 2006), 3:45 (cf. 72, 80, 87). Cf. Kristin A. Swanson, "A Reassessment of Hezekiah's Reform in Light of Jar Handles and Iconographic Evidence," *CBQ* 64 (2002): 460–69, esp. 464–66.

66. E.g., Lichtheim, *Ancient Egyptian Literature*, 2:54–58. See also Pinch, *Handbook*, 131.

67. Vernus and Yoyotte, *The Book of the Pharaohs*, 56. See also "shared in the nature of the blazing goddesses Sakhmet, Wadjit, and Nekhbet" (ibid.). See further Pierre P. Koemoth, "L'Atoum-serpent magicien de la stèle Metternich," *SAK* 36 (2007): 137–46; John Coleman Darnell, "The Apotropaic Goddess in the Eye," *SAK* 24 (1997): 35–48.

68. For an illustration, see de Buck, "La Fleur," 18–29. See also Goodyear, *Lotus*, 20–21; Rafael Frankel and Raphael Ventura, "The Miṣpe Yamim Bronzes," *BASOR* 311 (1998): 39–55, esp. 40.

69. For an illustration, see Andrews, *Book of the Dead*, 182–83. The female supplicant has a mounted lotus as a frontal. See also Goodyear, *Lotus*, 391; Goody, *Flowers*, 41.

The offering of lotuses is vital, because this act vicariously shares in Neferetum's identity, status, and role.[70] Neferetum, represented as a lion-headed man wearing a lotus headdress,[71] is identified as the lotus god who is located at the nose of Ra,[72] pacifying the high god with the pleasing aroma of the flower.[73]

The Book of the Dead is representative at this juncture; ch. 81a reads, "I am the holy lotus that cometh forth from the light which belongeth to the nostrils of Rā, and which belongeth to the head of Hathor. I have made my way, and I seek after him, that is to say, Horus. I am the pure lotus that cometh forth from the field [of Rā]."[74] Therefore, based on the cyclical opening and closing of lotuses caused by the sun, along with its surrounding mythology,[75] "[l]e lotus, qui se trouve au nez du dieu-soleil lorsque celui-ci se lève et quitte triomphant le royaume des morts, est également symbole de vie."[76] This sort of resurrection is also represented in Egyptian iconography where the four sons of Horus, "the genii of the dead," stand on a lotus.[77]

Therefore, the correspondences between the headdress of Israel's high priest and Egypt's king include a golden ornament surmounted on the frontal (rosette || uraeus), a symbol of the deity also on the headdress (*YHWH* written on plate ||

---

70. For other gods associated with the lotus, see Alice Grenfell, "The Rarer Scarabs, etc., of the New Kingdom," in *Recueil de Travaux Relatifs à la Philologie et à l'Archéologie Égyptiennes et Assyriennes*, Fascicules 3–4, ed. Gaston Maspero (Paris: Librairie Honoré Champion, 1910), 132–33.

71. Lichtheim, *Ancient Egyptian Literature*, 2:189; Pinch, *Handbook*, 158; William C. Hayes, "The Egyptian God of the Lotus: A Bronze Statuette," *BMMA* 33 (1938): 182–84.

72. E.A. Wallis Budge, *The Book of the Dead* (Secaucus, NJ: University Books, 1960), 557–58 (ch. 81b); Lichtheim, *Ancient Egyptian Literature*, 1:54. See also H.W.F. Saggs, "The Branch to the Nose," *JTS* 11 (1960): 318–29; Keel and Uehlinger, *Gods, Goddesses, and Images of God*, 86–88; Germer, "Flowers," 541.

73. Flora was widely used in funerary rites to drive off the scent of decay; see, e.g., Goody, *Flowers*, 31–33; Germer, *OEAE* 2:542–43. A variation of the physical lotus or the iconographic personified lotus is the Egyptian blossom scepter; see Goodyear, *Lotus*, 43–65; Keel and Uehlinger, *Gods, Goddesses, and Images of God*, 39–43, 66–68, 86–87. This appears to have conceptual overlay with Aaron's staff that blossoms; cf. Nahman Avigad, "The Inscribed Pomegranate from the 'House of the Lord,'" *BA* 53 (1990): 157–66.

74. Budge, *Book of the Dead*, 557 (ch. 81a).

75. Goodyear, *Lotus*, 3–41; Grenfell, "The Rarer Scarabs," 132. Cf. W. Benson Harer, Jr., "Lotus," *OEAE* 2:304–05.

76. De Buck, "La Fleur," 25. For a blooming lotus as a sign of resurrection, see Paul Pierret, *Le Panthéon Égyptien* (Paris: Leroux, 1881), 62; de Buck, "La Fleur," 27; Goodyear, *Lotus*, 4.

77. For illustration, see Budge, *Book of the Dead*, xxx; see also Goodyear, *Flowers*, 64–65. Cf. Andrews, *Book of the Dead*, 80. See also (the head of) Horus rising out of the open lotus bloom; e.g., Andrews, *Book of the Dead*, 79. Goodyear (*Lotus*, 102) states: "The rosette form belongs, however, to the series of mortuary amulets, among which it is very frequent, and it can be dated as an amulet to the XIIth Dynasty."

image representing Ra),⁷⁸ a particular piece of flora nearby (rosette on the forehead || lotus in the throne-room), and matching design colors (blue and white, and gold)—all of which underscore life and the cultic sustenance thereof.

Mesopotamian

Whether the genesis of the rosette was from Assyria or whether it migrated and morphed from Egypt,⁷⁹ "[i]n Mesopotamian iconography the most common type of head ornament with apotropaic function is the rosette, a blossom-shaped decoration on a miter or the like, or on a headband."⁸⁰ In addition to kings and royalty, Mesopotamian divine (winged) figures also wear rosettes on their wrists and sometimes heads.⁸¹

A widespread Assyrian scene features (with variation⁸²) a stylized, sacred tree with winged genii on either side,⁸³ often holding a bucket in one hand and a sacred cone in the other.⁸⁴ Paul Haupt explicates the winged genii are "carrying

---

78. For the association of the Egyptian lotus and (gold) uraeus in relation to the Israelite golden rosette both placed on the foreheads and representing, in symbol or epitaph, the god(s), see de Buck, "La Fleur," 18–29; cf. also, László Török, *The Image of the Ordered World in Ancient Nubian Art: The Construction of the Kushite Mind (800 BC–300 AD)* (Leiden: Brill, 2002), 153–54, 181.

79. So Goodyear, *Lotus*, 101–07; Goody, *Flowers*, 33; cf. also Charles Jaret, *Les Plantes dans l'Antiquité et au Moyen Age: Histoire, Usages et Symbolisme* (Paris: Bouillon, 1897), 426–45. I am inclined to accept Goodyear's thesis. Whereas Cahill ("Royal Rosettes," 57) argues the Hittites invented the rosette, Goodyear (*Lotus*, 150 [cf. 99 n.1]) documents how the rosette came to Assyria via the Phoenician and Hittite interaction with Egypt.

80. Pope and Tigay, "A Description of Baal," 126.

81. See, e.g., *ANEP*, pl. 614 (p. 323); Layard, *Monuments*, pls. 34, 35, 37.

82. In the variations, there are animals (usually bulls) attending the tree, or if it is a human-like figure it may instead hold a small animal (goat or ibex) for what seems like a sacrificial preparation (e.g., Layard, *Monuments*, pls. 6, 45, 50.6); other times a sacred cone is present without the sacred tree (e.g., Layard, *Monuments*, pl. 5).

83. Layard, *Monuments*, pls. 6, 7, 7a, 25, 39, 44.2, 47.4. Cf. Mariana Giovino, *The Assyrian Sacred Tree: A History of Interpretations*, OBO 230 (London: Academic Press; Göttingen: Vandenhoeck & Ruprecht, 2007).

84. See Layard, *Monuments*, pl. 39 A; Tylor, "Winged Figures," pls. I, II, III; Frankfort, *Art and Architecture*, pl. 83; Perrot and Chipiez, *Chaldæa & Assyria*, 1:42, 63–64.

It is often described as a fir or pine cone; see, e.g., Frederick R. Grace, "An Assyrian Winged Genius," *BFAM* 9 (1940): 22–28; Albert Tobias Clay, "Bas-reliefs of Ashurnasirpal," *BMMA* 7 (1912): 72–73; Tylor, "Winged Figures," 384–85. Layard, *Discoveries*, 115. But Layard (*Discoveries*, 289, 549) has instead suggested it is a piece of fruit, likely pomegranate; cf. pomegranates in the HB, particularly as design in clothing (Exod 28:33–34; 39:24–26) and temple architecture (1 Kgs 7:18, 20, 42; 2 Kgs 25:17; 2 Chr 3:16; 4:13; Jer 52:22–23). See again, Avigad, "Inscribed Pomegranate," 157–66.

the pollen of the male palm-inflorescences to the female date-palm. The cone-shaped object with which they touch the branches of the sacred tree is ... a male palm-inflorescence stripped of its spathe."[85] This artificial fertilization of a tree of life by divine figures connotes that the "significance is in some degree apotropaic or purificatory."[86]

Simo Parpola avers that the sacred tree "represents the divine world order maintained by the king as the representative of the god Aššur, embodied in the winged disk hovering above the Tree."[87] Thus, when the king takes the place of the sacred tree, in the scene, and is flanked by winged genii, this implies that he—as the ideal human—is an omnipotent sovereign.[88] If this is the case,[89] there could be similar ideological reverberations in the HB.

Notably, the high priest is portrayed, in the texts mentioning the rosette (Exod 28:36–38; 39:30–31; Lev 8:9) and Num 17 (see below), as a sort of sacred (almond) tree, achieving the equilibrium between heaven and earth by expiating the sins of the people before God. Thus, it is God, or the high priest as a stand-in,[90] who pollinates the people's rosette-like tassels to stimulate obedience to covenantal observance—a perpetual fertility or flourishing; and, in turn, the nation is to operate outwardly as a kingdom of priests (Exod 19:6).

In Assyria, rosettes decorate architecture; they are located, for example, on the exterior of Sargon's palace at Khorsabad.[91] It is through Assyrian influence, further, that the Phoenicians of Tyre designed Solomon's temple with, specifically, "carved engravings of cherubim, palm trees, and open flowers" (1 Kgs 6:29 NRSV).[92] That there are cherubim in the holy of holies, one on each side of the ark of the covenant, is striking—since, according to Heb 9:4, Aaron's tree-like staff was in the ark (cf.

---

85. Paul Haupt, "The Visions of Zechariah," *JBL* 32 (1913): 116. See further Charles S. Dolley, "The Thyrsos of Dionysos and the Palm Inflorescence of the Winged Figures of Assyrian Monuments," *PAPS* 31 (1893): 109–16.

86. Grace, "Winged Genius," 25. Cf. Barbara Nevling Porter, *Trees, Kings, and Politics: Studies in Assyrian Iconography*, OBO 197 (London: Academic Press; Göttingen: Vandenhoeck & Ruprecht, 2003).

87. Simo Parpola, "The Assyrian Tree of Life: Tracing the Origins of Jewish Monotheism and Greek Philosophy," *JNES* 52 (1993): 167.

88. Parpola, "Assyrian Tree of Life," 167–68.

89. Hittite renditions from Assyrian inspiration appear to incorporate an expression whereby the sacred tree is the goddess Asherah. So Steve A. Wiggins, "Of Asherahs and Trees: Some Methodological Questions," *JANER* 1 (2001): 158–87; contra Ward, "The Asherah," 44.

90. Previously, the winged genii have been taken for priests because of their projected mediatory and intercessory roles; see, e.g., *ANEP*, 323.

91. Perrot and Chipiez, *Chaldæa & Assyria*, 1:255. See further Goodyear, "Egyptian Origin of the Ionic Capital and of the Anthemion," *AJA* 3 (1887): 271–302; Goodyear, *Lotus*, 67–79; Goody, *Flowers*, 43–44; Frankfort, *Art and Architecture*.

92. Tylor, "Winged Figures," 391.

Num 17:10).[93] So, are the Israelite cherubim a counterpart of the winged genii who flank the tree of life or sacred tree? The parallelism is tempting.

Israelite

The tassels legislation (Num 15:37–41) is soon followed by Aaron's blooming staff (Num 17:23 MT). The intervening material of Num 16:1–17:15 (MT; Num 16 ET) portrays the contested communalization of the high priest's holiness among the other Levites and the ensuing conflict with Korah and his 250 followers. Numbers 16:3—"all the congregation are holy, every one of them" (RSV)—thus serves as a linking verse to Num 15:37–41, where the people's holiness (conditional upon covenantal obedience prompted by the tassel observance) is underscored.[94] Even though, as many surmise, there is no authentic connection between the tassel legislation and the subsequent so-called rebellion narrative(s) of Num 16–17*,[95] they have been fused together in the final redaction nonetheless.[96]

Aaron's staff,[97] which budded, ויצץ ציץ, *wayyāṣēṣ ṣîṣ*, blossomed, and borne almonds (Num 17:23 MT),[98] serves as a sign (against the insurrectionists) confirming the Aaronites as the high priestly family (Num 17:25–28 MT).[99] It was formerly Aaron's incense offering alone that did *ward off* (כפר, *kpr*)[100] YHWH's קצף, *qeṣep*, wrath and consequent נגף, *negep*, plague/מגפה, *maggēpâ*, plague (Num 17:1–15 MT). Hence, Aaron mediated in an ostensibly apotropaic manner, standing in between the living and the dead (Num 17:13 MT; cf. Exod 28:38). Aaron himself is

---

93. For the historicity of Aaron's budded staff, see Noth, *Numbers*, 131. Cf. Karel van der Toorn, "Did Jeremiah See Aaron's Staff?" *JSOT* 43 (1989): 83–94.

94. Numbers 15:37–41 has two redactional *leitworte*; תור, *tûr*, reconnoiter, is retrospective to the exploration narrative(s) of Num 13–14 (cf. Ezek 20:6) and ציצת is prospective to the aftermath of the rebellion narrative(s) of Num 17:23 MT (ויצץ ציץ, *wayyāṣēṣ ṣîṣ*, blossomed).

95. See Knierim and Coats, *Numbers*, 202–03; Baden, "Numbers 15," 351–67; Baden, "The Original Place of the Priestly Manna Story in Exodus 16," *ZAW* 122 (2010): 491–504.

96. Numbers 16–17, while mostly P, is complex on a source critical level. See, e.g., Reinhard G. Kratz, *The Composition of the Narrative Books of the Old Testament*, trans. John Bowden (London: T&T Clark, 2005), 102–03, 106–08; Joel S. Baden, *The Composition of the Pentateuch: Renewing the Documentary Hypothesis*, AYBRL (New Haven: Yale University Press, 2012), 162–63, 175–76. Cf. also Baruch A. Levine, *Numbers 1–20*, AB 4 (New York: Doubleday, 1993), 405; Donald James Taylor, *A Narrative Critical Analysis of Korah's Rebellion in Numbers 16 and 17* (Ph.D. diss; University of South Africa, 2010).

97. Aaron's staff, it should be remembered, had previously transformed into a serpent (Exod 7:8–13); on the convergence of flowers, staffs, and snakes, cf. A.L. Frothingham, "Babylonian Origin of Hermes the Snake-God, and of the Caduceus I," *AJA* 20 (1916): 175–211, esp. 176–79.

98. צוץ I (*ṣwṣ*): blossom, bloom, gleam (*HALOT* 2:1013); flourish, shine (BDB, 847).

99. Cf. Gordon J. Wenham, "Aaron's Rod (Numbers 17:16–28)," *ZAW* 93 (1981): 280–81.

100. In Isa 47:11, NRSV renders כפר as *ward off*, a synonym of *apotropaic*.

imaged as a bloom, with the rosette (ציץ) on his forehead (if he is there envisaged in full regalia) just as there is a blossom (ציץ) on his staff.[101] Thus, the blossom's fruitfulness is a symbol of life even as the high priest is granted access to the sphere of life, namely, the deity's sanctuary,[102] where life is (re)generated before the presence of YHWH and the ark of the covenant, as represented by the undying blossom (Num 17:19, 22 MT).

The שקדים, šəqēdîm, *almonds* borne by Aaron's staff (Num 17:23 MT) is reminiscent of the cups of the lampstand (*menorah*), which is patterned after the משקד, məšūqqad, *almond blossom* (Exod 25:33–34; 37:19–20).[103] The instructions regarding the construction of the lampstand tell of its accompanying מחתה, *maḥəttâ*, *censers* (Exod 25:38; 37:23),[104] which too is reminiscent of the Levites' and Aaron's censures (מחתה) in Num 17:1–15 MT (cf. also Lev 16:12). In the temple, the ten lampstands, of the same design, are part of its décor (1 Kgs 7:49–50; cf. Zech 4:2–3);[105] and this, once more, coincides with the floral engravings (1 Kgs 6:18, 29, 32, 35) of the temple itself, as well as its capitals fashioned in the image of a שׁוּשַׁן/שׁוֹשָׁן, *šûšan/šôšān*, *lotus* (1 Kgs 7:19/1 Kgs 7:22, 26; cf. 2 Chr 4:5).[106] Therefore, the *menorah* (one in the tabernacle or ten in the temple), which is a refraction of the almond tree, could ideologically be seen as representing the sacred tree[107]—even a paradisiac tree of life (cf. Gen 2; cf. also Ps 92:12–14).[108]

Since "la fleur est, par excellence, le symbole de la mortalité et de la fragilité" (cf. Isa 28:1–4),[109] it is therefore suggestive that there are a few immortal blooms

---

101. Cf. See Noth, *Numbers*, 131; de Buck, "La Fleur," 18–19. Cf. Steins, *TDOT* 12:367–68, 372. See further *ANEP*, 197 (272), for a tree branch staff, and similarly Frankfort, *Art and Architecture*, 30 (pl. 28).

102. Othmar Keel, *Symbolism of the Biblical World: Ancient Near Eastern Iconography and the Book of Psalms*, trans. Timothy J. Hallett (Winona Lake, IN: Eisenbrauns, 1997), 116–20.

103. These are the only occurrences of משקד in the HB. Cf. שקד, *šāqad*, *almond tree* is in Gen 43:11; Num 17:23; Eccl 12:5; Isa 29:20; Jer 1:11. Cf. further, Goodyear, *Lotus*, 64–65, for seven-stemmed lotus budded décor.

104. See further the censers at the altar of burnt offering in Exod 27:3; 38:3 (cf. Lev 10:1).

105. The תמרה, *timōrâ*, *palm tree* also figures in the Solomonic Temple (1 Kgs 6:29, 32, 35; 7:36; 2 Chr 3:5) and the temple envisioned by Ezekiel (Ezek 40:16, 22, 26, 31, 34, 37; 41:18–20, 25–26).

106. See Blažej Štrba, "שׁוֹשַׁנָּה of the Canticle," *Bib* 85 (2004): 475–502; W. Derek Suderman, "Modest or Magnificent? Lotus versus Lily in Canticles," *CBQ* 67 (2005): 42–58. Cf. also Goodyear, "Ionic Capital," 271–302; Keel, *Symbolism of the Biblical World*, 163–71. Egyptian *ssn* means *lotus* (Harer, Jr., *OEAE* 2:305).

107. Joan E. Taylor, "The Asherah, The Menorah and The Sacred Tree," *JSOT* 66 (1995): 29–54; cf. also William Hayes Ward, "The Asserted Seven-Fold Division of the Sacred Tree," *JBL* 8 (1888): 151–55.

108. Keel, *Symbolism of the Biblical World*, 140–44; Rahmani, "Nahariyya," 387–90.

109. De Buck, "La Fleur," 18.

in the HB. Aaron's bloomed (ויצץ ציץ) staff, the high priest's calyx designed (Josephus, *Ant.* 3:178) golden rosette (ציץ), and the people's floral-patterned tassels (ציצת), as well as the aforementioned temple/tabernacle furniture and engravings, are all enduring, nature defying, and hence sacred flowers/trees. Thus, from an ideological–theological point of view, the sanctuary of YHWH's presence and the mediation of the high priest wards off evil (cf. Exod 28:33–38), and the apotropaic emanations are transported beyond the sanctuary by the tasseled people of Israel.

Insights from the comparative analysis of the ideological–theological constellation
Extrapolating the elements of the foregoing constellation, a few deductions can be made relating to the ideological–theological interfacing between Israelite religion and that of Egypt and Assyria. Regarding a floral element to a royal headdress, Israel is, in this respect, more reminiscent of Egyptian culture; and, regarding the sacred tree aspect with the quasi-divine figures ritually attending it, Israel is, in this way, more evoking Assyrian ideology. Primarily, each region has a god or divine figure who sustains the fertility of a certain piece of flora. In Egypt, Ra, as the sun god, draws out the lotus from the water's surface, causing a bloom every new day.[110] In Assyria, the winged genii fertilize, via inflorescence, the stylized, sacred tree with sacred cones.[111] Similarly, YHWH perpetually sustains Israel's life, via atonement of sin, symbolized by the floral accoutrement: both the rosette and tassels.

Inversely, the flora in focus is also presented back to the god/deity as an offering. In Egyptian iconography, lotuses are commonly held out or placed atop an altar, with other gifts, to the gods. In Assyrian reliefs, the tree responds to the sacred cone, yielding fruit, an image of order and prosperity. With Israel, the covenantal faithfulness of the people (Num 15:37–41) and the cultic ritual performed by the high priest (Exod 28:36–38) may themselves be ideology seen as a floral offering to YHWH, since flower-like items (ציץ/ציצת) are affixed to their clothing.

Seals, amulets, and apotropaism

At this juncture, I will adduce the apotropaic function of tassels and rosettes based on their concomitant use for seals and amulets. The purpose of my investigation will be to propose that based on the broader ideology of covenantal faithfulness tassels and rosettes functioned amuletically, as evil-averting mechanisms.

---

110. For the lotus, or water lily, blooming every 24 hours—hence being a symbol of (new) life—see Goodyear, *Lotus*, 3–41; Grenfell, "The Rarer Scarabs," 132; Harer, Jr., "Lotus," 304–05.
111. Cf. also Layard, *Discoveries*, 135–36.

Seal (Rosette)

Returning to the high priest's rosette described in Exod,[112] I will explore the significance of the inscription *holy to YHWH* that is "engrave[d] on it, like the engraving of a signet" (Exod 28:36 NRSV; also Exod 28:11, 21; 39:6, 14, 30). Signets appear in two major forms in the Levant, cylinder and seal, and were used for legal purposes, including—but not limited to—identity and authorization.[113] Both of these purposes are served by the high priest's rosette when he enters the holy of holies: the high priest, *identified* as belonging to YHWH and representing the people of Israel,[114] performs an *authorized* ritual for atonement.[115]

Rosettes (of various amounts of petals)[116] were common patterns for seals in ancient Judah. Archaeological excavations have unearthed approximately 250 rosette-stamped seals, mainly on ovoid storage jars and in a couple cases on the handles of wine decanters; these findings can be dated to the late seventh to early sixth centuries BCE, contemporary to Josiah and the remaining kings of Judah.[117] Prior to the rosette, the *lmlk* inscriptions (accompanied by the four-winged scarab or the two-winged disk) of the eighth century BCE served as the equivalent seal during the reign of Hezekiah.[118] Yet, in one extant instance there is an intersection of these two seal designs; on a double handled jar, both rosettes and the inscription *lmlk*, (belonging) to (the) king, are found.[119]

---

112. Leviticus 8:9, though mentioning the rosette, does not specify an inscription.

113. Bonnie S. Magness-Gardiner, "Seals, Mesopotamian," *ABD* 5 (1992): 1062–64; Arthur C. Mace, "The Murch Collection of Egyptian Antiquities," *BMMA* 6 (1911): 1–28.

114. Other items in the Tetrateuch which has names engraved on them include the names of the tribes of Israel on the Umin and Thummin (Exod 28:9–12; 39:6), on the various stones of the breastpiece (Exod 28:21, 29; 39:14), and on the staffs deposited before YHWH in the tent of meeting (Num 17:16–22 MT). See further Imes, "Between Two Worlds," in this volume, 55–7.

115. Kings and governors, and sometimes nobility, are also portrayed in the HB wearing a *signet ring* (חותם/חתם, *hôtam/ḥōtam*); see, e.g., Gen 38:18; 1 Kgs 21:8; Jer 22:24; Hag 2:23 (cf. also Job 38:14; 41:7; Song 8:6).

116. Keel and Uehlinger, *Gods, Goddesses, and Images of God*, 353. See also the seal with a rosette and two surrounding buds (ibid., 356–57).

117. Cahill, "Royal Rosettes," 51. See also Keel and Uehlinger, *Gods, Goddesses, and Images of God*, 353–54; Jane M. Cahill, "Rosette Stamp Seal Impressions from Ancient Judah," *IEJ* 45 (1995): 230–52.

118. Cahill, "Royal Rosettes," 56. Cf. Keel and Uehlinger, *Gods, Goddesses, and Images of God*, 353–55. Cf. also Meir Lubetski, "King Hezekiah's Seal Revisited," *BAR* 27 (2001): 44–51, esp. 44; Raz Kletter, "Pots and Polities: Material Remains of Late Iron Age Judah in relation to Its Political Borders," *BASOR* 314 (1999): 34–38.

119. Cahill, "Royal Rosettes," 51. Cf. also Gordon J. Hamilton ("A Proposal to Read the Legend of a Seal-Amulet from Deir Rifa, Egypt as an Early West Semitic Alphabetic Inscription," *JSS* 54 [2009]: 51–79) where the item in question reads: *l qn ḥz* "(Belonging) to Qn, (the) Seer" (75).

This description bears a striking resemblance to the high priest's crown, where both the rosette and the dedicatory or possessive inscription (≈ *lyhwh*) are present. Thus, the imbued apotropaic nature of the high priest's composite headdress—seen especially in the atonement ritual—may also be theologically interpreted as applying to the people's tassels via "secondary transference," as Martin Noth puts it,[120] by virtue of it comprising the same materiality, design, and purpose. This would imply the tassels likewise are a sign of YHWH's possession of the Israelites (Num 15:41) and, in turn, the Israelites' dedication to YHWH (Num 15:40).

Curiously, there is a real possibility that tassels were used, on occasion, as a substitute for a seal. Clay impressions from a bristly cloth item of a *sisiktu* garment, that is, the vestment decorated with tassels (Assyr. *ṣiṣṣtu* ≈ Heb. *ṣiṣit*), are found from lower Mesopotamia from *c.* 1650 to 1100 BCE.[121] If the tassel was used as a seal, then, in addition to identity, it may also portent to be a symbol of authority and authorization.

Furthermore, just as *YHWH* is engraved like a signet on the high priest's forehead, so also is the Tetragrammaton sealed, as it were, upon the people of Israel when receiving the high priestly blessing (Num 6:24–26).[122] Whereupon the Divine Name is spoken over the Israelites thrice, the Aaronide priests are said, by YHWH, to have "put my name on the Israelites, and I will bless them" (Num 6:27 NRSV). This wearing of the Divine Name, for both the high priest literally and the people figuratively via blessings, has significant religious implications.[123]

Therefore, whereas engraved rosettes were a common pattern for seals, stamped upon important, even royal, items, YHWH inversely mandates the engraving of the Tetragrammaton upon a golden rosette for the high priest's headdress; and that ownership/identity and authority is transmitted to the populous in the rosette-templated tassels, and ritually so, by the high priest's blessing.[124]

---

120. Noth, *Exodus*, 225.

121. See Albert Tobias Clay, *Light on the Old Testament from Babel* (Philadelphia: Sunday School Times, 1907), 175–76; Ferris J. Stephens, "The Ancient Significance of *Ṣiṣith*," *JBL* 50 (1931): 59–70.

122. See Jeremy D. Smoak, *The Priestly Blessing in Inscription and Scripture: The Early History of Numbers 6:24–26* (Oxford: Oxford University Press, 2015). Cf. Imes, "Between Two Worlds," in this volume, 60–61.

123. Swartz, "The Aesthetics of Blessings and Cursing," 187–211; Wojciech Kosior, "'The Name of Yahveh is Called Upon You.' Deuteronomy 28:10 and the Apotropaic Qualities of Tefillin in the Early Rabbinic Literature," *StR* 48 (2015): 143–54, esp. 146–48.

124. Barat Ellman (*Memory and Covenant: The Role of Israel's and God's Memory in Sustaining the Deuteronomic and Priestly Covenants*, Emerging Scholars [Minneapolis: Fortress, 2013], 107–11, 150–52) argues that the high priestly ציץ, and other engraved things, are to evoke God's memory, while the ציצת are to evoke the people's memory—all toward covenantal fulfillment.

Amulets

The high priestly blessing is the chief inscription engraved on so-called phylacteries (or *tefillin*).[125] This is evidenced by the late sixth century BCE Ketef Hinnom amulets,[126] which were discovered alongside a "seal with branch and lotus bud decorations."[127] Consequently, there are two apotropaic items in this grave:[128] the amulet/phylactery and the seal with "the lotus [which] was used amuletically to protect" and preserve life, ideologically speaking (see above).[129]

When the high priestly blessing is cited in the DSS there is also corresponding acknowledgment of the blessing's life-restoring affect; 4Q374 reads: "'When He caused His face to shine upon them' (Num. 6:25) for healing, they were made strong once again."[130] Later, during the third–seventh centuries CE, Hebrew and Aramaic inscriptions utilize the contents of Num 6:24-26 for amulets with the purpose of healing.[131] Amulet T-S K 1.127 takes five out of a 38-line incantation to quote the high priestly blessing; this recitation—redolent with the Tetragrammaton "to add potency to the charm"—"is intended to bring about the healing the amulet

---

125. The word *phylacteries* (φυλακτήρια, *phulaktēria*) appears in the NT (Matt 23:5) as a technical term; also, in the same verse is reference to *tassel/fringe* (κράσπεδα, *kraspeda*). See further, Jeffery H. Tigay, "On the Term Phylacteries (Matt 23:5)," *HTR* 72 (1979): 45–53.

126. Cf. Ada Yardeni, "Remarks on the Priestly Blessing on Two Ancient Amulets from Jerusalem," *VT* 41 (1991): 176–85; Gabriel Barkay et al., "The Amulets from Ketef Hinnom: A New Edition and Evaluation," *BASOR* 334 (2004): 41–71; Angelika Berlejung, "Ein Programm fürs Leben: theologisches Wort und anthropologischer Ort der Silberamulette von Ketef Hinnom," *ZAW* 120 (2008): 204–30.

127. Keel and Uehlinger, *Gods, Goddesses, and Images of God*, 366 (365 for image). This is analogous to other seal-amulets with floral elements; see, e.g., an amulet with Horus on a lotus wearing an *atef*-crown in Philip C. Schmitz, "Reconsidering a Phoenician Inscribed Amulet from the Vicinity of Tyre," *JAOS* 122 (2002): 817–23.

128. Alissa M. Whitmore ("Fascinating Fascina: Apotropaic Magic and How to Wear a Penis," in *What Shall I Say of Clothes? Theoretical and Methodological Approaches to the Study of Dress in Antiquity*, ed. Megan Cifarelli and Laura Gawlinski, SPAAA 3 [Boston: Archaeological Institute of America, 2017], 53) finds similar phenomenon in her study of phallic pendants: "Since other amulets also appear in burials, it seems likely that any apotropaic function that phallic pendants had in life continued in death." Cf. John Strange, "The Idea of Afterlife in Ancient Israel: Some Remarks on the Iconography in Solomon's Temple," *PEQ* 117 (1985): 35–39.

129. Grenfell, "The Rarer Scarabs," 133.

130. Michael Wise, Martin Abegg, Jr., and Edward Cook, *The Dead Sea Scrolls: A New Translation* (San Francisco: HarperSanFrancisco, 1996), 335–36. See also Kosior, "Apotropaic Qualities of Tefillin," 144–45.

131. For citation of the *Shema*, Deut 6:4, which is the first line of the phylactery periscope, in several incantations, see Naveh and Shaked, *Amulets and Magic Bowls*, 184–87; Schiffman and Swartz, *Hebrew and Aramaic Incantation Texts*, 78.

seeks."[132] Lawrence Schiffman and Michael Swartz believe "the magician took Num. 6.27 literally ... that the divine name, or Priestly Blessing, is actually to be placed on the person in the form of an amulet."[133]

Initially, the legislation of the phylacteries, which (eventually) double as amulets, reads: "Bind them as a sign [אות, 'ôt] on your hand, fix them as an emblem [טטפת(ו), ṭō(ô)ṭāpōt] on your forehead" (Deut 6:8/11:18 NRSV; cf. Exod 13:16).[134] Like tassels, phylacteries too were used as mnemonic devices to remember YHWH, YHWH's laws, and to love YHWH.[135] Reinhard Achenbach deduces, "Num 15:37–41 thus represents a realistic interpretation of the symbolism of Deut 6:8–9 and 11:18–19."[136] So likewise, "the amulet functions not only as a physical object of power, it is a mnemonic, or script, for oral recitation."[137]

The command to bind (קשר) phylacteries in Deut 6:8 and 11:18 parallels Prov 6:20–26,[138] which bids one to bind (קשר) mitzvah and torah to one's heart and neck (vv. 20–21) so that it might lead, guard, and inculcate the individual (v. 22) for the purpose of living righteously (v. 23),[139] not being seduced by immorality who is (either figuratively personified as or literally) a promiscuous woman

---

132. Schiffman and Swartz, *Hebrew and Aramaic Incantation Texts*, 113, 38; see also Naveh and Shaked, *Amulets and Magic Bowls*, 237–38.

133. Schiffman and Swartz, *Hebrew and Aramaic Incantation Texts*, 122. Cf. Joshua Trachtenberg, *Jewish Magic and Superstition: A Study in Folk Religion* (New York: Behrman's Jewish Book House, 1939; repr. Philadelphia: University of Pennsylvania Press, 2004), 92.

134. "The word *ṭoṭepet* is used in the mishna (*Šabb.* 6:1) as an article of women's jewelry and in Mandaic in the sense of 'amulet'" (Moshe Weinfled, *Deuteronomy 1–11*, AB 6 [Garden City, NY: Doubleday, 1995], 334). See also Tigay, "*T(W)ṬPT*," 321–31, esp. 328 n. 46, and E.A. Speiser, "Ṭwṭpt," *JQR* 48 (1957): 208–17.

Regarding these being a *sign*, Wilhelm Rudolph, BHS editor of Numbers, proposes the text/scribe meant לאות instead of לציצת in Num 15:39; this suggestion might have arisen from predilections to harmonize it with Deut 6:8 and 11:18 and perhaps even Num 17:25 (MT).

135. Umberto Cassuto, *A Commentary on the Book of Exodus*, trans. Israel Abrahams (Jerusalem: Magnes, 1967), 384–85.

136. Reinhard Achenbach, "Complementary Reading of the Torah in the Priestly Texts of Numbers 15," in *Torah and the Book of Numbers*, eds. Christian Frevel, Thomas Pola, and Aaron Schart, FAT 2/62 (Tübingen: Mohr Seibeck, 2013), 229. Cf. Gray, *Numbers*, 183–84.

137. Swartz, "Scribal Magic," 166.

138. See Patrick D. Miller Jr., "Apotropaic Imagery in Proverbs 6:20–22," *JNES* 29 (1970): 129–30.

139. Richard D. Nelson (*Deuteronomy: A Commentary*, OTL [Louisville: Westminster John Knox, 2002], 92) takes the phrase "'[u]pon your heart'" in Deut 6:6 as "suggest[ing] texts hung around a learner's neck as an instructional aid (Prov 3:3; 6:21–22) or as an apotropaic amulet (cf. Exod 28:29)."

(vv. 24–26).[140] The *seductress* (זונה, *zônâ*) of Prov (6:26) has the same proclivities toward unfaithfulness as do the Israelites, as stated in the tassels legislation (Num 15:39b: אשר־אתם זנים אחריהם, *'ăšer 'attem zōnîm 'aḥărêhem, after which you whore*)—and each mnemonic, apotropaic object representing Torah is envisaged to expel this malicious spirit.[141] In this way also are the tassels (ציצת) "jouant le rôle de breloques et d'amulettes."[142]

Consequently, the high priestly blessing is the material for phylacteries which in Jewish tradition are utilized as amulets to preserve health and elongate life, warding off anything sinister that would compromise it; the tassel likewise, which represents Torah and the obedience of Torah which leads to sustained life, may be seen in an apotropaic light.

Conclusion

In the course of this chapter, I have set out to explore the apotropaic functions of the people's tassels and high priest's rosette in the HB, and their apotropaic counterparts in Levantine culture and religion, clothing design, and accoutrements. In the iconography of the ANE, only gods or divine figures and kings are (re)presented wearing rosettes on some sort of headdress. As a Persian colony (during the formation and finalization of the HB), the Jews consequently could not have a king bedazzled in rosettes (contra Ps 132:17–18). Instead, the characteristic feature of the kingly/godly headdress is (re)appropriated for the high priest, who, like the divine figures of the Levant, would serve as a propitiatory mediator on behalf of the people before YHWH. Furthermore, through the ideological–theological priestly outlook of H and P, the Israelites also shared in the role of the high priest (i.e., a kingdom of priests [Exod 19:6]) as represented in wearing tassels of mixed fabrics (Num 15:37–41; cf. Deut 22:12), as per the high priest's regalia (Exod 28). As a result, the communalization of an otherwise royal, sovereign emblem to the common person, in the form of tassels, is fairly unique to Israelite culture and religion.

---

140. Cf. *ANET*, 427. The location of heart and neck, in Prov 6:21, is a deviation from arm and forehead, in Deut 6:8 and 11:18b; although Deut 11:18a reads, "You shall put these words of mine in your heart and soul" (NRSV), *soul* (נפש, *nepeš*) sometimes meaning *neck* (Pss 69:2; 105:18; 124:4; Jonah 2:6; cf. *HALOT* 1:712).

141. So E.A. Speiser, "Palil and Congeners: A Sampling of Apotropaic Symbols," in *Studies in Honor of Benno Landsberger*, AS 16 (Chicago: University of Chicago Press, 1965), 391; Blau, *JE* 1:546. Cf. Michael V. Fox, *Proverbs 1–9*, AB 18A (New York: Doubleday, 2000), 228–29: "The metaphor also suggests amulet-like protection.... This does not mean that the teachings *are* an amulet, but that they are a *substitute* for one."

142. Bottéro, "Les Inventaires de Qanta," 15. See also Noth, *Numbers*, 117–18; Noth, *Exodus*, 225; Gerhard von Rad, *Deuteronomy: A Commentary*, trans. Dorothea Barton, OTL (Philadelphia: Westminster, 1966), 141.

I have argued that the connection between the rosette/tassels and their purported apotropaic function lies in their concomitant function as amulets. Amulets, also protective and evil-averting in nature, come in two relevant forms. First are floral-designed seals, because flowers are a sign of life (since they have an ongoing affect even after they are uprooted); second are amuletic objects such as phylacteries which have a mnemonic purpose and can be something worn and visible for use. The function of the rosette design and a mnemonic item, moreover, is found in the tassel. A subsidiary reinforcement for the aforementioned connection is the role of the high priestly blessing (Num 6:24–26); its contents are the material for amulets (e.g., Ketef Hinnom) and for apotropaic activity (i.e., incantations). Thus, apotropaism and the floral design of rosette/tassels (*ציץ) converge.

Therefore, by *gazing* (צוץ II) at the *flower* (ציץ ≈ ציצת) to *remember* (≈ צוץ II) the commandments of YHWH, the result is human *flourishing* or *blossoming* (צוץ I; see Ps 72:16; Isa 27:6), namely a life guarded from evil by means of covenantal faithfulness. As a consequence, the tassels (ציצת), and the rosette (ציץ), are apotropaic adornments to clothing so that Israel, like the high priest, might be(come) holy unto YHWH their God (Exod 28:38; 39:30; Num 15:39–40).

4

TAMAR AND TAMAR: CLOTHING AS DECEPTION AND DEFIANCE

Sara M. Koenig

There are two Tamars in the HB, and at first glance their stories seem quite different. Tamar in Genesis is the daughter-in-law of Judah, and she takes surprising initiative after Judah lied to her about giving her one of his sons as a husband. Through Judah, she becomes the mother of twins Perez and Zerah; Perez is the ancestor of King David. Tamar in 2 Samuel is the daughter of King David who is raped by her half-brother Amnon (who is killed two years later by her full brother Absalom). One could read the stories as having an inverse relationship to each other. For example, the story of Tamar in Genesis contains elements of comedy,[1] while the story of Tamar in 2 Samuel is tragic. One takes initiative sexually but the other is victimized.[2] The name Tamar means "date palm," though only the Tamar in Genesis is "fertile and fruitful" to bear sons; the Tamar in 2 Samuel is "fruitless and barren."[3] However, upon closer examination, the two stories share much more than just the names of the women, as both stories deal with patriarchal injustice.[4] Of special interest to this study, both characters wear specific clothing

---

1. Cf. Melissa Jackson, "Lot's Daughters and Tamar as Tricksters and the Patriarchal Narratives as Feminist Theology," *JSOT* 98 (2002): 29–46, Victor Matthews, *More Than Meets the Ear* (Grand Rapids, MI: Eerdmans, 2008), etc.

2. In fact, Fokkelein van Dijk Hemmes argues that the Tamar in Genesis is a midrash on the Tamar in Samuel, pointing out that women can and should take initiative in sexual situations and victimization is not the only model. "'Tamar and the Limits of Patriarchy': Between Rape and Seduction (2 Samuel 13 and Genesis 38)," in *Anti-Covenant*, ed. Mieke Bal (Sheffield: The Almond, 1989).

3. Tikvah Frymer Kensky makes the point that a date palm "must be pollinated by direct human action," in *Reading the Women of the Bible: A New Interpretation of Their Stories* (New York: Schocken Books, 2002), 266.

4. Both stories also share men (Judah and Absalom) who are influenced by other men (Hirah and Jonadab). Both involve some sort of deception: Amnon pretends to be sick, and Tamar's disguise involves some sort of pretense and deception. Both chapters use the verb

that they use as tools of agency, tools that turn them from passive recipients to active agents. Both Tamars use their clothing to defy the simplistic social roles of their environment. Both women are trapped, and what they do with their clothes leads to a level of liberation.[5] Based on the function of clothing in each story, the apparent differences between the two are subverted in light of their underlying similarity.

Clothing plays an important narratological role in each story.[6] Tamar of Genesis takes off her widow's clothes and covers herself with a veil as a disguise. This disguise is successful, and Judah understands her to be a prostitute. After Tamar sleeps with Judah, she takes off her veil and puts on her widow's clothes again. Tamar in 2 Samuel is dressed in an ornate robe, the kind of robe worn by "virgin daughters" of the king. After she is raped by Amnon, she puts ashes on her head and tears the ornate robe. Their garments are clearly part of the characterization of both Tamars, reflecting the various roles of widows, harlots, and virgin daughters. In fact, materialist readings would suggest that the garments themselves have force of their own, and the line between what the garments do and what the women do with their garments is blurred.[7] As the women engage in embodied practice with their clothing, their action is doubly communicative. The acts—of veiling

---

ראה, *r'h*, "to see," as the cakes Tamar makes are to be seen by Absalom (13:5–6) and sight and seeing is a *leitmotif* throughout Gen 38. Both chapters also include the time of sheep shearing, though it is the setting for Absalom's revenge on Amnon at the end of the chapter of 2 Sam 13 and happens in the middle of the chapter of Gen 38. Richard Elliot Friedman proposes that both texts are from the same author. He compares Absalom's vengeance on Amnon with the story of Simeon and Levi's vengeance on Shechem in Gen 34, noting how in both, brothers are avenging a sexual violation of their sister (15–16), but also affirms, "J has a Tamar also, the ancestor of the latter Tamar. Both are stories about sexual relations within a family. Revenge is taken for the Court History's Tamar when they are shearing (2 Sam 13:24); revenge is taken for J's Tamar when they are shearing (Gen 38:12)." *The Hidden Book in the Bible* (San Francisco, CA: HarperSanFrancisco, 1998), 17.

5. Of course, the liberation experienced by the Genesis Tamar is more complete than that of the 2 Samuel Tamar, which contributes to the tragedy of the latter story.

6. Ora Horn Prousser defines the narratological use of clothing as involving "the way in which dress is used to enhance the narrative … while each use of clothing may be symbolic on its own, the use of dress in the narrative as a whole is literary in character, paralleling, focusing and enriching the narrative text." "Suited to the Throne: The Symbolic Use of Clothing in the David and Saul Narratives," *JSOT* 71 (1996): 28.

7. Indeed, a materialist reading of the garments of Tamar and Tamar could extend certain ideas in this chapter. A phenomenological approach would also be complimentary to this narratology, highlighting the Tamars' embodied practice of wearing and changing clothing. My focus on the agency of the female characters is certainly not the only lens through which to read this narrative; as Shawn Flynn explains, in addition to understanding the communicative function of clothing in the narrative, one can also identify the constitutive function of clothing. In this volume, 17, 33–36.

and unveiling, of tearing—communicate, and the clothing—the veil, the widow's garments, the torn robe—also communicates. Specifically, the alteration of the garments allows both to protest their situations. What they both do with their clothing exposes the patriarchal injustices they have experienced; the actions of veiling and tearing are ultimately revealing.

Dress is one aspect of characterization, though typically the HB will not give detailed descriptions of a character's clothing.[8] Shimon Bar-Efrat notes that when clothing is mentioned, it is often done so to advance the plot; he writes, "In most of the instances in which clothing is specified, we are told what is *done* with it."[9] This is true for both of the Tamar stories: there is little detail as to the description of the garments, aside from their social role. And to Bar-Efrat's point, what is done with the garments is narrated: the widow's clothes are removed, and traded for a veil before being put on again. The robes are torn. These women—who have less social agency than the males in their stories—use their clothes as tools to further the plot, or to express and expose what has happened to them.[10]

Barbara Green suggests that dress in the HB can itself be understood as text to be read. She writes:

> Clothing is significant at the spatial and temporal plane of a narrative, communicating in space and time. It matters whether clothing is on or off, and to change it signifies fresh choices. Clothing is apt or not, depending on situation and context. At the psychological plane, making and giving clothing, receiving and returning it, wearing it and seeing it worn give clues to character's perceptions. And at the phraseological plane, clothing can be discussed, and it can communicate. Clothing functions as text, as richly polyvalent text. Clothes are not just given, received and worn but written, read variously, rewritten, reread variously, by characters and by the reader of the narrative.[11]

---

8. This lack of detail about clothing is entirely commensurate with the HB's typical lack of detail about physical appearance. In contrast, a novel like *Jane Eyre* has the title character observing the specifics of the garments worn by women who come to visit Thornfield, as follows, "Lady Lynn was a large and stout personage of about forty, very erect, very haughty-looking, richly dressed in a satin robe of changeful sheen … Mrs. Colonel Dent was less showy; but I thought, more ladylike. She had a slight figure, a pale, gentle face, and fair hair. Her black satin dress, her scarf of rich foreign lace, and her pearl ornaments, pleased me better than the rainbow radiance of the titled dame." Charlotte Bronte, *Jane Eyre* (London: McMillian Collector's Library, 2003), 231. Insofar as these two characters' clothing is part of their physical appearance, it expresses aspects of their characters.

9. Shimon Bar Efrat, *Narrative Art in the Bible* (JSOTSup 70; Sheffield: Almond, 1989), 51.

10. Kate Wilkinson quotes anthropologist Sherry Ortner to make the point that "agency" ought not be limited to the typical lens of Western individualism, with the agent as an autonomous actor. *Women and Modesty in Late Antiquity* (Cambridge: Cambridge University Press, 2015), 21.

11. Barbara Green, *What Profit for Us? Remembering the Story of Joseph* (Lanham, MD: University Press of America, 1996), 73–74.

Attentive reading and re-reading of the clothing of Tamars in light of the larger surrounding narratives may highlight how clothing functions differently for men and for women. In the larger Joseph story, clothing functions as markers of status, authority, and identity,[12] and in the David and Saul narratives, garments symbolize Saul's fall and David's rise.[13] For the Tamars, clothing goes beyond symbolic markers of status to catalyze their action, deception, and defiance. Both are entrapped, and their actions with their garments yield a level of liberation. This chapter will consider the individual accounts of each Tamar before examining how both narratives contribute to a larger understanding of the role garments play for women in the HB.

Tamar in Genesis

The account of Tamar and Judah is sometimes seen as an interruption within the Joseph narrative of Gen 37–50, but in fact it is integral to the larger story. In Gen 38:1 and 39:1 the same verb introduces the series of events; both Judah and Joseph וירד, *wyrd* and הורד, *hwrd* (respectively) "go down" before the rest of the family will go down to Egypt.[14] At the end of Gen 37, Jacob is in mourning for Joseph, and his refusal to be comforted[15] is in marked contrast with Judah, whose period of mourning for his wife has a definitive end. Moreover, as mentioned above, clothing plays a significant role throughout Gen 37–50. Jacob gave Joseph a specific garment to signal his favoritism, and the other brothers subsequently deceive their father with that bloodied and torn robe. Joseph leaves his cloak in the hands of Potiphar's wife (39:12–13), changes his clothes before meeting with the Pharaoh (41:14), and finally gets clothed with garments befitting his high status (41:42).

Tamar's garments play an important role in what happens to her, as can be observed in the structure of the narrative. Tamar's actions with Judah are enveloped by her dressing and undressing: she takes off her widow's garments and puts on a veil (38:14) before she goes out to meet Judah, and after their encounter, she takes off her veil and puts on her widow's garments (38:19). Within this story, it is—largely—clear what Tamar does: she changes her garments, she sleeps with Judah, and gets pregnant. It is less clear *why* she does it, even with the relatively good insight into motivations within this narrative as compared with other biblical narratives. Between the "what" and the "why" is Tamar's clothing, which becomes

---

12. See Victor Matthews, "The Anthropology of Clothing in the Joseph Narrative," *JSOT* 65 (1995): 25–36 and John R. Huddlestun, "Divesture, Deception and Demotion: The Garment Motif in Genesis 37–39," *JSOT* 98 (2002): 47–62.

13. Prousser, "Suited to the Throne," 28ff. Cf. also Sean Cook's chapter in this volume, where he argues that the narrator of 1 Samuel refers to Saul's garments and battle gear in ways that communicate Saul's progressive alienation and justifies his downfall.

14. Green, *What Profit for Us*, 63.

15. Gen 37:35. Jacob's beloved wife and the mother of Joseph, Rachel, is also said to refuse to be comforted in Jer 31:15.

almost a character in itself. At the least, Tamar's clothing is an "actant"[16] in the larger story, with "power to modulate and alter societal interactions."[17]

Tamar: Entrapment

Before Tamar enters the scene, it is set by Judah "descending" from his brothers and settling "near a certain Adullamite named Hirah." The fabula[18] of the story proceeds rapidly: Judah finds a wife, begets three sons, and takes a wife—Tamar—for his eldest son in the narrative space of four short verses. Story time does not match real time. Beginning in verse 7, time slows down, but the slower pace does not include longer explanations. For example, Er, Judah's firstborn son, is evil in God's sight and is killed. Er's name ער, ʿr is an anagram with his moral quality, רע, rʿ "evil," but no other details are given. After Er's brief and barely explained death, Judah commands his second son to perform Levirate duties toward his dead brother by "going in to Tamar" and "raising up offspring" for her. Onan does not, and is killed. Onan's death is introduced with the same phrase that introduced Er's death in 38:7; רע בעיני יהוה, rʿ bʿyny yhwh, "evil in the eyes of YHWH." But in v. 10 there is the added specification that אשר עשה, ʾšr ʿśh, "what [Onan] did" was the reason he was killed, and the previous verse ascribes motive; Onan saw that the heir would not be his own, so he spilled his semen on the ground. That is why YHWH killed him.

The text says nothing about the relationship between Tamar and Er, including whether or not that marriage was consummated, nor does the text give details about Tamar and Onan's relationship. But we ought not miss the fact that though Tamar will take initiative to become pregnant by Judah, she, like the Tamar in 2 Samuel, is sexually violated and trapped. Certainly Tamar in 2 Samuel is violated grievously and egregiously when she is raped by Amnon. But Tamar in Genesis is also violated by Onan's practice of coitus interruptus. Even if he only practiced it once before he was killed, there had to have been enough to have been interrupted. Hillel Milgrim agrees that we are not told how long Onan's practice continues, but writes, "This gives Onan the best of both worlds: he has full and frequent sexual use of Tamar but also prevents her from producing an heir to her late husband."[19]

---

16. This term is borrowed from A. J. Greimas' semiological model of narratives, where there are six possible facets or "actants" involved in the action of a plot: (1) the subject who relates to (2) the object; (3) the sender, who will send to (4) the receiver; (5) the helper who helps accomplish the action, who is contrasted with (6) the opponent who hinders it. In *Sémantique Structurale* (Paris: Presse universitaires de France, 1986).

17. Cf. Heather McKay, "Clothing, Adornment and Accouterments," in *Samuel, Kings and Chronicles, I: Texts@Contexts*, ed. Athalya Brenner-Idan and Archie C.C. Lee (London: Bloomsbury T&T Clark, 2017), 240.

18. This is a term from Russian Formalism, and refers to the chronological events of the story, as distinct from the "*sujet*," which refers to how the story is told.

19. Hillel Milgram, *Four Biblical Heroines and the Case for Female Authorship: An Analysis of the Women of Ruth, Esther and Genesis 38* (Jefferson, NC: McFarland & Company, 2007), 80.

After Onan's death, Tamar is trapped in the social status of widowhood, wearing the trappings that mark her social role. Not until she changes her garments will her social status and role also change.

Onan's death means that Judah has only one living son by the end of 38:10, whereas five verses earlier he had three sons. Judah's future, as Green comments, "appears severely diminished; not since Abraham and Sarah has an ancestral pair been reliant on merely one son."[20] Judah then speaks to Tamar, who is identified by the narrator as "his daughter-in-law." He commands her to remain a widow in her own father's house until Shelah grows up. Nothing in the text defines Shelah's age and how long Tamar will ostensibly need to wait. In fact, such a detail is irrelevant in light of Judah's fear that Shelah may also die; Judah will not give Shelah to Tamar (Gen 38:11). Two things related to Judah are striking. First, he—incorrectly—sees Tamar as the danger to his sons. T. J. Wray explains it as follows:

> Judah thinks Tamar is a toxic bride and fears losing another son (Gen 38:11). It is clear that he has no intention of allowing Shelah anywhere near Bridezilla, not now, not ever. While the reader knows the truth behind Judah's actions, Tamar does not. This makes her a sad victim of Judah's fears.[21]

Indeed, the readers of the story know that it is not Tamar, but YHWH who caused the sons' deaths, and if any human is to blame, it is the sons themselves for their "evil." Second, as Wray notes, Judah's words are a lie; he has no intention of giving Shelah to Tamar. He will not do what he says he will do, for his fears prevent him from doing so. Green notes the analogy between Judah and Onan as both attempt to "stop time, appearing to do what is needed while simultaneously vitiating the action the family owes."[22] Green describes Tamar as being placed "on hold,"[23] but that description may be too soft. Rather, Tamar is trapped. As she goes to live with her father (38:11), she still legally belongs to Judah, and is supposed to perpetually wait for something that will not happen, not free to marry another, continually wearing the garments of widowhood.

The next event in the story is another death. It is not Shelah who dies, as Judah feared, but Judah's unnamed wife.[24] Now with the death of his wife, Shelah is all that Judah has. Again, there are no details, just the fact of her death.[25] Moreover,

---

20. Green, *What Profit for Us*, 64.
21. T.J. Wray, *Good Girls, Bad Girls* (Lanham, MD: Rowman & Littlefield, 2008), 104–05.
22. Green, *What Profit for Us*, 65.
23. Ibid.
24. She is the "daughter of Shua," so there is some possibility that she is linked with Bathshua, identified in 1 Chronicles 3:5 as Bathsheba.
25. Green comments, "Given that Judah suspects their partner as the cause of the death of his two sons, the reader may wonder who is the culprit when another spouse dies. In a story where Judah projects onto others deeds that he is slow to see himself doing, the suspicion is not unfounded." *What Profit for Us*, 64–65.

there is no narrative space between Judah's wife's death and his comfort, for a single sentence announces both: "The wife of Judah died and Judah was comforted" (38:12).²⁶ The chapter began with Judah ירד, *yrd*, "going down," and now he עלה, *'lh* "goes up" to the particular location of Timnah, for the time of sheep-shearing (38:12).²⁷ All these specific details—the where, the what, and the when—are important because they are the catalyst for Tamar's clothing change.

Tamar: Action

Green asserted that the wearing of clothing and seeing clothing worn give "clues to character's perceptions,"²⁸ and this is particularly true for Tamar. Her actions of changing her clothing are enveloped by her perceptions of hearing and seeing. Before she takes off her widow's garment and puts on a veil she hears about Judah,²⁹ and after she goes to Petah Enaim, the text explains "for she saw that Shelah had grown, but she had not been given to him as a wife" (38:14). In other words, Tamar's clothing change was preceded by her hearing and followed by her seeing. The location where she stations herself suggests more perception, as Petah Enaim means "opening of the eyes" in Hebrew.³⁰ Tamar sees things clearly, with open eyes.

Judah's sight, by contrast, is myopic. When Judah sees her, "he thought her to be a prostitute, for she כסה, *ksh* covered her face" (38:15). Bar-Efrat asserts, "The object of changing her clothes is clear: Tamar does not want Judah to recognize her, and even wants him to think she is a harlot."³¹ The specific verb translated as

---

26. The verse begins with the temporal description, "in the fullness of days." If this refers to both events in the sentence, and not simply the wife's death, then Judah could be understood to have mourned for a certain, full amount of time after which he is comforted. Nevertheless, there is a stark contrast between Judah's comfort here, and his father Jacob's refusal to be comforted in the previous chapter (37:35).

27. Tammi Schneider suggests that "sheep-shearing" is a euphemism for "having sex," which would explain some of the specifics of what transpires between Judah and Tamar. *Mothers of Promise: Women in the Book of Genesis* (Grand Rapids, MI: Baker Academic, 2008), 137. Green notes how the time is the reason why Tamar must act so swiftly: even if Judah is (only) going to shear sheep, such an event happens only once a year, and perhaps it is an opportune time of the month for Tamar to do what she will do. *What Profit for Us*, 66.

28. Green, *What Profit for Us*, 74.

29. Literally ויגד, *wygd*, she "was told," 38:13.

30. In the Midrash Rabbah, the rabbis explain the name of the place as follows, "It teaches that she lifted up her eyes to the gate (*petha*ḥ) to which all eyes (*'enayim*) are directed and prayed: 'May it be Thy will that I do not leave this house with nought.'" Freedman, *Midrash Rabbah Genesis* (London: The Soncino, 1983), 794.

31. Bar Efrat, *Narrative Art*, 51. Bar Efrat also uses Gen 38:15 as one of his examples of "cognition," saying that Judah's thinking Tamar to be a prostitute is a place where the narrator knows the inner workings of the human character. *Narrative Art*, 20.

"thought" is חשב, ḥšb, a word that can be used for false assessments.[32] Both the LXX and Vulgate of 38:15 add the phrase that Judah did not recognize Tamar.[33] Such a detail—not in the MT— emphasizes his lack of recognition, and suggests that the veil has more to do with Tamar's hiding her true identity than portraying her as a prostitute. And yet, it is not only the veil which leads to Judah's misperception, it is also her location and her solitude. Joan Goodnick Westenholz asserts that the veil by itself only serves as a physical disguise, and may not have other significance to the story. She argues that it is the location that defines Tamar's "social status as a prostitute."[34] Victor Matthews explains, "Judah is unable to see Tamar as anything but a prostitute because his cognitive perception has been channeled by her clothing, her physical location and that she is unaccompanied."[35] Moreover, Judah is the only person who "sees" Tamar dressed up as a prostitute; as the inquiries by Hirah the Adullamite demonstrate (38:20–22), no one else saw her.[36] Tikvah Frymer Kensky describes what happens as follows: "Using her veil as an anti-recognition strategy, sitting at the 'opening of the eyes,' she draws a veil across Judah's eyes and prevents him from seeing her identity."[37]

Though Judah perceives Tamar to be a זנה, znh, "prostitute" (38:15, cf. v. 24), he later refers to her as אשה, 'šh, "woman/wife" (38:20) when he sends Hirah to give her a kid in exchange for the items he gave her in pledge.[38] Hirah, in turn, refers to her as קדשה, qdšh, "temple prostitute" (38:21, 22). Phyllis Bird understands this as an "issue of opprobrium … Hirah knows how to handle the situation; he uses a euphemism."[39] By contrast, Westenholz explains that Hirah is "denying the affair

---

32. Maren Niehoff, "Do Biblical Characters Talk to Themselves?" *JBL* 111 (1992): 579. The word can be understood as "thought," or "reckoned" in situations that may or may not be true. It can also be translated as "regard" as in Isa 33:8, or to "devise" works, as in the Tabernacle instructions in Ex 26. It is also used in Gen 15:6, when after Abram sees the stars in the sky, God "thinks him righteous."

33. Huddlestun, "Divesture, Deception and Demotion," 58.

34. Joan Goodnick Westenholz, "Tamar, *Qedesa*, *Qadistu*, and Sacred Prostitution in Mesopotamia," *HTR* 82 (1989): 247.

35. Matthews, *More Than Meets the Ear*, 47.

36. Green, *What Profit for Us*, 68.

37. Frymer-Kensky, *Reading the Women of the Bible*, 270.

38. These items are tantamount to handing over a driver's license, passport, and social security card; things incredibly personal to Judah. Green asserts that Judah's "staff, cord and seal are his equivalent of clothing." *What Profit for Us*, 77–78. Wray describes the transaction as follows: she asserts that Judah, as recently widowed, "lacks experience with the protocols of the sex trade. Not so with Tamar, who has apparently done her homework. We can almost see her smirking under her veil as Judah hands over his identifying accoutrements." *Good Girls, Bad Girls*, 107.

39. Phyllis Bird, "The Harlot as Heroine," *Semeia* 46 (1989): 126.

and pretending to take the kid to the קדשׁה [qĕdēšā] for a sacrifice, as in Hos 4:14."[40] Matthews responds by writing:

> This is possible, but it would erode the comic character of the episode. Compounding the rhetorical game playing, Judah chooses to use a term that means both woman and wife. Hirah, who may be making a value judgment on the affair, uses a cultic term, as do the people of Enaim, who are pleased to be able to deny any such person exists as a way of staying out of the whole thing.[41]

Tamar: Liberation

Green also asserts, as mentioned above, that changing clothing signifies fresh choices.[42] Tamar's actions, more closely considered, show three verbs associated with her clothing: she סור, *swr* "takes off" her widow's garment, כסה, *ksh* "covers" herself with a veil, and עלף, *ʿlp* "wraps" herself. In 38:19 she will again סור, *swr* "take off" the veil, but this time she will לבשׁ, *lbš* "dress" herself, in the garments of widowhood. Matthews notes that when clothing is changed, social markers also shift. He argues that without a legal change of status (like remarriage) it was a socially inappropriate act for Tamar to take off her widow's clothes and put on a veil.[43] Yet, it is precisely the socially inappropriate nature of Tamar's act which indicates her defiance and subversion of the social norms. Moreover, Tamar worked within the social codes of clothing to subvert larger social codes, such as those governing marriage and remarriage. Nelly Furman describes Tamar's actions as calling attention to two differing social functions of garments: their use as symbols in sexual code, and as masks and disguises. Furman understands Tamar to be making use of these social codes for her own purposes.[44]

Tamar's specific garment צעלף, *ṣʿlp*, the "veil," deserves attention.[45] When Judah sees her, "he thought her to be a prostitute, for she כסה, *ksh* 'covered' her face" (38:15). Many commentators focus on the veil—not the action of covering her face—and assume that the veil is the garment of a prostitute, that prostitutes cover

---

40. Westenholz, "Tamar, *Qedesa*, *Qadistu*, and Sacred Prostitution in Mesopotamia," 248.
41. Matthews, *More Than Meets the Ear*, 60.
42. Green, *What Profit for Us*, 73.
43. Matthews, *More Than Meets the Ear*, 39.
44. Furman, "His Story versus Her Story: Male Genealogy versus Female Strategy in the Jacob Cycle," in *Women in the Hebrew Bible: A Reader*, ed. Alice Bach, 122-24 (New York: Routledge, 1999).
45. Wilkinson reviews the significance of veiling in a variety of places and contexts, including in New Testament texts, the Christian patristic era, Islam, etc. *Women and Modesty in Late Antiquity*, 48-56.

their faces with a veil.⁴⁶ Certain cognate ANE texts might call this assumption into question. Hittite Marriage Laws state that a man whose wife has committed adultery can veil her as a way to make a public proclamation that he wants to reinstate her as his wife. Thus, veiling confirms or reconfirms the marital status of a woman whose position as a wife has been brought into question.⁴⁷ In the Middle Assyrian law, the veil was a mark of distinction for a free woman; married women did not typically wear veils. Linguistic evidence suggests that veiling is part of the marriage ceremony: in Akkadia, a bride was called *kallatu kutumtu*, "the veiled bride." *Pussumtu*, "the veiled one" is another term for *kallatu*, "bride." Another Middle Assyrian law prohibited a prostitute from wearing a veil: if she was found veiled, she would be flogged fifty times and have hot tar poured on her head. Bird asserts, "It is useless to argue from the Middle Assyrian Laws to practices in Canaan since dress is a matter of local or regional custom," though she notes how the reference to the "prostitute's forehead" in Jer 3:3 suggests that prostitutes in Canaan are not always veiled.⁴⁸ The only other place in the MT that the word צעלף, *ṣʿlp*, "veil" occurs is with Rebekah in Gen 24:65, who covers her face with a veil in preparation to meet—and marry—Isaac.⁴⁹ David Gunn and Danna Nolan Fewell suggest that Tamar's intent is to publically present herself as a bride to indicate that Judah has failed to uphold her rights and those of her dead husband.⁵⁰

The בגדי אלמנות, *bgdy ʾlmnwt*, "widow's garments" do not occur much more frequently than the "veil." However, another woman who "took off her widow's garments" is Judith, who does so in order to adorn herself so that she may seduce—and ultimately behead—the Assyrian general Holofernes. Unlike Tamar, Judith has not covered her face; in Jdt 10:23 the text says, "When Judith came into the presence of Holofernes and his servants, they all marveled at the beauty of her face." Judith's song in chapter 16 highlights the motivation for her clothing

---

46. For example, Matthew Henry explains, "It should seem, it was the custom of harlots, in those times, to cover their faces, that, though they were not ashamed, yet they might seem to be so. The sin of uncleanness did not then go so barefaced as it does now." http://www.biblestudytools.com/commentaries/matthew-henry-complete/genesis/38.html

47. Tsevat, "The Husband Veils a Wife," *Journal of Cuneiform Studies* 27.4 (October 1975): 238.

48. Bird, "The Harlot as Heroine," 135 n. 15.

49. Some assume that Leah was veiled in Gen 29, which is why Jacob didn't recognize her, though the word צעלף does not occur there. The Midrash Rabbah explains that Rebekah and Tamar were the two who, "covered themselves with a veil and gave birth to twins." *Midrash Rabbah Genesis*, 794.

50. David Gunn and Danna Nolan Fewell, *Gender, Power and Promise: The Subject of the Bible's First Story* (Nashville, TN: Abingdon, 1992), 87–89. In her midrash on Tamar, Nancy Bowen suggests that one benefit of the veil is hiding Tamar's lack of tears for Er's death. "Women, Violence, and the Bible," in *Engaging the Bible in a Gendered World: An Introduction to Feminist Biblical Interpretation in Honor of Katharine Doob Sakenfeld*, ed. Linda Day and Carolyn Pressler (Louisville, KY: Westminster John Knox, 2006), 196.

change; "For she put away her widow's clothing to exalt the oppressed in Israel" (Jdt 16:7). Erin K. Vearncombe notes the irony of how this story has been received, for women are typically assessed negatively when they dress in order to seduce. Judith, however, is praised by early male Christian interpreters who positively evaluate Judith's action. Vearncombe writes:

> We see clearly that dress defines the identity of Judith and structures the movement of the narrative. We know Judith from beginning to end through dress, and it is Judith's use of dress, her careful construction and presentation of her body, that brings about the climax of text: the murder of Holofernes, and the resulting salvation of her people. Judith, in "dressing to kill," actually dresses to preserve and save.[51]

In Isa 54:4, a time is promised when the חרפת אלמנות, ḥrpt 'lmnwt, "reproach of widowhood" will no longer be remembered. Though the reference is not specifically to בגדי אלמנות, bgdy 'lmnwt, "garments of widowhood," the chapter in Isaiah also uses other words that occur in the story of 2 Samuel Tamar. When Tamar implores Amnon to talk to their father the king, she asks, "where could I cause my חרפה, ḥrpt reproach to go?" (2 Sam 13:13). In Isa 54:1, the children of the שׁמם, šmm, "desolate one" are affirmed to be more numerous than the children of the בעלה, b'lh, "married wife." That promise does not come true for the Tamar in 2 Samuel, who remains שׁממ, šmm, "desolate" in her brother Absalom's house (2 Sam 13:20). It is the Tamar in Genesis whose widowhood is not permanent, who will give birth to twins, "more numerous" than a typical birth. Those twins, of course, provide two more sons to Judah after his first two were killed. Tamar's actions of deception and defiance are ultimately redemptive to preserve the line of Judah, and his descendants David and Jesus, whose actions are also redemptive.

Tamar's clear perceptions and fresh, bold choices are enacted through her dress. As Tamar changes her garments, she is a character who does something with her clothing. But the reverse is also true, where her clothing allows her do to something: her veil allowed her to encounter Judah in a way she would not have otherwise had she remained in her father's house wearing the garments of widowhood. This aspect of Tamar's clothing illustrates how clothing can be costume, helping a person to act in a way she might not otherwise if she were not wearing the specific garments. Tamar's change of clothing made her effective in procuring offspring, something she would not have otherwise been able to do.

Additionally, Tamar's specific garments illustrate aspects of her character, and are suggestive of her identity as widow or prostitute, but in complicated ways. The external trappings identify her, but she also uses the misidentification for her own purposes. External trappings similarly identify people today, but we must be wary

---

51. Erin K. Vearncombe, "Adorning the Protagonist: The Use of Dress in the Book of Judith," in *Dressing Judeans and Christians in Antiquity*, ed. Kristi Upson-Saia, Carly Daniel-Hughes, Alicia J. Batten (Farnham, Surrey, England; Burlington, VT: Ashgate, 2014), 3.

of falling into simplistic traps of thinking that a garment is definitive. For example, someone may wear camouflage to indicate their membership in a military group, or as an ironic comment on such group membership, or simply because it is on the fashion runways this season.[52] Tamar—and her clothing—serves as a reminder that appearance may be deceptive[53]: the one whom Judah (mis)understood to be a prostitute was the one whom he declared as more righteous than himself (Gen 38:26).[54]

Tamar in 2 Samuel

Dress plays less of a narratological role in 2 Sam 13 than it did in Gen 38. In the tragic tale in 2 Samuel, Tamar tears her robe after Amnon rapes her and sends her away. In Genesis, clothing changes enveloped the action of sleeping with Judah (38:14 and 19), while in 2 Samuel, the clothing is altered in response to the action (13:18–19). But clothing is still significant in the later pericope, and highlights a connection between the two accounts: as mentioned above, the words describing 2 Samuel Tamar's robe are the same used to describe Joseph's garment in Gen 37:3, 23, 32, in the chapter immediately preceding the story of the Genesis Tamar. Though 2 Samuel Tamar's garment is less crucial for the plot, and what she does with her robe does not ultimately liberate her, her robe still conveys her entrapment, her action, and her attempts at liberation.

Tamar: Entrapment

In the very first verse of 2 Sam 13, where Tamar is introduced she is entrapped in a literary structure that Phyllis Trible describes as a "ring composition," within which "circular patterns reflect the whole."[55] In 13:1, Tamar is introduced in the center of the verse, after "Absalom son of David" and before "Amnon son of David"; Tamar is identified as Absalom's sister. Literarily, the two men surround Tamar. In 13:2 there is another circle, but here only Amnon encircles Tamar. The first clause explains that Amnon is so tormented that he makes himself ill on account

---

52. Ann Margaret Brach, "Identity and Intersubjectivity," in *Identities through Fashion: A Multi-Disciplinary Approach*, ed. Ana Marta González and Laura Bovone (London: Bloomsbury Academic, 2012), 117.

53. Huddlestun highlights the deceptive aspects of Tamar's veiling, describing it as "trickery," in "Divesture, Deception and Demotion," 56.

54. Obviously, this is a relative righteousness, and Judah has hardly been a paragon of righteousness thus far. In the Midrash Rabbah, R. Jeremiah interpreted in the name of R. Samuel b. R. Isaac that it was not Judah who said this, but "it was the Holy Spirit that exclaimed, Through me (*mimmeni*) did these things occur." *Midrash Rabbah Genesis*, 797.

55. Phyllis Trible, *Texts of Terror: Literary-Feminist Readings of Biblical Narratives* (Minneapolis, MN: Fortress, 1984), 38.

of Tamar, and after she is named, the final clause explains that it was impossible in Amnon's eyes to do anything to her.

In addition to being described as sister to Absalom, there are two other descriptions in the center of the ring compositions: in 13:1, Tamar is described as יפה, *yph*, "beautiful" and in 13:2, she is identified as בתולה, *btwlh*, "a virgin."[56] Both those descriptors help build the trap, and will be discussed in turn. First, the adjective "beautiful" is applied to a number of characters in the HB.[57] Bar-Efrat notes that while Hebrew narrative does not often give details about a character's appearance, most often a description is connected with the plot; for example, Absalom's abundant hair (2 Sam 14:26) will play a part in his death (2 Sam 18:9).[58] Matthew Henry makes the connection between Tamar's beauty and the danger she is in, saying:

> Beauty is a snare to many; it was so to her. She was fair, and therefore Amnon coveted her, v. 1. Those that are peculiarly handsome have no reason, on that account, to be proud, but great reason to stand upon their watch.[59]

Henry's language of "snare" highlights how Tamar's beauty was a kind of a trap.[60] Second, Tamar's virginity is mentioned twice: first, in 2 Sam 13:2, and a second time in 2 Sam 13:18, in connection with the garment she wears. Frank Yamada explains that as a virgin, Tamar is in a prized position in terms of her sexuality and relation to marriage,[61] but the prized position turns out to be problematic. As noted, the clause כי בתולה היא, *ky btwlh hy'*, "for she was a virgin" in 2 Sam 13:2 is sandwiched between two others: it is preceded by the clause that explains that Amnon was so tormented that he became ill, "for she was a virgin," and following it is the statement "and it was difficult in Amnon's eyes to do anything to her." Scholars are divided on which of the two surrounding clauses relates most closely

---

56. The word sometimes includes the qualifying phrase, "who has never known a man" (Gen 24:16, Num 31:18), it does not do so here. בתולה more precisely can be translated as "young woman." Cf. Schmitt, "Virgin," ABD VI, 853–54.

57. These include Sarai in Gen 12, Rachel in Gen 27, Joseph in Gen 39, Abigail in 1 Sam 25, David in 1 Sam 16, both Absalom and his daughter Tamar in 2 Sam 14, Abishag in 1 Kgs 1, Job's daughters in Job 42, the beloved in Song 4 and 6, etc.

58. Bar-Efrat, *Narrative Art*, 48–50.

59. http://www.biblestudytools.com/commentaries/matthew-henry-complete/2-samuel/13.html

60. By saying this, I do not in any way want to suggest that Tamar's beauty is at fault; such an implication is too close to blaming the victim. Bar-Efrat, for example, writes that Bathsheba's beauty "is mentioned solely because it plays the central role in the course of events, providing the motivation for David's … licentious behavior." *Narrative Art*, p. 49. While Bathsheba's beauty is significant, it in no way excuses David for what he does after seeing her. Similarly, Tamar's beauty cannot excuse Amnon for his sickness and violence.

61. Frank Yamada, *Configurations of Rape in the Hebrew Bible: A Literary Analysis of Three Rape Narratives* (New York: Peter Lang, 2008), 109.

to the identification of Tamar as a virgin. Many commentators have seen that Tamar's status as a virgin is what makes it difficult for Amnon because as a virgin, Tamar was ostensibly protected and guarded. That is, it was difficult for Amnon to have access to her because she was a virgin. Bar-Efrat, however, argues that the clause about Tamar's virginity is an explanation for what precedes it in the verse: the fact that Tamar is a virgin is what causes Amnon to be so tormented that he makes himself ill.[62] Yamada agrees with Bar-Efrat that Tamar's virginity is not connected with her inaccessibility, pointing out that the ease with which David sent Tamar to Amnon would belie such an understanding.[63] But Yamada also suggests that it is not only her sexual status that causes Amnon torment; it is also her status as a sister of Absalom, a potential successor—and therefore a rival of Amnon—for their father's throne.[64]

Yamada's suggestion illustrates how Tamar is trapped not only literally, and in her beauty and virginity, but also in the social world of monarchy. This can be seen more clearly in comparing the Genesis Tamar with the 2 Samuel Tamar: the Genesis Tamar moves from one space to another and back; she has a relative freedom of decision making. In contrast, the 2 Samuel Tamar does not travel long distances, nor have freedom to make her own decisions. These differences can be seen to reflect a difference between the structures of the בת אב, *bt 'b*, "house of the father" and the monarchy. Though the patriarchal "house of the father" is no bastion of egalitarianism for women, the matriarchs in Genesis frequently exercise a level of autonomy to affect the events that occur. The head of the family, as powerful as he may be, is not a king. In contrast, the monarchy and palace are arguably less flexible and more restrictive for the women. Tamar in 2 Samuel is trapped by her brothers, the princes, but also trapped by the king.

The constrictions and confines of the monarchy are exemplified in Tamar's garment, which is described in 2 Sam 13:18 with the words כתנת פסים, *kĕtōnet passim*. This term only appears here, and in Gen 37:3. P. Kyle McCarter explains that the traditional translation as "coat of many colors" comes from the LXX translation of Gen 37:3 as *chitōna poikilon*, either an "embroidered" or a "variegated" garment. In 2 Sam 13:18, the LXX either translates it as a garment with sleeves reaching to the wrists (*chitōn karpōtos*, LXX[B]) or a garment reaching to the ankles (*chitōn astragalōtos*, LXX[L]).[65] Mendenhall describes *kĕtōnet passîm* as "a garment …

---

62. Bar-Efrat, *Narrative Art*, 243.
63. Yamada, *Configurations of Rape*, 109–10.
64. Ibid., 110.
65. P. Kyle McCarter, *II Samuel* (Garden City, NY: Doubleday, 1984), 325. The Genesis translation, McCarter posits, "may have been a guess based on one meaning of *pas* in Rabbinic Hebrew, viz. 'strip, stripe,'—thus *kĕtōnet passîm*, 'gown of strips' or 'striped gown.' Another postbiblical meaning of *pas* was 'palm (of the hand)' or 'sole (of the foot)'; hence the Septuagint's reading." Ibid. Adrien Bledstein explains that rabbic commentators described the garment as "so light and delicate that it could be crushed and concealed in the closed palm of one hand." "Tamar and the 'Coat of Many Colors'" in *Samuel and Kings, A Feminist Companion to the Bible*, ed. A. Brenner (Sheffield: Sheffield Academic Press, 2000), 66.

associated with the highest social or political status. In other words, the term does not describe the form of the garment, but its social function."⁶⁶ McCarter critiques Mendenhall's philology, and offers his own argument, that the term פס, *pas*, refers to extremities, and because it is plural, not dual, it means that the garment reaches to both the hands and feet, thus "a long gown with sleeves."⁶⁷ When Josephus describes Tamar's outfit, he explains, "for the virgins of the old times wore such loose coats tied at the hands and let down to the ankles, that the inner coats might not be seen."⁶⁸ This garment was meant to cover, and even confine Tamar, but it did not protect her.

The two words, *kĕtōnet passîm*, that describe the garment are modified with other terms, including מעילים, *m'ylym*, "robes," used in the end of 2 Sam 13:18. Kirkpatrick explains that the narrative is clarifying the two garments, so there is not "confusion between the robe or mantle (*mĕ'îl*) and the garment or tunic (*c'thōneth*) which were distinct."⁶⁹ A number of emendations, however, are proposed. Wellhausen proposes to emend MT's מעילים, *m'ylym*, "robes" to מעולם, *m'wlm*, "from eternity" based on Josephus' wording, "for in ancient times (*tōn archaiōn*) virgins wore ... "⁷⁰ Such an emendation is reflected in the NRSV translation of the verse, "this is how the virgin daughters of the king were clothed in earlier times." McCarter proposes, instead, an emendation of *mē'lôm* or *mē'ălûmîm* derived from the verb עלם, *'lm*, "to be sexually mature," thus translating it as "from puberty."⁷¹ Adrien Bledstein argues that no emendation is necessary, and the *kĕtōnet passîm* itself was a priestly robe because Tamar was a priestess.⁷²

As Scott Starbuck argues in this volume, a מעיל, *m'yl*, "robe" reflects an elite, royal status.⁷³ Tamar is a princess, and her connection to David is clarified in 2 Sam 13:18 when the verse explains that her clothing is worn by the בנות־המלך הבתולת, *bnwt-hmlk hbtwlt*, "virgin daughters of the king." Green comments, "Clothing

---

66. Mendenhall 1973:54–55. Mendenhall's argument rests on his identification of *kĕtōnet passim*, and specifically the Hebrew *pas* with the Ugaritic word *pd*. Mendenhall then associates the Ugaritic term and its parallel *'nn* with the Akkadian *melammū* and *puluḫtu* and the Hebrew *kābôd*, the later terms are used to refer to the "glory" of a god or king, "the refulgent envelope that surrounded the divine or royal body." McCarter critiques Mendenhall's argument because Mendenhall does not cite any parallels for the presumed philological correspondence of the letters. *II Samuel*, 325.

67. McCarter, *II Samuel*, 326.

68. *Antiquities,* book 7, chapter 8.

69. A. F. Kirkpatrick, *The Second Book of Samuel with Notes and Introduction* (Cambridge: Cambridge University Press, 1919), 344.

70. McCarter, *II Samuel*, 319.

71. Ibid.

72. Bledstein, "Tamar and the 'Coat of Many Colors,'" 70–73. Carmen Imes discusses the כתנת, *ktnt*, "tunic," worn by the high priest, in this volume, 57–58.

73. Cf. Starbuck, in this volume, 242.

is apt or not, depending on situation and context."[74] Tamar's clothing—worn by virgin daughters *of the king*—might suggest that she had David's favor, but there turns out to be a gap between the sign and what it signifies. In fact, in contrast to Joseph who was given his garment—the same as the one Tamar wore—as a sign of his father Jacob's favor, Tamar seems to have the favor not of her father, David, but of her brother Absalom. This can be seen in two places in the narrative: first, in the interactions, or lack thereof, between David and Tamar, and second, in the ways the text describes the relationships. First, the only interactions between Tamar and David are indirect. He does not speak directly to her, but sends a message to her to go to Amnon (13:7). That message is brief and focused, using imperative verbs. Bar-Efrat notes that David does utilize the polite expression, נא, *n'*, "pray," and asserts that David therefore is giving Tamar a request rather than a command, but Bar-Efrat also explains that "as a father (and king) [David] is in a position to command without needing to explain and justify himself."[75] The only other possible interaction between David and Tamar is in 13:21, after Tamar has been raped, when the text says that David "heard about all these things and was very angry." The MT ends there, but the LXX adds, "but he would not punish his son Amnon, because he loved him, for he was his firstborn."[76] The relational focus is therefore between father and son, not father and daughter. Second, the very first verse of 2 Sam 13 highlights the relationship between the men, as both Amnon and Absalom are introduced as David's sons, but Tamar is the sister of Absalom, not David's daughter. Even when Tamar speaks of David she refers to him not as father, but as "the king" (2 Sam 13:13).[77] Tamar's garment turns out to be not apt in her status as virgin, nor is it an apt mark of the favor of her father. David's favor for his son—and not his daughter—seems to be why David does nothing in response to Tamar's trauma.[78] Even Judah, the father-in-law whose actions are in no way exemplary, eventually does right by his daughter-in-law. David, the beloved anointed of YHWH, does not.

Tamar: Action

Tamar's entrapment sets the scene, but Tamar continues to be trapped by the action done against her, as Trible notes; Trible analyzes 2 Sam 13:9d-18 as a chiasm

---

74. Green, *What Profit for Us?*, 74.
75. Bar-Efrat, *Narrative Art*, 254–55.
76. This is also attested in the Samuel scroll from Qumran.
77. It is likely that this reference is an appeal not to the paternal connection, but to the authority that David—as king—would have to give Tamar to Amnon as a wife.
78. A contrast with Joseph is instructive here: when Jacob hears the report of Joseph's death and sees the "evidence" of the bloodstained כתנת פסים, *kětōnet passîm*, he refuses to be comforted. However, Jacob is as passive as David when it comes to responding to Dinah's rape. In both cases, the fathers do not act, and it is the brothers who seek to avenge their sisters.

with rape at the center. Trible comments, "Tamar is entrapped for rape."⁷⁹ While the action done against Tamar must not be minimized, Tamar's own action should not be overlooked. Before she is raped, she follows the command of her father and prepares food for her brother, and she speaks at length, (unsuccessfully) attempting to persuade Amnon not to rape her. After she is raped, she again (unsuccessfully) attempts to persuade Amnon not to throw her out, and then she tears her garment, puts ashes on her head, and זעקה, *zʿqh*, "cries out." The narration of the action of the rape is quite terse; Tamar's actions are narrated at much more length and in much more detail.

Tamar's litany of reasons why Amnon should not do את־הנבלה הזאת, *ʾt-hnblh hzʾt*, "this folly" (2 Sam 13:12) is systematic and extensive, wise and reasonable. Henry explains it as follows:

> We may well imagine what a surprise and terror it was to the young lady to be thus attacked, how she blushed and how she trembled; yet, in this great confusion, nothing could be said more pertinently, nor with greater strength of argument, than what she said to him ... But all her arts and all her arguments availed not.⁸⁰

---

79. Trible, *Texts of Terror*, 44. Trible describes the chiasm as follows: (a) Amnon's command to the servants and their response (13:9de); (b) Amnon's command to Tamar and her response (13:10–11a); (c) Conversation between Amnon and Tamar (13:11b chiasm 14a); (d) Rape (13:14b chiasm 15b); c' chiasm b': conversation between Amnon and Tamar; Amnon's command to Tamar and her response; a': Amnon's command to a servant and his response.

80. http://www.biblestudytools.com/commentaries/matthew-henry-complete/2-samuel/13.html. Henry explains Tamar's speech at length, and his list highlights the "pertinent" and systematic nature of Tamar's argument. He writes, "1. She calls him brother, reminding him of the nearness of the relation, which made it unlawful for him to marry her, much more to debauch her. It was expressly forbidden (Lev. 18:9) ... 2. She entreats him not to force her, which intimates that she would never consent to it in any degree; and what satisfaction could he take in offering violence? 3. She lays before him the great wickedness of it. It is folly; all sin is so, especially uncleanness. It is wickedness of the worst kind ... 4. She represents to him the shame of it, which perhaps might influence him more than the sin of it ... that is, "Thou wilt be looked upon as an atrocious debauchee, the worst of men; thou wilt lose thy interest in the esteem of all that are wise and good, and so wilt be set aside as unfit to rule, though the first-born; for Israel will never submit to the government of such a fool" ... 5. To divert him from his wicked purpose at this time, and (if possible) to get clear of him, she intimates to him that probably the king, rather than he should die for love of her, would dispense with the divine law and let him marry her: not as if she thought he had such a dispensing power, or would pretend to it; but she was confident that, upon notice given to the king by himself of this wicked desire, which he would scarcely have believed from any one else, he would take an effectual course to protect her from him."

Even if contemporary readers do not share Henry's certainty that Tamar would be able, in the actual scenario, to respond so systematically, the rhetoric of the narrative is no less powerful. In fact, Tamar's reasonable, articulate speech only heightens the horror of what Amnon does to her.[81] Her words would seem to empower her, but Amnon's violation of her shows how relatively powerless she is. Additionally, Tamar was a king's daughter who had enjoyed privilege, and likely, shelter. It might not have occurred to her that when she attempted to set boundaries, they—and she—would be violated.

The rape is narrated quickly, with just two words in Hebrew ויּשׁכב וענה, w'nh wyškb, but has a prolonged affect. After raping Tamar, Amnon's feelings change from love to loathing, and he adds insult to injury by casting Tamar out and locking the door.[82] In response, Tamar rips her garment. The explanatory gloss in 13:18 about the robe being worn by the virgin daughters of the king interrupts the flow of the plot,[83] but adds an important explanation for the significance of the act of tearing it. While a number of scholars suggest that Tamar rips her garment as a typical act of grief,[84] others understand the symbolism of the act. Tamar's alteration of her robe marks the change in her status: a virgin at the beginning of the narrative, she is not one at the end. Yamada explains, "Tamar's virginal status has been shattered by her half-brother."[85] Keil and Delitzsch add that the mention of Tamar's royal dress accentuates the harshness of Tamar's treatment, because the servant was able to see Tamar's status by her garment. They write, "Notwithstanding this dress, by which a king's daughter could at once be recognized, Amnon's servant treated Tamar

---

81. A number of places give detailed accounts of how she responded to Amnon with "wise words" (Trible, *Texts of Terror*, 56) and emphatic speech. Cf. Yamada, *Configurations of Rape*, 115–16; Bar-Efrat, *Narrative Art*, 261; Frymer-Kensky, *Reading the Women of the Bible*, 161–63; etc.

82. Though the scale is hardly a great one, Shechem would nonetheless appear to be better than Amnon, for he asked for Dinah's hand in marriage after raping her (Gen 34:4, 8).

83. Yamada, *Configurations of Rape*, 121, fn. 35, argues, "This intrusion to the narrative is most certainly an ancient misplaced gloss, intended to explain the significance of the robe that Tamar tears in v. 19."

84. For example, Lange writes, "She had on a garment with long sleeves (פַּסִּים); the usual undergarment covered only the upper arm, while this covered the whole arm, and took the place of the armless *meil* (outer garment or robe). Translate: **thus were the king's daughters, the virgins, clothed with robes;** such long-sleeved mantles distinguished the princesses—Ver. 19. Her indication of grief at the shame done her. The hands clasped above the head or laid on the head, are a sign of grief at the shame that has come on the head as the bearer of one's personal honor. Comp. Jer. ii. 37." 485. Indeed, tearing garments to signify grief occurs in a number of places, such as Gen 37:29, 34; Num 14:6; Josh 7:6; Judg 11:35; 2 Sam 3:31, etc. Interestingly, David does not tear his clothes in response to the death of the first child with Bathsheba in 2 Sam 12 (though he changes his clothes after he hears the news), or in response to Absalom's death in 2 Sam 19.

85. Yamada, *Configurations of Rape*, 121.

like a common woman, and turned her out of the house."[86] And Bar-Efrat asserts, "The tear symbolizes the drastic change which has taken place in her situation: she is no longer a virgin and has also been cast out by Amnon and his servant, in contrast to the treatment which should be accorded a king's daughter."[87] Tamar's act of tearing her garment was in part an act of protest against the monarchy and her royal status, as if to say that because the insignia of royalty meant nothing, she would destroy it. Additionally, if the kĕtōnet passîm was a modestly long garment that covered Tamar's arms and legs, her tearing of it is a protest against modesty, implying that there is no point in covering what had been uncovered.

Trible described Tamar as "a victim of shame that her clothes cannot hide,"[88] but that seems to be exactly the point: Tamar's torn garment does not hide her shame, but exposes it. Recent statistics suggest that 2/3 of rapes go unreported,[89] and often victims of trauma are so traumatized that they cannot voice what happened. Tamar, however, speaks through her actions. In addition to tearing her garment in 2 Sam 13:19, she places ashes on her head, places her hands on her head and goes walking around and crying out. Frymer-Kensky notes the similarity between Tamar's actions and the actions of those who see a ruin, according to Ezek 27:30: raising voices and crying out and placing dust and ashes upon themselves. She writes, "Tamar creates a public spectacle. She draws attention to her own devastation by openly revealing her plight. Not trying to hide her shame, she performs an act of grief and lament."[90] Centuries earlier, when he preached on Tamar, John Calvin had a similar interpretation of Tamar's actions as a declaration of her innocence: "The sum total of all this is that she wanted to declare to everyone that she had been violently taken by force, and that she had not consented to evil."[91]

But Tamar's declaration is stifled by her brother Absalom, who tells her in 2 Sam 13:20 to "be silent" and "consider not this thing." Yamada notes the incongruity between the cruelty of the rape and Absalom's response, and explains

---

86. Carl Friedrich Keil and F. Delitzsch, *Biblical Commentary on the Books of Samuel*, trans. James Martin (Edinburgh: T. & T. Clark, 1868), 400. Similarly, Yamada writes, "Once again, the use of this language to describe the coat is ironic. Amnon refused to listen to Tamar after the rape and has sent her away. Hence, he has treated this royal daughter of the king like a prostitute. This frock of honor cannot cover the humiliation of Tamar. Hence, though the narrator's description of the coat interrupts the action of the story, the meaning of the כתנת פסים functions rhetorically to fuel even further the reader's judgment of Amnon's crime. The royal robe is set in stark contrast to both the humiliation that Tamar experienced at the hands of her half-brother and the shame that she now feels as she is being escorted out by one of his servants." *Configurations of Rape*, 121.

87. Bar-Efrat, *Narrative Art*, 52.

88. Trible, *Texts of Terror*, 49.

89. According to the "Rape, Abuse and Incest National Network," only 32 percent of rapes are reported. https://rainn.org/get-information/statistics/reporting-rates

90. Frymer-Kensky, *Reading the Women of the Bible*, 165.

91. John Calvin, *Sermons on 2 Samuel* (Edinburgh: Banner of Truth Trust, 1992), 354.

it as Absalom's desire to carry out his plans for revenge in secret.⁹² Frymer-Kensky, however, reads it as Absalom silencing her, writing:

> But for Tamar to hush means that she will forgo any chance that she can be vindicated and her honor restored. She herself will be complicit in covering up Amnon's crime, and she will be denied the satisfaction of retribution and revenge. Absalom makes her stifle her rage and leave her grief unassuaged.⁹³

Tamar has been referred to as "sister" eight times in the narrative, either in reference to Amnon or Absalom. And it is Absalom who takes Tamar into his house, who punishes Amnon for what he had done to Tamar, who names his own beautiful daughter after Tamar. But whatever Absalom's reasons for silencing his sister, this eloquent woman has no more say in the text.

Wray offers a midrash of sorts as she writes, "At the end of her story, she is sequestered away in the home of her doomed brother, Absalom, her royal robes torn asunder."⁹⁴ There is nothing in the text that indicates whether or not Tamar is still wearing her torn robe at the end of the account, but the riches-to-rags image is evocative. A Tamar who remains garbed in her ripped *kětōnet passim* would be continually reminded of her loss of status. Changing her robe—the robe that marked her as a virgin daughter of the king—would indicate, perhaps more accurately, her change of position and status. If Tamar kept wearing her robe despite its deceptive symbolism, that too could be a type of defiance.

Tamar: Liberation?

Wray's midrash is based on the text of 2 Sam 13:20 which, as mentioned above, describes Tamar as שׁמם, *šmm*, "desolate." The woman with the courage to defy, to speak out, is desolate. She tore her garment as an indication of the tearing of her virginity, protection, and privilege, but this is a liberation without joy. Tamar may be freed from the things her garment represented, but she is not free for anything, apparently, except to remain in her brother's house. Trible attempts to notice what is positive in this narrative and explains,

> In [his daughter] Absalom has created a living memorial for his sister. A further note enhances the poignancy of his act. Tamar, the daughter of Absalom, "Became a woman beautiful (*yph*) to behold." From aunt to niece have passed name and beauty so that rape and desolation have not the final word in the story of Tamar.⁹⁵

---

92. Yamada writes, "The veil of secrecy that Absalom has created, combined with his deep hatred of Amnon, suggests to the reader that revenge is forthcoming from Tamar's blood brother, even if the plans for retaliation are not explicit." *Configurations of Rape*, 124.
93. Frymer-Kensky, *Reading the Women of the Bible*, 167.
94. Wray, *Good Girls, Bad Girls*, 144.
95. Trible, *Texts of Terror*, 55.

But if rape and desolation do not have the final word, they are close. Even after Absalom kills Amnon, Tamar is not mentioned again. Perhaps it is only Tamar's torn garment that speaks, that bears witness to what happened to her, long after she has been silenced, and even after the text is silent about her.

Conclusions

Both narratives about Tamar contribute to a larger understanding of the role that garments play in the HB. Narratologically, clothing moves the plot. For characterization, clothing tells us about the identity of the characters and what they do. And the Tamars use their clothing to respond—in defiance and protest—to the patriarchal systems that have abused them. The Tamars' use of clothing echoes into other situations, even today. Clothing can disguise, as in the Civil War when Frances Clayton disguised herself as "Frances Clalin" in order to fight with the Confederate soldiers.[96] Clothing can empower: Amelia Michele Joiner, a lawyer who was interviewed about what she wore that made her feel powerful, described a "power navy suit and pearls" that she would put on when going to court.[97] An assistant professor explained, "Sometimes I put things on so that they can almost be armor. For example, when I go to a scholarly conference and I have to give a paper, ... I wear my glasses and suit so that I can feel like I'm a serious academic."[98] Clothing can identify status. In Margaret Atwood's *The Handmaid's Tale*, the color of the clothing reveals the status of the various characters: powder-blue is worn by the Commander's Wife, while a handmaid wears red.[99] Lauren Winner writes:

---

96. http://www.smithsonianmag.com/ist/?next=/history-archaeology/The-Women-Who-Fought-in-the-Civil-War.html

97. Tiffany Ludwig and Renee Piechocki, *Trappings: Stories of Women, Power and Clothing* (New Brunswick, NJ: Rutgers University Press, 2007), 215. In a follow up interview, however, Joiner explained that she let her suit go, because she had been empowered by her experiences. "I might have to wear [the suit] when I write this really awful opinion I have to write this week, but for the most part, I feel the power all by myself, so I don't necessarily need the clothes anymore. I got 'em, though. I still have my good bag. The pearls—I can't let 'em go." Ibid., 215.

98. Ibid., 125.

99. The titular character describes her clothes as follows: "Red shoes, flat heeled to save the spine and not for dancing. The red gloves are lying on the bed. I pick them up, pull them onto my hands, finger by finger. Everything except the wings around my face is red: the color of blood, which defines us. The skirt is ankle-length, full, gathered to a flat yoke that extends over the breasts, the sleeves are full. The white wings too are prescribed issue; they are to keep us from seeing, but also from being seen." Margaret Atwood, *The Handmaid's Tale* (New York: Alfred A. Knopf, 2006), 14.

> "Fashion" is a noun, calling to mind Paris runways, models in Jean Paul Gaultier creations, *Elle* and *Marie Claire* magazines. But "fashion" is also a verb. It means "to mold or to shape." ... This is why some of us enjoy clothes so much, why we love changing our clothes and trying out a different look—every time we change into a different kind of clothing, we can play at being a different kind of self.[100]

In the social world of the HB, women likely were the ones who created fabric and garments, weaving the cloth and sewing it together. Clothing, therefore, is women's work. In these texts, the women used their fabric garments to mark symbolic unraveling of the social structures. In the case of the Genesis Tamar, she wove new possibilities through how she changed her garments. In the case of the 2 Samuel Tamar, the tearing of her garments marked the destruction of her royalty, her modesty, and her virginity.

M. Meg 4:10 refers to two types of biblical texts: those that are to be read aloud in the synagogues but not translated, and those that are to be neither read nor translated. The story of Tamar in 2 Samuel falls into the second group, along with other texts that refer to suspicious or improper sexual encounters, such as David's adultery with Bathsheba in 2 Sam 11 or Reuben's sleeping with Bilhah in Gen 35. The story of Tamar in Genesis, however, falls into the first group: it is not to be translated, but is to be read aloud. Susan Niditch comments that the texts not read nor translated "are destructive of the social fabric ... In contrast, the union between Judah and Tamar does not mar the social fabric, but repairs it."[101] Perhaps it is more accurate to say that this "social fabric" can be seen more clearly through the garments worn and utilized by both Tamars. When the Tamar in 2 Samuel tears her robe, this is not just destroying the social fabric, but illuminating it, in ways analogous to what is revealed when the Tamar in Genesis changes her clothing. Both women use their garments to express and enact what is possible in their social world. Tamar and Tamar actively respond to violation and victimization, using their clothes in defiance to reclaim their agency.[102]

---

100. Lauren Winner, *Wearing God: Clothing, Laughter, Fire, and Other Overlooked Ways of Meeting God* (New York: HarperOne, 2015), 38.

101. Niditch, "The Wronged Woman Righted: An Analysis of Genesis 38," 149.

102. I'm grateful to Nancy Bowen, whose e-mail correspondence with me about Tamar was both clarifying and inspiring. I also thank my colleagues in this PNWSBL Hebrew Bible working group, especially Tony Finitsis, Shawn Flynn, Carmen Imes, Ehud Ben Zvi and Scott Starbuck, for their thoughtful suggestions and enthusiastic support. It has been a privilege to work with such fine scholars and people.

5

IS SAUL AMONG THE PHILISTINES? A PORTRAYAL OF ISRAEL'S FIRST AND FLAWED KING

Sean E. Cook

The stern verdict regarding the future of Israel's first king in 1 Samuel comes soon after his rise to power. After the prophet Samuel anointed Saul (1 Sam 10) and following a great military victory at the hand of Israel's new king (1 Sam 11), Saul is told that his kingdom will not endure (13:13–14) and is then rejected as king by YHWH (15:23). Many have wrestled with Saul's swift condemnation and harsh judgment. Sternberg, for example, asks, "Does Saul's sparing of 'Agag and the best of his sheep and the oxen' justify God's tearing the kingdom from him?"[1] "Isn't there a glaring disproportion between achievement and reward, sin and penalty?"[2]

The narrator of Samuel works out the prophetic word regarding Saul's fate in the events that follow Saul's rejection in 1 Sam 15. Saul's sins, early in his reign, are followed by a long downward decline eventually leading to his tragic death (1 Sam 16–31); thus Samuel's word is fulfilled.[3] While David is certainly an important figure in these chapters (1 Sam 16–31), the focus is not entirely on him as we are also given many glimpses of Saul.[4] These glimpses of Saul reveal a clearer picture of

---

1. Meir Sternberg, "The Bible's Art of Persuasion: Ideology, Rhetoric, and Poetics in Saul's Fall," HUCA 54 (1983): 48.

2. Ibid. Keith Bodner, *1 Samuel: A Narrative Commentary*, Hebrew Bible Monographs 19 (Sheffield: Sheffield Phoenix, 2008), 121–27, surveys a number of different interpretations of Saul's initial failures in 1 Samuel 13.

3. Little is said regarding the reason for Saul's rejection after 1 Sam 15. Just before Saul's death in 1 Sam 31, he seeks counsel from the dead Samuel (by means of a medium) who reminds him of his sins from chapter 15 where Saul did not carry out YHWH's wrath against the Amalekites (1 Sam 28:18).

4. The focus on David in 1 Sam 16–31 is understandable. Von Rad, for example, comments that the stories of Saul and David in the book of 1 Samuel are really stories about David, Gerhard von Rad, *Old Testament Theology*, vol. 1 (Edinburgh: Oliver and Boyd, 1963), 324. Steven McKenzie notes that Saul is a one-dimensional character who provides a contrast to David, Steven L. McKenzie, "Saul in the Deuteronomistic History," in *Saul in*

him where our narrator does not simply describe his decline; he rather continues to shape our view of him. A complete picture of Saul (i.e., Saul's rejection along with how he is shown in 1 Sam 16–31) helps ease the apparent inequity that many scholars have felt regarding Saul's sins and harsh judgment of him all of which lead to his tragic death.[5]

An important means by which Saul's story is shaped in 1 Sam 16–31 is through his dress including his battle garments and gear.[6] One of the unique features of 1 Samuel (especially when compared with 2 Samuel) is the frequent use of or reference to various sorts of dress including battle garments.[7] Clothing

---

Story and Tradition, ed. Carl S. Ehrlich and Marsha C. White, FAT 47 (Tübingen: Mohr Siebeck, 2006), 68. One can even understand why 1 Sam 16–2 Sam 5 is often referred to as the History of David's Rise, cf. Walter Dietrich and Thomas Naumann, "The David-Saul Narrative," in *Reconsidering Israel and Judah: Recent Studies on the Deuteronomistic History*, ed. G.N. Knoppers and J.G. McConville (Winona Lake, IN: Eisenbrauns, 2000), 276–318; N.P. Lemche "David's Rise," *JSOT* 10 (1978): 2–25; P.K., McCarter, Jr., "The Apology of David," *JBL* 99 (1980): 489–504. Even though David is important and even a central focus in these chapters, I want to emphasize that the figure of Saul does not disappear in 1 Sam 16–31 and continues to be shown in different ways and not for the sole purpose of contrast to David. There is much that is said about Saul following his rejection.

5. Many scholars have wrestled with ideas of "fate" and "tragedy" within the Saul narratives. Among them von Rad draws our attention to the tension of Saul as a flawed hero (thus creating his own fate) versus seeing him as a "special tool of the will of Jahweh in history" (thus emphasizing a tragic component to the narrative), von Rad, *Old Testament Theology*, 324–27. Cf. also J. Cheryl Exum, *Tragedy and Biblical Narrative* (Cambridge: Cambridge University Press, 1992), 16–41; David Gunn, *The Fate of King Saul*, JSOT 14 (Sheffield: JSOT, 1980), 23–31; Yairah Amit, "The Delicate Balance in the Image of Saul and Its Place in the Deuteronomistic History," in *Saul in Story and Tradition*, ed. Carl S. Ehrlich and Marsha C. White, FAT 47 (Tübingen: Mohr Siebeck, 2006), 71–79.

6. In this chapter, I will refer to clothing and garments in the broadest of terms to include battle garments and gear. While a sword or a spear is technically not a garment, they are a part of one's battle gear which would include actual battle apparel. Saul, for example, "clothed (לבשמד) David with his garments (שלב), and put a bronze helmet on his head, and he clothed (לבש) him with armor (שריון)," 1 Sam 17:38. David then straps on a sword over his armor (מד), 1 Sam 17:38–39. There are a number of studies that describe clothing in the HB including these particular items. Cf. *ABD*, s.v., "Dress and Ornamentation"; Alicia J. Batten, "Clothing and Adornment," *Biblical Theology Bulletin* 40.3 (2010): 148–59; Philip J. King and Lawrence E. Stager, "Culture and Expressive Life," in *Life in Biblical Israel*, ed. Philip J. King and Lawrence E. Stager (Louisville: Westminster John Knox, 2001), 259–318.

7. A few examples of this are "robe" (מעיל) occurs 7 times in 1 Samuel and once in 2 Samuel, "cloth garment" (מד) occurs 4 times in 1 Samuel and once in 2 Samuel, "ephod" (אפד) occurs 9 times in 1 Samuel and once in 2 Samuel, "garment" (בגד) occurs 4 times in 1 Samuel and 9 times in 2 Samuel, "helmet" (קבע) occurs once in 1 Samuel and 0 times in

in 1 Samuel is used in different ways and for different purposes. For example, at times our author may invite the reader to consider the possible symbolic significance of how clothing is used.⁸ Prouser examines in an essay the role of clothing in the Saul–David narratives as a whole. He argues that clothes in these narratives are a narratological device that highlights "David's rise to power and Saul's fall from grace."⁹ David's rise and Saul's fall are highlighted through an asymmetrical exchange. David continually receives clothes from different sources, and Saul continually discards clothing.¹⁰ In this chapter, I want to further Prouser's observations focusing in on Saul's various garments and argue that the narrator of Samuel has intentionally highlighted Saul's garments and has done so in order to encourage the reader's rejection of him. The inequity and perhaps injustice of Saul's initial rejection observed by scholars are keenly felt if one focuses solely in on 1 Sam 13 and 15. But our narrator has much more to say about Saul following these chapters. Here, I will argue that by means of Saul's garments, Saul is shown to look more like a foreigner rather than an Israelite.

In stating that Saul is shown to look more like a foreigner than an Israelite, I am not saying anything about Saul's ethnicity or ancestry. He is indeed an Israelite, the son of Kish (1 Sam 9:1–2). What I want to suggest is that while Saul is among the elect, God's chosen people of Israel, Saul is symbolically Othered in the narratives of 1 Samuel. What I mean by this is that he is shown in such a way that puts him in the category of the "anti-elect" which Kaminsky defines as "those few groups who are deemed to be enemies of God and whom Israel is commanded to

---

2 Samuel, "sword" (חרב) occurs 24 times in 1 Samuel and 15 in 2 Samuel, "spear" (חנית) occurs 21 times in 1 Samuel and 9 times in 2 Samuel, and finally "armor" or "clothing" (שריון) occurs 3 times in 1 Samuel and 0 times in 2 Samuel.

8. An explicit example of this is found in 1 Sam 15:27–28. After Samuel delivers the news to Saul that YHWH has rejected him as king over Israel, Samuel turns to leave and Saul immediately grasps the edge of Samuel's robe (מעיל) and it tears (קרע). Samuel's response to Saul's action is clear: "The Lord has torn (קרע) the kingdom of Israel from you this very day, and has given it to a neighbor of yours, who is better than you" (1 Sam 15:28).

9. Ora Horn Prouser, *Suited to the Throne: The Symbolic Use of Clothing in the David and Saul Narratives*, JSOT 71 (1996): 29. Prouser does not deny that particular references to clothing may be symbolic (e.g., 1 Sam 24). His focus is rather on clothing in the narrative as a whole and how dress is used to enhance the narrative. Bar-Efrat and Berlin also note how outward appearance (including clothing) is used by biblical writers to advance the plot of a narrative and to explain its course. Cf. Shimon Bar-Efrat, *Narrative Art in the Bible*, JSOTSup 70 (Sheffield: Sheffield Academic Press), 48; Adele Berlin, *Poetics and Interpretation of Biblical Narrative* (Winona Lake, Indiana: Eisenbrauns, 1983), 34.

10. Prouser, *Suited to the Throne*, 30. According to Prouser, the accumulation or receiving of garments in the Bible is considered a positive indicator, while the loss of clothing or nakedness is seen as something negative.

annihilate, such as the Canaanites and the Amalekites."[11] Again to be clear, Saul is not a Canaanite or an Amalekite, for example. He rather fits in the category of the anti-elect whereby God works against him (resulting eventually in his death) in a similar way that God works against Israel's enemies such as the Philistines or the Amalekites.[12] The task of Othering in the HB is often used to "set the religious community of Israel apart from the surrounding nations and groups in the larger ancient Near East."[13] But as Edelmman suggests, the task of Othering in the HB is also used "to argue that YHWH will reject or has rejected or Othered Israel, his otherwise treasured, selected people, making them an outside group rather than an inside one."[14] Saul is depicted like a foreigner, and the manner in which this is shown in 1 Samuel is through his clothing and armor.[15] Given all of this, my chapter will proceed to examine the various references to Saul's different garments and will show how these references work together to reveal the ways in which Saul is Othered, looking more like a Philistine than an Israelite. In what follows, I will use the method that Moshe Garsiel calls a "literary synchronic approach."[16]

---

11. Joel S. Kaminsky, "Israel's Election and the Other," in *The "Other" in Second Temple Judaism: Essays in Honor of John J. Collins*, ed. Daniel C. Harlow, Karina Martin Hogan, Matthew Goff, and Joel S. Kaminsky (Grand Rapids: William B. Eerdmans Publishing Company, 2011), 17–30.

12. Kaminsky, "Israel's Election and the Other," also notes that there are exceptions to this where biology and ethnicity do not determine those who are among the anti-elect. Examples of exceptions are figures such as Rahab or Achan, an Israelite who is treated like a Canaanite and wiped out for his violating the warn ban (Joshua 7). Saul is an example of an exception in a similar way as that of Achan.

13. Diana V. Edelman, "YHWH's Othering of Israel," in *Imagining the Other and Constructing Israelite Identity in the Early Second Temple Period*, ed. Ehud Ben Zvi and Diana V. Edelman, LHBOTS 456 (London: Bloomsbury, 2014), 41.

14. Ibid., 41. Edelman goes on to show in her essay the strategies used in the HB whereby YHWH Others Israel.

15. For the narratological function of clothing, see Sara M. Koenig's contribution, in this volume, 146–49. Clothing in the ancient world was not only a sign of one's wealth, status, and religion, it was also a signpost of one's ethnicity and group identity, cf. *ABD*, s.v., "Dress and Ornamentation"; Batten, "Clothing and Adornment," 148; King and Stager, "Culture and Expressive Life," 259. Some recent studies that explain how clothing and dress can function as an alterity category include S. Baizerman, Joanne B. Eicher, and C. Cerny, "Eurocentrism in the Study of Ethnic Dress," in *Visible Self: Global Perspectives on Dress, Culture and Society*, ed. Joanne B. Eicher, Sandra L. Evenson, and Hazel A. Lutz (New York: Fairchild Publications, 2008), 123–32; Will Rollason, "Counterparts: Clothing, Value and the Sites of Otherness in Panapompom Ethnographic Encounters," *Anthropological Forum* 18 (2008): 17–35.

16. Moshe Garshiel, *The First Book of Samuel: A Literary Study of Comparative Structures, Analogies and Parallels* (Jerusalem: Revivim, 1983), 16.

Appearances matter (1 Sam 9:1–2; 10:23–24)

It is worth noting that the first time Saul is introduced we are given a description of his appearance. While clothing is not mentioned in Saul's introduction (chapter 9), his outward appearance is important from the outset and it will later include his garments.

Saul's impressive genealogy in 9:1 is followed by two details. Saul as the son of Kish is first described as "choice and good," בחור וטוב (9:2).[17] Saul is not only chosen and good, he is better than the sons of Israel.[18] The next thing we are told about Saul is that he was a "head taller than any of the others" (9:2). A description of Saul's height is also mentioned at the end of chapter 10 when he is chosen as king at Mizpah: "as he stood among the people he was a head taller than any of them." Even Samuel takes notice of Saul's stature; after Saul stood before the people in 10:23–24, Samuel remarks, "do you see (ראה) the one whom the Lord has chosen? There is no one like him from among all the people."[19] Thus, the way that Saul is introduced is by means of his appearance and the fact that he looks different and stands apart from others. This standing apart from others will later result in him being isolated and eventually separated from those around him.

As we seek answers to questions related to Saul's harsh rejection and his difficult downward spiral after his rejection, I suggest that our author has given us a clue as to one of the ways in which he will portray Saul and he does so right at the

---

17. Following Auld's translation of בחור וטוב, cf. Graeme Auld, *I & II Samuel*, OTL (Louisville: Westminster John Knox, 2011), 10. Ralph W. Klein, *1 Samuel*, WBC 10 (Waco: Word Books, 1983), 80, translates בחור וטוב as "a fine young man" while P. Kyle McCarter, Jr., *I Samuel*, AB (New York: Doubleday and Company, 1980), 164, as "handsome young man." McCarter notes that the "attribution of good looks is a traditional part of the biblical presentation of an Israelite hero or heroine, e.g. Joseph (Gen 39:6), Esther (Esther 2:7), the infant Moses (Ex. 2:2) and so on," Ibid., 173.

18. Auld, *I & II Samuel*, 102. Robert Rezetko, *Source and Revision in the Narratives of David's Transfer of the Ark: Text, Language, and Story in 2 Samuel 6 and 1 Chronicles 13, 15–16*, LHBOTS 470 (New York: T&T Clark, 2007), 46, notes that only Saul and Absalom are described as the most handsome "in all of Israel" and it is only their description that focus on their shoulders upward.

19. It seems reasonable to assume that Samuel is referring to Saul's height in 10:24 as his height is mentioned just before Samuel asks the people this question. Samuel also reacts to the outward appearance of Eliab in 16:6. Here it is made explicit in YHWH's comments that Samuel has reacted to Eliab's appearance and/or height (cf. 16:7). The irony of Samuel's statement is poignant as we see Saul's foreboding physical appearance contrasted with his timid behavior, for the people have to go looking for Saul because he was hiding among the baggage (10:22–23). Auld, *I & II Samuel*, 115, comments that we are given no indication that whether Saul's hiding himself is demonstrating commendable modesty or a flaw in his character. Cf. the story of Gideon (Judges 6–7) who also presents a picture of a similar reluctance despite all attempts of divine assurance.

outset of his reign. One of the ways Saul will be shown is by means of his outward appearance and this will later include his clothing and battle garments. Saul is not the only figure within 1–2 Samuel where a character's outer appearance is described,[20] and given the many references to clothing in 1 Samuel, I will show that these are clues that serve the plot of the narrative.

Saul armed

Saul, David, and Goliath (1 Sam 17:32-40)

1 Samuel 17 is one of the most well-known stories within Samuel and even the HB. Just prior to the battle scene between David and Goliath (17:41–48), a conversation takes place between Saul and David that not only increases tension leading up to the battle, but it also slows down the narrative enough to reveal several comparisons between Saul, David, and Goliath.[21] In the first part of their conversation (17:32–37), Saul and David debate whether or not David is able to go out and fight the giant Philistine. Here Saul creates the first of two obstacles for David, as David considers a duel with the giant.[22] In 17:33 Saul initially refuses to let David go up against the Philistine because David is a "boy" or a "youth" (נער) and the Philistine has been fighting since his youth (מנעוריו). This elicits a major speech from David (17:34–37) after which Saul relents and allows him to fight. Given David's experience battling lions and bears, and after David mentions that it is YHWH who will fight this battle on his behalf (17:37), Saul acknowledges David's words, but as Klein notes, Saul does not fully perceive their implications.[23]

The second part of their conversation (17:38–40) focuses on what David will wear for this duel and within this conversation Saul creates a second obstacle for David. Immediately after David's speech, Saul "clothes" (לבש) David with his own "garments" (מד), sets a "bronze helmet" (קובע נחשת) on his head, and finally clothes (לבש) David with "armor" (שריון). David then fastens Saul's "sword" (חרב) over his "armor" (מד). While Saul's battle garments are not said to be heavy, it is perceived

---

20. Examples of the personal appearance of characters in Samuel (aside from references to a character's clothing) include Eliab (1 Sam 16:6–7); David (16:12; 17:42); Abigail (25:3); Tamar I (2 Sam 13:1); Absalom (14:25, 26); Tamar II (14:27); and an Egyptian (23:21), cf. Auld, *I & II Samuel*, 102.

21. Antony F. Campbell, *1 Samuel*, FOTL 7 (Grand Rapids: William B. Eerdmans Publishing, 2003), 182.

22. Fokkelman states that the two obstacles are Saul refusing David to fight and Saul dressing David in his armor. He also comments that Saul wants to act as David's helper but he is acting as his opponent instead. J.P. Fokkelman, *Narrative Art and Poetry in the Books of Samuel*, vol. II, *The Crossing Fates* (Assen/Maastricht: Van Gorcum, 1986), 167.

23. Klein, *1 Samuel*, 179.

that David is unable to walk and as Auld indicates, "what else could a bronze helmet be but heavy?"[24] David then sets aside Saul's armor and chooses items that are not called "light," but "the name of everything he (David) does select (v. 40) plays on and hints at *qal*, the Hebrew adjective for 'light' and 'fast': most obviously his "stick" (מקל) and "sling" (קלע), but also (with key consonants reversed) the "smooth" [stones] (חלק) and his "pouch" (ילקוט)." The sharp difference between Saul and David is highlighted through their contrasting choices in battle gear, as David engages in battle with the Philistine.[25] As Campbell notes, David must stay light in battle with the giant, he has to be fast and get close enough to be sure not to miss.[26] The cumbersome nature of Goliath's armor proves to be no match for David's light weapons as Goliath soon finds out; there is no mention of Goliath reaching for his shield or having the opportunity to react in any way to David's choice of weapons (17:48–49).[27]

David's victory in battle without Saul's armor does more than highlight the differences between their respective choice of battle gear, and these contrasts may also reveal the similarities between Saul and Goliath's armor. In fact, "the pieces of armed protection provided by Saul correspond strikingly to the elements of Goliath's armor (vv. 5–7)."[28] Both not only wear similar gear ("bronze helmet," קובע נחשת, "armor," שריון) but also everything about their respective armor and weapons is emphasized as being heavy. David cannot stand under Saul's armor while most of Goliath's equipment is made of bronze (helmet, scale armor, greaves, javelin). The weight of Goliath's iron spear tip is also mentioned and he even has a shield bearer carry his shield. Saul's solution for David to fight the giant is, thus, to match armor with armor and in this way Saul looks like the Philistine enemy. The similarities between Saul and Goliath are also seen in references to each of their stature. Leading up to 1 Samuel 17, Saul is twice referred to as a head taller than any of the others (1 Sam. 9:2; 10:23), while the Philistine's height is described to

---

24. Auld, *I & II Samuel*, 211.
25. The use of different types of defensive and offensive battle gear in the ancient Near East is outlined in detail in Philip J. King and Lawrence E. Stager, *Life in Biblical Israel* (Louisville: Westminster John Knox, 2001), 223–30; and Charlie Trimm, *Fighting for the Gods: A Survey of Warfare in the Ancient Near East* (Atlanta: SBL, 2017), 513–52. King, Stager, and Trimm give a number of examples of both long- and short-range weapons as well as defensive type of equipment. The contrast between David and Goliath's battle gear is not only seen in their weight (as noted above); it is also seen in the type of equipment used for different battle situations. Goliath carries weapons that were largely used for hand-to-hand or short-range combat (e.g., a scimitar, כידון, and a javelin or spear, חנית) while David carries weapons that was used for long-range combat (a sling, קלע, and slingstones, אבן), cf. King and Stager, *Life in Biblical Israel*, 228.
26. Campbell, *1 Samuel*, 181.
27. Ibid.
28. Auld, *I & II Samuel*, 211.

be six cubits and a span (17:4).[29] To be sure, the language that is used to describe both Saul and the giant Philistine differs, but the point still remains; both are very tall men. And, thus, here we begin to see how appearances (and particularly battle gear) are shown to be important in the Othering of Saul. David, who is chosen to lead Israel over Saul, is different from Goliath and Saul. Saul, however, the rejected king over Israel, is not only different from David; he resembles a foreigner, the sworn enemy of Israel.

David, Jonathan, Saul, and Goliath (1Sam 18:1–4)

The contrasts and similarities between Saul, David, and Goliath seen thus far in their choice of garments and weapons, and hence their different approaches to battle, continue into chapter 18. In fact, immediately after David defeats the Philistine, 18:1–4 describes the deep friendship that ensues between Saul's son Jonathan and David. In 18:1–4 we are told a number of things about Jonathan and David: Jonathan becomes one in spirit/soul with David,[30] Jonathan makes a covenant (ברית) with David because he loved him as himself, and finally, Jonathan gives David his robe (מעיל) along with his fighting garments (מד), including a sword (חרב), bow (קשׁת), and a belt (חגור). While this exchange between David and Jonathan has been the focus of much discussion,[31] of interest here is the further use of battle garments and gear as a means by which to continue to compare and contrast the narrative's characters. Here in 18:1–4, Jonathan dresses David like himself and David, YHWH's anointed, becomes in clothes a prince of Israel.

This comparing and contrasting continues to be seen as we consider 18:1–4 together with chapter 17, and more to the point, as we compare the battle garments and gear that both Saul and Jonathan give to David. Fokkelman notes: "Jonathan's four pieces of equipment contrast with the four useless items that Saul wanted

---

29. Some Greek witnesses, Josephus, and 4QSam[a] read "four cubits and a span" which is approximately 6 feet 9 inches tall. The difference between these witnesses and the MT might be due to exaggeration, cf. McCarter, *I Samuel*, 286. Cf. also, J. Daniel Hays, "Reconsidering the Height of Goliath," *JETS* 48 (2005): 701–14.

30. Literally, "the soul of Jonathan was bound with the soul of David," ונפש יהונתן נקשרה בנפש דוד.

31. For example, scholars have debated whether or not the transfer of clothing and battle gear from Jonathan to David is in a way Jonathan transferring his claim to the throne to David. Fokkelman, *Narrative Art*, 199, argues just this and says that clothing in 18:1–4 is a "metonym and symbol for the person himself, therefore with his cloak, Jonathan is conveying to David the crown prince's rights and claims to the throne." Cf. also, Walter Brueggemann, *First and Second Samuel*, Interpretation (Louisville: John Knox, 1990), 136; Campbell, *1 Samuel*, 183; Klein, *1 Samuel*, 182. J.A. Thomson, "The Significance of the Verb Love in the David-Jonathan Narratives in 1 Samuel," *VT* 24 (1974): 334–38, comments that the lesser person passes his arms on to the greater.

to lend David, a contrast of transparent symbolism."³² The contrast is shown by means of how both sets of battle garments fit David. Jonathan's gifts of clothing to David fit him like a glove, while we are very well aware that Saul's clothing did not fit David.³³ To highlight this contrast (i.e., how each set of clothes fit) even further, we find that David's rejection of Saul's clothing is followed by great success (i.e., with Goliath), while his acceptance of Jonathan's clothing is also followed by great success.³⁴ This latter success is immediately apparent in 18:5 where it states "whatever Saul sent him to do, David did it so successfully that Saul gave him a high rank in the army." All of this certainly plays into the narrative's favorability of David over Saul, but my particular concern here is with Saul's disfavor and its depiction.

To help us see how Saul is being portrayed disfavorably, Fokkelman draws our attention to how the story in chapters 17 and 18:1–4 contrasts two negative series of arms (those of Goliath and Saul) with two positive series of arms (those of David and Jonathan).³⁵ The two negative series of arms are in a sense rejected (Goliath's defeat in battle and Saul's armor by David), while the two positive series of arms are elected (David's use of his shepherd's tools and acceptance of Jonathan's armor).³⁶ Furthermore, looking at the different descriptions and exchanges of armor more closely, one sees that two of Saul's four items of equipment give us a miserable reminder of Goliath: bronze helmet and armor; and it is precisely these two which do not occur in 18:4.³⁷ All of this is evidence of a growing division between David and Saul. While our author clearly favors David, Saul is aligned with the Philistine, Goliath. This point is made stronger by looking at two of Goliath's pieces of battle gear, particularly his sword and spear, and how these become a symbol of both Goliath's death (17:51) and Saul's downfall (cf. 1 Sam 31:4–5; 2 Sam 1:6; and also 1 Sam 18:10–11; 19:9–10). Saul's alignment with Goliath and the Philistines will also

---

32. Fokkelman, *Narrative Art*, 199. Jonathan's "four pieces of equipment" are a robe (מעיל), a sword (חרב), a bow (קשת), and a belt (חגור). Saul's "four pieces of equipment" are a garment (מד), a bronze helmet (קובע נחשת), armor (שריון), and a sword (חרב) put on over his garment/armor (מד).

33. Fokkelman, *Narrative Art*, 199. While we are not told that David actually put on the gifts of clothing from Jonathan (as he explicitly puts on Saul's armor in 17:38–39), this may very well be implied in 18:4–5.

34. Fokkelman, *Narrative Art*, 199, comments that there is no polemic against the use of weapons in this narrative. The use of weapons here is not thought to be taboo. "What is involved is the spirit in which they are used: whether one relies on the living God of Israel or on the magic of numbers and armour."

35. Ibid., 200.

36. Ibid.

37. Ibid. "Tunic" and "sword" are found in both 17:39 and 18:4. The addition of the "bow" in 18:4 is significant as it precedes Saul's sword in David's lament (2 Sam 1:22) and it is also present when the two friends depart from one another in 1 Sam 20. Saul's spear plays a large part in his portrayal. He never leaves it and even dies by it.

be seen in the narrative that follows. For the remainder of 1 Samuel, Saul will not make great efforts to fight against his enemy (the Philistines) as an Israelite king ought to do. Instead, Saul will pursue David whom he perceives as an enemy and create division among his own people. In this manner, Saul, who resembles the Philistine in 1 Samuel 17, is separated from his people by attempting to take the life of one of his own people.

Saul's spear and David (1 Sam 18:10–11; 19:9–10)

The division between David and Saul continued to grow following David's battle with the giant Philistine. Saul's "spear" (חנית), which may signify his kingship (much like a scepter, cf. 1 Sam 22:6–7),[38] is one means by which we see his antagonism toward David. Twice we are told (1 Samuel 18:10–11; 19:9–10) that an evil spirit from YHWH came over Saul, provoking his attempts to pin David to the wall with his "spear" (חנית).[39] Both times David eludes disaster by narrowly escaping Saul's madness. Whatever one makes of Saul's madness in these circumstances including an evil (רעה) spirit from YHWH (cf. also 16:14), it is clear that Saul's anger and particularly his jealousy results in him twice attempting to take David's life.

The cause for both outbreaks against David is seen in what precedes each episode. Immediately before each attempt on David's life, we are told of David's victory in battle (18:5–7; 19:8). Before the first attempt in chapter 18 and immediately after hearing the people's refrain about David's great victory (18:7), Saul's anger leads him to keep a watchful eye on David (18:9). This "eyeing" of David involves fearing him (18:12) and fearing him leads him to remove David from court by giving him a commission.[40] The new commission results again in David's battle victory, and the cycle of Saul fearing David (18:15) and later attempting to take his life (19:9–10) continues. These attempts on David's life are, as I have just indicated, used to separate Saul from David and from his own people.

While much could be said about these pericopes, Saul's choice of weapon against David is of particular interest. In chapter 17 we have just seen that Saul's armor and weapons were offered to David to fight against the Philistine giant. These were then quickly rejected. Saul's weapons, and particularly his spear (portrayed as a symbol of his kingship, cf. 1 Sam 19:9; 22:6–7), is now used to fight against the very man who is fighting Saul's real battles against the enemies of his people (cf. 19:4–5). Perhaps, though, as Saul twice uses his spear (חנית) to make an attempt on David's life, we are meant to think of the giant Philistine Goliath who also stood before David with his spear (חנית) in his hand ready to battle (17:7, 45, 47). Thus Saul, by means of his spear (1 Sam 18:10–11; 19:9–10), acts exactly like a Philistine by attacking David an Israelite. Later in 1 Sam 26, as Saul continues

---

38. Klein, *1 Samuel*, 188.
39. It is thought by some that 18:10–11 is a duplicate incident modeled after 19:9–10, Ibid.
40. Auld, *I & II Samuel*, 217.

to seek to find David to kill him, David and Abishai sneak into Saul's camp and steal Saul's spear (חנית). Rather than using the spear to kill Saul (which Abishai encourages), David refrains from doing so because Saul is YHWH's anointed (1 Sam 26:7–12). These sharply contrasting uses of a spear further underline Saul's rejection and David's election.

Saul and the cult

Saul disrobed (1 Sam 19:23-24)

As the narrative proceeds, references to Saul's clothing now focus on Israel's prophets and cult rather than his battle garments. The first of three references is found in 1 Samuel 19:23–24, where Saul prophecies "naked" before Samuel. Here we see that Saul is Othered by YHWH, who works actively against the king. YHWH is often shown to work against Israel's enemies.

After David escapes Saul's second spearing attempt, Saul continues in hot pursuit of David by sending men to David's home to kill him. Michal urges David to save himself and flee from Saul, and she not only helps David to escape but uses a "garment" (בגד) to deceive Saul's men, allowing the escape to take place (19:13). After Saul learns that David has gone to Naioth at Ramah, he sends three groups of men, all of whom see a group of prophets prophesying (with Samuel among them) and all of whom end up prophesying in the presence of Samuel. Word comes to Saul about this and Saul himself ends up going to Ramah. Upon arriving, the spirit of God also comes over Saul and he, too, walks around prophesying, having stripped off his "clothes" (בגד) and prophesying "naked" (ערם) all day and night (19:24).[41]

Saul's experience prophesying naked before YHWH's prophet all day and night is significant in at least two ways. The first is that Saul's ecstatic experience involving nakedness is likely meant to portray him in a negative manner. This is seen in two ways. The first is that generally in the Bible, nakedness is something negative and even shameful.[42] Furthermore, if we compare this ecstatic experience in 19:23–24 with Saul's similar ecstatic experience in chapter 10, we see two very different pictures of him. In chapter 10, the spirit of God also comes over Saul and he prophecies among a group of prophets, but Saul's first prophetic experience takes place after he has been anointed, and he is fully clothed. This is one of the divine signs to confirm his kingship (1 Sam 10:9), whereas in 19:23–24, Saul lays

---

41. Klein, *1 Samuel*, 199, argues that even though we are told only that Saul stripped off his garments, the two glosses in MT (19:24a and 19:24b) suggest that the messengers did the same. Bodner, *1 Samuel*, 210, suggests that Saul may very well be wearing his royal robe as he makes the journey to Ramah.

42. Klein, *1 Samuel*, 199; Genesis 2–3 is a good example of this, cf. Dietmar Neufeld, "The Rhetoric of Body, Clothing and Identity in the *Vita* and Genesis," *Scriptura* 90 (2005): 679–84.

naked while David escapes his pursuit.[43] These two experiences contrast one another and the first is often thought to be something positive, while the second in 19:23–24, something negative.[44]

Saul's negative experience in prophesying before Samuel is also significant because YHWH is acting against Saul. In chapter 19, Saul is forced to make the same journey to Ramah that his men made. It is very clear that the purpose of Saul's journey (along with those of his men) to Ramah is to find David, but it is also clear that their ecstatic state and prophesying prevents them from doing so (cf. 1 Sam 20:1). It is important to note that when Saul sheds his garments, he does so in the presence of Samuel, YHWH's prophet. In doing this, not only is Saul shown to be out of control, lying helpless on the ground, he is also under divine control. Saul's first experience coming under divine control (10:2–4) showed us that he has limits to his royal discretion and "beyond these he cannot go."[45] Saul's second experience coming under divine control (10:23–24) is a vivid picture that has YHWH set limits for Israel's first king, and is in fact acting against Saul to prevent him from finding and killing YHWH's newly anointed (David). This is symbolized through the use of clothing and gear. Thus, not only did we see Saul's spear revealing his fight against YHWH's anointed; we also see Saul's nakedness revealing YHWH's fight against Saul.

There may be an additional way in which this episode Others Saul. Reflecting on Saul's prophetic experience and YHWH's control of him as he seeks to kill one of his own people, one may very well be reminded of Balaam's similar experience (Num 22–24). As Balak king of Moab sought to defeat God's chosen people, he enlisted Balaam, a non-Israelite prophet, to curse the Israelites. Balaam is prevented from doing so as he comes under YHWH's control and is made to prophecy, but not against Israel. As we read about Saul in 1 Samuel 19, perhaps we as readers are meant to be thinking of the foreign figures of Balaam and Balak who are trying to work against YHWH's people and are prevented from doing so through a prophetic experience.

Saul kills the priests (1 Sam 22)

1 Sam 22 is a disturbing chapter wherein Saul continues in hot pursuit of David. The whole focus of chapter 22 is on Saul's retribution against the priests (Ahimelech and his father's family) who have aided David as he flees from Saul. Details about Ahimelech having given refuge and food as well as Goliath's sword are all found in 1 Sam 21. Because of this, Ahimelech and the priests pay a steep

---

43. Driver proposed that Saul was not naked, but only stripped off his outer garment, leaving a long tunic beneath (Isaiah 20:2–4; Micah 1:8), S.R. Driver, *Notes on the Hebrew Test and the Topography of the Books of Samuel* (Oxford: Clarendon, 1913), 160.

44. Ian D. Wilson, "The Emperor and His Clothing: David Robed and Unrobed before the Ark and Michal," in the present volume, 214–16; Klein, *1 Samuel*, 199.

45. Auld, *I & II Samuel*, 229.

price for aiding David and not telling Saul of his whereabouts. Of interest here are two things, first what Ahimelech and the priests are wearing and second the function or significance of these garments.

Saul's brutal act of reprisal is an act of desperation because he remains in the dark concerning David. Not only have Ahimelech and the priests not told Saul about David's visit (22:13), even Saul's own men do not tell him details concerning David's covenant with Jonathan (22:7–8). Saul's words betray his frustration as he accuses his own men that they have conspired against him (22:8).

As a result, Saul turns to his guards and orders them to kill the priests of YHWH. The insanity of such a command prompts even Saul's own men to refuse his order (22:17). Because everyone around Saul appears to be acting against him, Saul turns to a foreigner (Doeg the Edomite) to do his work and kill the priests, which he does indeed do. It appears that Saul's only hope is this foreigner who has just given him details about David's visit to Ahimelech.

As Doeg strikes down eighty-five of YHWH's priests, we are not simply told that the priests were killed. We are given information about what the priests were wearing or carrying: "he killed that day eighty-five men who carried the linen ephod" (אפוד בד). One might suggest that this reference to the priests' "linen ephod" was simply part of the priestly vestments and attach no further significance to its mention here. While this is certainly possible, I would like to suggest that this particular priestly garment, which is so often associated with the task of hearing the will of YHWH (cf. Ex 28:30; Judg 20:27; 1 Sam 14:18, 41), draws our attention to themes of hearing and communication seen throughout this chapter (and even in chapter 21). While David receives aid from the priest Ahimelech (and perhaps a word from YHWH, cf. 22:10), Saul continues to remain in the dark, hearing nothing from YHWH, his priests, and his own men. In desperation, Saul sides himself with a foreigner who tells him what he wants to hear, and in an act of great irony he has the priests killed, the very ones who are able to hear a word from YHWH. Again, Saul's actions alienate him from his own people and his god. These very themes seen in 1 Sam 22 continue in what follows as we now look to an attempt where Saul again seeks counsel.

Saul robed (1 Sam 28)

1 Sam 28 continues to narrate Saul's hopelessness. This time, however, it relates not to his search for David but to the presence of the Philistines. In this chapter the Philistines come out to fight against Israel (28:1), and David, whom Saul has been relentlessly pursuing, is present among the Philistines and even fights on their behalf (28:1–2, cf. also chapter 27). Adding to this bleak situation, Samuel has died (28:3).

In response to these circumstances, Saul does what YHWH's anointed ought to do; he inquires of YHWH and he does so by dreams, Urim, and prophets (28:6).[46]

---

46. Klein, *1 Samuel*, 271, notes that the Hebrew contains a pun in 28:6 where "Saul sauled (asked) YHWH. YHWH did not answer, just as he had not in 14:37."

These attempts, however, are unsuccessful. This should not be surprising given that Saul has just killed 85 priests all carrying an ephod (1 Sam 22:6–23). McCarter notes that Saul's actions in chapter 22 now lead to the oracle being silent for him.[47] As a result, Saul seeks the aid of necromancy and turns to a medium for direction.

Saul's seeking of a necromancer to bring up the dead for counsel violates the holiness rules (cf. Lev 19:31) and the stipulations forbidding the imitation of the abhorrent practices of other nations (cf. Deut 18:11), and we even find that the later tradition has remembered these particular actions of Saul as the cause of his downfall (cf. 1 Chr 10:13). My particular interest in this episode with the woman of Endor is to highlight how Saul continues to be shown. The practice of divination and the consulting of the dead (among other practices) are of course strictly forbidden in the law (Deut 18:9–13). These are the detestable (תועבה) practices of the nations and by engaging in them, one becomes תועבה to YHWH. Clearly Saul was aware of YHWH's instructions on this matter as he had previously expelled the mediums (אבות) and the spiritists (ידענים) from the land (28:3). This said, given the grave situation Saul finds himself in including YHWH's silence (28:6), Saul immediately turns to the services of one of the very mediums he has already expelled (28:7). Again, Saul's clothing is mentioned. He disguises himself from the woman at Endor by putting on a "garment" or a "robe" (בגד). Saul's awareness of what he is doing is further seen in the fact that he and two men approach the woman "at night."[48]

While clothing is used to conceal Saul's actions, it is also used to reveal his guilt and thus his fate. After the woman brings up Samuel, she sees him and immediately not only recognizes him (no mention of clothing here), but her reaction to seeing Samuel is actually directed toward Saul ("you are Saul") whom she now recognizes even while wearing his robe.[49] After Saul assures the medium of her safety, he asks the woman about the spirit coming up out of the ground and says, "what does he look like?" She answers, an old man wearing a robe (בגד) is coming up and immediately Saul knew it was Samuel. Saul sees the old cloak of his nemesis and is reminded of his past and thus his fate is sealed.[50]

The main thrust of 1 Sam 28 is on Saul's seeking counsel and direction given the imminent threat of the Philistines and he does indeed receive a word from Samuel. While we do not find any explicit assessment of Saul's actions in this chapter, his garment gives him away. In Saul's desperate attempt to hear from YHWH, he disguises himself and takes part in the abhorrent and forbidden practices of the nations. Saul's Othering proceeds until he embraces a foreign identity. This is

---

47. McCarter, *I Samuel*, 422.

48. Bodner, *1 Samuel*, 295, comments: "Over the course of his career, one recalls that Saul often does things under the cover of darkness; here, the temporal setting symbolizes a lack of spiritual perception, just like the nearly blind Eli in chaps. 3 and 4."

49. No explanation is given as to how the medium knows that it is Saul after seeing Samuel. LXX has "Saul" for "Samuel" in 28:12.

50. McCarter, *I Samuel*, 422.

emphasized by his request in 28:8 to "conjure up" or "bring up" (קסם) the prophet Samuel. The only other time this word is used in Samuel is in 1 Sam 6:2 where the Philistines priests and diviners (קסם) also seek counsel on what they should do with the stolen ark. Thus, in a sense "Saul's anxious inquiry of the woman aligns him with the desperate Philistines consulting their priests and diviners."[51] Saul's identity as a Philistine is almost complete.

Saul disarmed (1 Sam 31)

The final chapter of 1 Samuel narrates the end of Saul's life in a way consistent with the picture that has been painted thus far of Israel's first king. As the Philistines advance, and after killing Saul's sons including Jonathan, Saul is wounded in battle. Saul then urges his armor bearer to run him through and the reason for this final request is that he does not want to fall into the hands of the "uncircumcised" (ערל). These final words of Saul reveal an irony in that while the Philistines do not kill him, he is in a way portrayed in their likeness (or at least aligned with them) even after his death. This is seen in the following ways.

After Saul takes his own life, the Philistines continue to advance and the Israelites abandon their towns and flee. The day following this great battle, the Philistines find Saul among the dead and do two things to his body. They first cut off his head and then strip off his weapons (כלי) and put these in the temple of the Ashtoreths (31:9–10).[52] As we read about these final details of Saul's life, we are reminded of similar events earlier in the narrative. In 1 Sam 17 Saul was also faced with the threat of the Philistines, including the giant Goliath, against whom David won a great victory. After killing Goliath, David cut off Goliath's head with Goliath's own sword (17:51). Given the alignment between Saul and Goliath seen previously in their choice for battle garments and gear, perhaps our narrator once again reminds us of this alignment through their beheadings.

The placement of Saul's weapons in a (foreign) temple is also significant. After David cuts off the head of the Philistine, we find the reverse take place where he takes Goliath's weapons (כלי) and puts them first in his own tent (17:54) while later we read that Goliath's sword was put in the sanctuary (21:9–10). The only other time we are told of an Israelite item being put in a foreign temple is when the ark of YHWH had been deposited in the temple of Dagon (5:2). The difference between Saul's weapons and the ark being put into a foreign temple is that the ark of YHWH is sent back to Israel (due to YHWH's great display of power) while Saul's weapons remain in a foreign temple. YHWH who was present and working against the Philistines within the ark narrative now seems to be absent and there is no mention of Saul's weapons returning to Israel. Saul, now through his weapons

---

51. Auld, *I & II Samuel*, 327. Note also that Balaam was a קסם.
52. The NIV and NRSV render כלי as "armor" in 31:9–10.

that played such an important role in how he has been portrayed, belongs to the Philistines; he is now one of them.

Conclusion

The difficulty that many have had with Saul's initial failures and swift rejection as Israel's first king (1 Sam 13 and 15) is understandable. These events are indeed puzzling and there appears to be an inequity between Saul's achievements and his sins or penalties as Sternberg has noted above. Having said this, the reader must move on from this perplexing beginning to the remainder of 1 Samuel where our narrator continues his portrayal of Saul and adds to our understanding of why he was rejected by YHWH. One of the ways in which Saul is portrayed following YHWH's rejection of him is by means of his clothing and armor. By means of Saul's clothing and armor—in comparison and contrast with those around him— he is portrayed to look and act more and more like a foreigner, and in particular a Philistine. Thus, via the use of dress he is symbolically Othered. Coming to the end of 1 Sam, Saul's rejection is now complete. Saul, who initially rejected YHWH's commands is then rejected by YHWH, who in turn works against him as YHWH often works against foreigners. Saul looks and acts like a Philistine and is rejected as such.

After hearing the news of Saul's death, David mourns for Saul and Jonathan in a lament (2 Sam 1:17–27). In this lament David mentions how Saul dressed the daughters of Israel in luxury, like queens: "O daughters of Israel, weep for Saul, who clothed you in scarlet and finery, who adorned your garments with ornaments of gold." The use of dress in David's lament reveals an irony that draws together how Saul has been shown in 1 Samuel. Israel's first king who was once clothed in royalty and who also clothed YHWH's chosen daughters of Israel in luxury and finery is shown by means of his clothing to be among the anti-elect.

6

THE EMPEROR AND HIS CLOTHING: DAVID ROBED AND UNROBED BEFORE THE ARK AND MICHAL

Ian D. Wilson

The famous story of David dancing before YHWH's Ark as it enters Jerusalem has two distinct versions: one in 2 Samuel 6 and the other in 1 Chronicles 15.[1] In both versions, a grand procession bears the Ark into the City of David, the king dances wildly, and Michal observes the events from a window. The two versions are, however, remarkably different in many of their particulars. One such particular is the king's clothing. The version in 2 Samuel states that David "whirled with all his might" before the Ark while wearing a "linen ephod" (אפוד בד)—some kind of priestly clothing that is probably only a scant loincloth or undergarment (6:14).[2] Michal despises David for this behavior (6:16), and she chastises him for it, claiming that he exposed himself "as one of the riffraff might expose himself" (6:20). Michal thus condemns David's dancing but also his clothing (or lack thereof). In 2 Samuel's version of the story, David seems to have dressed down for the occasion. In 1 Chronicles, however, David is "wrapped in a robe of fine linen"

---

1. Psalm 132 contains another account of the Ark entering Jerusalem. It speaks of YHWH's/Zion's priests being "clothed" (לבש) in righteousness and victory (vv. 9, 16), and of David's enemies being clothed in disgrace (v. 18). The psalm, though, does not mention David's clothing, his dancing, or Michal's reaction—the main concerns of this chapter—so I do not discuss it here.

2. Cf. 1 Sam 2:18; 22:18; also Exod 28:42; 39:28; Lev 6:3; 16:4, 23, 32 (see בד [III] in *HALOT*; N.L. Tidwell, "The Linen Ephod: 1 Sam. II 18 and 2 Sam. VI 14," *VT* 24 [1974]: 505–07; and P. Kyle McCarter, Jr., *II Samuel*, AB 9 [New Haven: Yale University Press, 1984], 171). In 2 Sam 6:14 it is impossible to tell for sure the nature of the garment indicated. Michal's response to David's actions, however, strongly suggests that this particular garment, worn while dancing about, conceals very little. In 1 Sam 2:18–19, moreover, the text notes that young Samuel wore an אפוד בד and that his mother would bring him "a little robe" (קטן מעיל) every year, implying that the אפוד בד was to be accompanied by another, outer garment (cf. Exod 28:4, 31; 29:5; 39:22–23; also 1 Chr 15:27). See Carmen Imes' contribution for additional discussion of priestly garments, in this volume, 30–38.

(מכרבל במעיל בוץ) in addition to his priestly ephod (1 Chr 15:27).³ The narrative in Chronicles highlights Michal's distaste for David's whirling about (1 Chr 15:29), but it does not recount Michal's comments about indecent exposure. David's state of dress (and Michal's reaction to it) is a conspicuous difference in the versions, a difference that impacts potential readings of the narrative.

In this chapter, I want to work toward an understanding of how ancient Judean literati thought about David's (lack of) clothing and its (in)appropriateness at this momentous event. Judean readers in the early Second Temple era were conversant with the book of Samuel and the book of Chronicles. They read both, they contemplated both, and both played a part in their social remembering of Judah's monarchic past. Both books were, without a doubt, part of the intellectual repertoire of the literate community in and around the Jerusalem temple in the Late Persian period. The two books existed in this historical context in a discursive relationship, informing and balancing one another's narrative perspectives on Israel's past.⁴ When the discourse came to David and his state of dress before the Ark and Michal, what were the discursive possibilities? How did these texts contribute to the remembering of David and the Israelite monarchy in a postmonarchic milieu?

The first thing to consider is the broader cultural context of the narrative. The story of the Ark entering Jerusalem is a narrative that reflects ANE royal rituals and festivities. It depicts a civic event, a spectacle that puts royal and cultic functionaries and their accoutrements on full display for the purpose of celebrating the king and his deity and (re)affirming their relationship of power and the power of their relationship.⁵ Compare, for example, the annual Hittite festivals of the Late Bronze Age, which in some cases lasted for multiple weeks and which included ceremonies at the main temple in Hattusa as well as traveling processions to neighboring locales.⁶ "By maintaining the various cults in the

---

3. On the term "robe" (מעיל), see Scott Starbuck's contribution to this volume, 145–50.

4. Although the narrative in Samuel–Kings appears to have been the more authoritative version of the monarchic past, Chronicles also garnered some amount of authority for Judean readers, as later Second Temple-era literature evinces (Ehud Ben Zvi, *History, Literature and Theology in the Book of Chronicles* [London: Equinox, 2006], 243–68; Ian D. Wilson, "Chronicles and Utopia: Likely Bedfellows?" in *History, Memory, Hebrew Scriptures: A Festschrift for Ehud Ben Zvi*, ed. Ian D. Wilson and Diana V. Edelman [Winona Lake, IN: Eisenbrauns, 2015], 151–65).

5. Such rituals/celebrations were either one-time events (see, e.g., C.L. Seow, *Myth, Drama, and the Politics of David's Dance*, HSM 44 [Atlanta: Scholars Press, 1989]) or annual rites of commemoration (see, e.g., Daniel E. Fleming, *The Installation of Baal's High Priestess at Emar*, HSS 42 [Atlanta: Scholars Press, 1992]).

6. David P. Wright, "Anatolia: Hittites," in *Religions of the Ancient World: A Guide*, ed. Sarah Iles Johnston (Cambridge, MA: Belknap of Harvard University Press, 2007), 193; Billie Jean Collins, *The Hittites and Their World*, Archaeology and Biblical Studies 7 (Atlanta: SBL, 2007), 162–64.

kingdom," states David Wright, "the king shored up the unity of the kingdom and engendered support for his rule."[7] Indeed, for the Hittite king, there was no real distinction between political and cultic concerns.[8] More often than not, this was the case throughout the ANE world. With such things in mind, what broad cultural expectations might the Judeans have had with regard to a king's clothing in a civic celebration? Second, we should consider the implications of David's clothing within each narrative context: What potential meanings are at play in Samuel, in Chronicles, and in the interrelationship between the two? Drawing on research into social memory and "forgetting," I will argue that Judean readers of these texts would partially warrant Michal's distaste for David's dressing-down while still maintaining a critical stance toward the queen.

Kingly clothing and rituals/ceremonies in the ancient Near East

I begin with a few comments on representations of kingly dress and kingly ritual and ceremony in the ANE. From "prehistory" to the Persian period, there are numerous representations, visual and written, of kings in ritual procession or pious activity. In such representations the kings are, of course, clothed.

Take the Uruk vase, for example, from the late fourth millennium in southern Mesopotamia. It depicts a human ruler, followed by a long line of human offerers, presenting the produce of the land to the goddess Inanna. The offerers, carrying baskets of various goods, are completely nude. The image of the ruler is, unfortunately, only partially preserved, but it is nonetheless clear that he wears an ornate garment in stark contrast with his naked servants. Inanna, too, wears a headdress and a robe with marked trim.[9] In images from the Late Bronze Age, the Hittite king, mentioned above, appears in divine attire, either in the dress of the Sun-God or in battle gear of the warrior-gods.[10] Later, in the Iron Age, representations of the Assyrian king—in both the imperial center and its periphery—display the king in full royal garb, including robe, necklace and/or bracelet with divine icons, priestly headdress, as well as standard kingly weapons and other accoutrements.[11]

---

7. Wright, "Anatolia: Hittites," 193.

8. Collins, *Hittites and Their World*, 157–58.

9. For a discussion of the vase, its imagery, and its narrative, see Zainab Bahrani, "Performativity and the Image: Narrative, Representation, and the Uruk Vase," in *Leaving No Stones Unturned: Essays on the Ancient Near East in Honor of Donald P. Hansen*, ed. Erica Ehrenberg (Winona Lake, IN: Eisenbrauns, 2002), 15–22. For more on the clothing of deities, see the contributions of Ehud Ben Zvi and Shawn Flynn to this volume.

10. Collins, *Hittites and Their World*, 97–98.

11. For discussions of Assyrian imperial iconography, its ideology, and its creation—at both center and periphery—see Ann Shafer, "Assyrian Royal Monuments on the Periphery: Ritual and the Making of Imperial Space," in *Ancient Near Eastern Art in Context: Studies in Honor of Irene J. Winter by Her Students*, ed. Jack Cheng and Marian H. Feldman (Leiden:

In depictions of the Assyrian king—whether he is violently engaging and crushing an enemy horde, receiving supplication from subjects, or approaching the divine in reverence and solitude—he appears in full and typical Assyrian royal dress.[12] Examining the Persian Empire and its era, we find similar depictions of the king. From Bisitun to Susa to Persepolis, the king appears in full regalia, whether receiving blessing from Ahuramazda, grappling with a beast, or sitting on his throne. Although there are important distinctions in the respective iconographic ideologies of Assyria and Persia, for example,[13] throughout both empires the king was consistently portrayed as elaborately and fully clothed.[14]

Written texts depict the same sorts of imagery. Clothing (or lack of it) is a conspicuous marker of social standing and power. Nudity is dishonorable, a mark of shame and impoverishment. The poor have few clothes—the rich have lots. Similarly, the uncivilized and barbarous lack proper clothing or have none at all, while the civilized have clean and elegant attire. And the king, at the top of society, chosen by the gods to rule the peoples of the earth, has the most and the best.[15]

Brill, 2007), 133–59; also Irene J. Winter, "Art in Empire: The Royal Image and the Visual Dimensions of Assyrian Ideology," in *Assyria 1995: Proceedings of the 10th Anniversary Symposium of the Neo-Assyrian Text Corpus Project, Helsinki, September 7–11, 1995*, ed. S. Parpola and R.M. Whiting (Helsinki: The Neo-Assyrian Text Corpus Project, 1997), 359–81.

12. Notably, in Assyria, the king was an active participant in cultic duties; he had a definite priestly role. To be sure, all kings in the ANE had some connection to the cult, even if only as patron and ritual bystander (which was the case at Emar, for example; see Fleming, *Installation of Baal's High Priestess*, 99–102. On the pious king in general in Mesopotamia, see Caroline Waerzeggers, "The Pious King: Royal Patronage of Temples," in *The Oxford Handbook of Cuneiform Culture*, ed. Karen Radner and Eleanor Robson [Oxford: Oxford University Press, 2011], 725–51). But in Assyria the king had a remarkably close relationship to the cultus (see, e.g., Peter Machinist, "Kingship and Divinity in Imperial Assyria," in *Text, Artifact, and Image: Revealing Ancient Israelite Religion*, ed. Gary M. Beckman and Theodore J. Lewis [Providence, RI: Brown Judaic Studies, 2006], 156–59). This means that in depictions of Assyrian kingship in particular, priestly iconographic elements are regularly apparent (Ursula Magen, *Assyrische Königsdarstellungen—Apekte der Herrschaft: Eine Typoligie*, Baghdader Forschungen 9 [Mainz am Rhein: Philipp von Zabern, 1986], 65–69).

13. Margaret Cool Root, *The King and Kingship in Achaemenid Art: Essays on the Creation of an Iconography of Empire*, Acta Iranica 19 (Leiden: Brill, 1979); Erica Ehrenberg, "Dieu et Mon Droit: Kingship in the Late Babylonian and Early Persian Times," in *Religion and Power: Divine Kingship in the Ancient World and Beyond*, ed. Nicole Brisch, Oriental Institute Seminars 4 (Chicago: Oriental Institute of the University of Chicago, 2008), 103–31.

14. By "fully clothed" I do not necessarily mean fully *covered*. Kings are depicted sometimes with a bare shoulder or often with bare forearms and lower legs. What I mean is that kings are always dressed fully and appropriately for the setting.

15. Alicia J. Batten, "Clothing and Adornment," *BTB* 40 (2010): 149–50.

Consider, for example, a piece of Assyrian mythology probably related to Assyrian coronation hymns. The text reads:

> Ea began to speak, addressing Belet-ili:
> You are Belet-ili, lady of the great gods!
> It is you who have created *lullu-man*,
> now create a king, a man to be in control!
> Encircle the whole of his body with something fine.
> Finish perfectly his appearance, make his body beautiful![16]

The text goes on to describe how the gods gave the king his crown, his throne, his weapons, his terrifying splendor, his beautiful countenance, and so on.[17] These divine gifts prepare the king specifically for his role as divinely appointed warrior and subduer of all chaos.[18] But they also serve to set the king apart in general, to emphasize his special, superhuman status vis-à-vis the rest of creation: his body is encircled with "something fine"—within creation his beauty and appearance are beyond compare. These lines in particular refer to the king's body and to the magnificence of kingly appearance in general, not to his clothing per se. In the context of a civic ceremony such as a coronation rite or a ritual procession of divine artifacts or the sanctification of a new capital, however, the king's clothing and accoutrements, which conspicuously marked his actual physical appearance, would be the representations of his special status and aura. What he carried on his body symbolized the mythic status of the kingly body itself. Clothing is wrapped up, so to speak, with identification—with gender, ethnicity, socioeconomics and politics, and so forth.[19] At least in the case of Mesopotamian kings in the first millennium BCE, clothing not only identified kingship at the top of the socioeconomic and political hierarchies but also marked the interrelationship between royalty and the divine realm.[20] Given this sort of evidence, it is reasonable to argue that there was an expectation for the king to be clothed in exceptional style.[21] His body and its clothing were set apart, recognizably different from that of common humanity.

---

16. *COS* 1.146 (pp. 1:476–77); Werner Mayer, "Ein Mythos von der Erschaffung des Menschen und des Königs," *Orientalia* 56 (1987): 55–68.

17. Compare Assurbanipal's coronation hymn (*COS* 1.142 [pp. 1:473–74]).

18. C.L. Crouch, *War and Ethics in the Ancient Near East: Military Violence in Light of Cosmology and History*, BZAW 407 (Berlin: De Gruyter, 2009), 24–26.

19. Batten, "Clothing and Adornment," 148–49; Mary Harlow, "Dress and Identity: An Introduction," in *Dress and Identity*, ed. Mary Harlow, BAR International Series 2356 (Oxford: Archaeopress, 2012), 1–5.

20. A. Leo Oppenheim, "The Golden Garments of the Gods," *JNES* 8 (1949): 172–93.

21. On patterns and decorations on kingly garments in this era, see Eleanor Guralnick, "Neo-Assyrian Patterned Fabrics," *Iraq* 66 (2004): 221–32.

Interpreting David's (lack of) clothing

The above examples give us some idea as to expectations concerning kingly clothing in general, but what do we make of David's clothing (or lack of it) amid the Ark's procession into Jerusalem in 2 Samuel 6 and 1 Chronicles 15? What can we say about kingly clothing in such ritualistic or ceremonial contexts in ancient Israel and Judah? Scholars have offered a number of conjectural reconstructions of what sorts of ritual or ceremony the episode in 2 Samuel 6 and 1 Chronicles 15 might reflect—be it an enthronement rite or festival, a reenactment of the divine warrior's mythic victory over chaos, an introduction of a deity into a new city, an annual parading of divine images, a kingly fertility rite, or some combination of several of these options.[22] Unfortunately, though, there is little (if any) evidence that can help us understand the king's clothing in such contexts.

For instance, in a commonly cited work, C. L. Seow argues that the procession reflects the West Semitic divine warrior motif, and he illuminates some of the episode's apparent mythological background in its Levantine milieu. Regarding the king's specific actions and clothing, he suggests that David's whirling and prancing reflect animal-like cultic dancing evinced in the Levant and elsewhere in the ANE, and that David's scant clothing in 2 Samuel 6 is comparable to depictions of nude worshippers in ANE iconography.[23] David, however, is a king leading a cultic procession into his new capital; he is not a common cultic participant bringing regular offerings to a deity or performing special rites in a deity's sanctuary.[24] In the narrative, the king is subservient to the deity and worships him, to be sure. But comparing David's dancing with depictions of non-kingly worshippers fails to account for the king's prominent position in the social hierarchy. The worshippers on the Uruk vase, for example, are nude, but their king certainly is not.

In a more recent contribution, Bruce Rosenstock compares the episode in 2 Samuel 6 to Greek fertility rituals. His work perhaps sheds some light on the issue of David's self-exposure and Michal's response, especially with regard to ideological expectations in the overarching narrative. "In the case of this particular enthronement ritual," writes Rosenstock,

---

22. E.g., J.R. Porter, "The Interpretation of 2 Samuel VI and Psalm CXXXII," *JTS* 5 (1954): 161–73; Patrick D. Miller and J.J.M. Roberts, *The Hand of the Lord: A Reassessment of the "Ark Narrative" of 1 Samuel* (Baltimore: Johns Hopkins University Press, 1977); McCarter, *II Samuel*, 180–82; Seow, *Politics of David's Dance*; Allan Rosengren Petersen, *The Royal God: Enthronement Festivals in Ancient Israel and Ugarit?* JSOTSup 259 (Sheffield: Sheffield Academic, 1998); Gary N. Knoppers, *I Chronicles 10–29*, AB 12A (New Haven: Yale University Press, 2004), 629–33; Bruce Rosenstock, "David's Play: Fertility Rituals and the Glory of God in 2 Samuel 6," *JSOT* 31 (2006): 63–80.

23. Seow, *Politics of David's Dance*, 104–18.

24. McCarter, *II Samuel*, 180–82; Knoppers, *I Chronicles 10–29*, 629–30.

expectations about the "proper" behavior of the king were overturned. ... In effect, Michal and David have exchanged ritual roles. David seems to have been expected to play the serious role of victorious king and Michal was to enact the role of a "player" who engaged in jesting mockery. David, however, assumed the role of jesting "player," while Michal was cast in the role of serious disparager of the king's performance.[25]

Assuming that the procession into Jerusalem has to do with fertility ritual, he goes on to argue that David (and thus the story) is deliberately mocking any theological association between the king, the deity, and procreative success: the story points out Michal's "theological mistake" and thus critiques the "pan-Mediterranean veneration of divine/royal phallic power."[26]

It is not self-evident, however, that the activities in this episode necessarily have to do with securing "procreative fecundity," as Rosenstock assumes, so we cannot take for granted that David was actively exposing himself as he danced, in some kind of fertility rite, with the purpose of mocking "phallic power" with a carnivalesque gesture.[27] Rosenstock's argument places much weight on YHWH's blessing of Obed-edom's house and all his belongings (2 Sam 6:11-12; cf. 1 Chr 13:14; 26:5). This blessing functions as a major catalyst in 2 Samuel's version of the narrative: David decides to reinitiate the Ark's procession to Jerusalem when he hears of it, presumably because he wants the same sort of blessing for Jerusalem and his own household there.[28] The blessing may indeed imply fecundity in part: the narrator's comment concerning Michal's lack of children suggests as much (2 Sam 6:23),[29] so does the account of Obed-edom's posterity

---

25. Rosenstock, "David's Play," 73.
26. Ibid., 74, 78.
27. Ibid., 65. See McCarter, *II Samuel*, 188–89, who emphasizes that the procession does not reflect a sacred marriage rite or some other sexually charged event; rather, it reflects the entry of a god into its capital city.
28. This detail plays a lesser role in Chronicles' account, in which the story of the Ark's transfer includes notices concerning David's palace, his wives and children, his routing of the Philistines, and his activities in Jerusalem to prepare for the Ark's arrival (see 1 Chr 14:1–15:24). As "the Chronicler" is wont to do, in this case he has "repositioned material from his *Vorlage* of Samuel, recontextualized it, overwritten certain parts, furnished rubrics, introduced material from a variety of biblical psalms, and added new material" (Knoppers, *I Chronicles 10–29*, 589). Knoppers argues that, in this instance, Chronicles' presentation of the material relies upon the Zion-centered perspective of Ps 132 (*I Chronicles 10–29*, 590–91).
29. The statement in 2 Sam 6:23 is clear with regard to Michal's lack of progeny, but it gives no explicit reason for this lack. The syntax of the statement leaves the connection between it and the preceding narrative ambiguous. Some English translations are misleading here, reading a causal conjunction between vv. 22 and 23 (e.g., KJV, NJPS), but nothing in the Hebrew requires such a reading (Robert Alter, *The Art of Biblical Narrative* [New York: Basic Books, 1981], 125–26).

in 1 Chr 26:4–8. In other words, having children is one leitmotif in the passage. Successful procreation, however, is certainly not the only thing implied here in 2 Sam 6, nor is it even the most obvious within the context of Judean discourse on these matters. In a number of texts, a blessed household refers first and foremost to material possessions (e.g., Gen 30:30; 39:5; Job 1:10), and in any case the statement in 2 Sam 6:12 mentions outright that the blessing has to do with Obed-edom's household *and all his belongings*. Rosenstock's analysis, in addition, relies heavily upon Seow's, which has its own difficulties interpreting David's meager clothing and bodily exposure, as mentioned above. To be clear, I agree with Rosenstock that this narrative is concerned with ideological expectations for the glory of the king and his deity (more below), but I do not think that the procession and David's exposure has entirely or even mainly to do with fecundity or ritualistic "phallic display." Drawing analogies between David's dancing during the Ark's procession and ancient Mediterranean fertility rites is, therefore, something of a misstep and in the end helps little in our attempt to understand David's clothing in this episode and its potential import for the Judean readership.

In any case, I argue, the ancient Judean readers of 2 Samuel 6 would have understood David's clothing before the Ark and Michal—his wearing nothing but a skimpy linen ephod and exposing himself in the midst of civic celebration—as somewhat out of the ordinary. The fine linen robes worn by David and his attendants in 1 Chronicles 15 represent something closer to the convention for kingly clothing. David's clothing in 2 Samuel 6 was, with regard to ANE norms, abnormal for a king, despite attempts to argue otherwise. Wearing non-kingly garments—especially garments that might expose oneself during the civic celebration of a deity entering his chosen city—was not standard practice for a ruler in the Persian era or earlier. The king's garments were supposed to set him apart, to mark his divinely chosen and even sacred body, not to reveal his commonness. The question now becomes: What might this abnormality have signified in the context of Persian-period Judah, and what did Persian-period readers make of the abnormality in light of the narrative variant in 1 Chronicles?

David's (lack of) clothing and Michal's disgust

Thus far I have argued that, in the ANE, there was a general expectation that kingly clothing was exceptional and noteworthy. It stood out and marked the king's sociopolitical, economic, and even theological status, his position as a divinely chosen ruler of his people and even the world.

Given this expectation, and given the lack of good evidence suggesting otherwise, it is probable that David's priestly but scanty undergarment in 2 Samuel 6 would have stood out to readers as something out of the ordinary, as something not becoming of a king. Typically, kings did not dress down for rituals or ceremonies like the procession recounted in this text. In any case, nudity in general is associated with shame in Judean literature, Genesis 2–3 being the famous exemplar.³⁰ It is, for the most part, unbecoming for anyone to go about naked, given humanity's post-Edenic state of existence, let alone the king. Take, for example, Saul's naked prophesying (1 Sam 19:24)—the only other instance of an under- or undressed king in the Judean literature. The people regard this activity as unusual for their ruler: "Is Saul also among the prophets?," they ask. Although the text does not comment directly on Saul's removal of his clothing and his nudity in relation to the ecstatic utterances, it does point to the uncommonness of such actions for someone in his position. Learning of Saul's naked prophesying, the people are taken by surprise.³¹ Also notice that Isaiah's three-year nakedness (Isa 20:2–4), though commanded by YHWH, is an act meant to signify the coming defeat and humiliation of the Egyptians. Generally, nudity is marked as out-of-the-ordinary and even shameful. What, then, can we say about David's (non-)clothing and Michal's responses to it, in 2 Samuel 6 and 1 Chronicles 15, respectively, within Judean discourse in the early Second Temple era? And what might the discursive interrelationship of these texts tell us about Judean remembering of kingship?

It is important to reemphasize that this entire issue, the (in)appropriateness of David's clothing in relation to his behavior, is a product of Michal's reaction to the procession. The narrator offers no expositional comments on the issue of David's dance and clothing in particular, which "opens the gates to multiple interpretations" of Michal's response.³² In 2 Samuel 6 we read, simply, that Michal despised David for his dancing (6:16) and that, while dancing, David exposed himself in a way Michal considered to be dishonorable (6:20).

As Rosenstock's analysis evinces, it is not uncommon to regard Michal as theologically "mistaken" or somehow in the wrong on this issue. To wit: Antony Campbell comments that 2 Sam 6:16 "brings out Michal's self-imposed exclusion" and argues that Michal has (impiously) kept herself from "the inauguration of

---

30. Dietmar Neufeld, "The Rhetoric of Body, Clothing and Identity in the Vita and Genesis," *Scriptura* 90 (2005): 679–84.

31. Cf. 1 Sam 10:9–13. In that story, too, Saul prophesies ecstatically and the people respond by asking, "Is Saul also among the prophets?" But in that instance, there is no mention of nakedness. The story in 1 Samuel 10—even though it is notably ambivalent about Saul himself and the function of kingship in general—presents Saul's prophetic activity positively, as a sign of YHWH's spirit coming upon Israel's first king. In 1 Samuel 19, to the contrary, Saul's prophetic activity—and the nudity that goes along with it—is a negative sign, pointing to the removal of YHWH's favor. Saul's moment of naked ecstasy foils his attempt to seize David, the one whom YHWH has chosen to replace the failed king Saul. For more on Saul with regard to clothing, see Sean Cook's contribution to this volume.

32. Alter, *Art of Biblical Narrative*, 123. He comments further, "The biblical writer knows as well as any psychologically minded modern that one's emotional reaction to an immediate stimulus can have a complicated prehistory; and by suppressing any causal explanation in his initial statement of Michal's scorn, he beautifully suggests the 'overdetermined' nature of her contemptuous ire, how it bears the weight of everything that has not been said but obliquely intimated about the relation between Michal and David."

a momentous new epoch in the story of Israel."[33] In other words, according to Campbell's reading, David righteously guides and takes part in the festivities, blessing the people in YHWH's name (6:18), while the embittered Michal opts out. In such a reading, Michal's perspective reflects misunderstanding or ignorance or denial concerning these matters, and David's reflects proper understanding and knowledge: David is right—Michal is wrong.[34] A closer examination of the discourse, however, reveals that in the case of David's dancing and clothing and bodily exposure, the division between who is "right" and who is "wrong" is not so clear.

There is, without question, a strongly political aspect to the narrative in 2 Samuel 6. Michal's family, at least, does not come off well. Notice that Michal is identified throughout the passage as "the daughter of Saul" (vv. 16, 20, 23). In the passage's closing statement, in v. 23, this genealogical detail is clearly emphasized: the actual subject of the clause is ילד ("child"), but the clause begins with the prepositional phrase למיכל בת שאול ("as for Michal daughter of Saul"), making it quite clear that Saul's household—and thus any potential future Saulide claim to the throne—is at stake here.[35] The war between David's and Saul's houses is over, David has completely taken over the kingship, he has also taken Jerusalem and made it his capital, and now he is ushering YHWH's Ark into the city. It is a triumphant moment for Davidic rule indeed.

The exchange between Michal and David (vv. 20–23) highlights this political transition, to be sure, but it also subtly raises a number of other issues in the discourse, issues that would have complicated the readership's understandings of David's behavior and clothing and Michal's reactions to them. Michal, בת שאול, acknowledges David's kingship outright, referring to him as מלך ישראל, but she does so in the midst of a thickly sarcastic remark: "How the king of Israel is honored [כבד Niph.] today!—the one who has exposed himself today in the sight of his servants' maids, as one of the riffraff [הרקים][36] might expose himself!" This statement, while acknowledging David's rule, pulls no punches when it comes to David's behavior

---

33. Antony F. Campbell, *2 Samuel*, FOTL 8 (Grand Rapids, MI: Eerdmans, 2005), 67.

34. Ellen White, "Michal the Misinterpreted," *JSOT* 31 (2007): 451–64. See also David J.A. Clines, "Michal Observed: An Introduction to Reading Her Story," in *Telling Queen Michal's Story: An Experiment in Comparative Interpretation*, ed. David J.A. Clines and Tamara C. Eshkenazi, JSOTSup 119 (Sheffield: JSOT, 1991), 54–57, who surveys the common interpretation that Michal's "religious sensibilities are the inferior of David's" (54).

35. E.g., Seow, *Politics of David's Dance*, 130–31; Ina Willi-Plein, "Michal und die Anfänge des Königtums in Israel," in *Congress Volume: Cambridge 1995*, ed. J.A. Emerton (Leiden: Brill, 1997), 416–17; Campbell, *2 Samuel*, 67; A. Graeme Auld, *I & II Samuel: A Commentary*, OTL (Louisville, KY: Westminster John Knox, 2011), 415; and Joel Baden, *The Historical David: The Real Life of an Invented Hero* (New York: HarperCollins, 2013), 190.

36. Literally "the empty ones" (from the Hebrew adjective ריק), implying persons that are unprincipled or lacking in character (cf. Judg 9:4; 11:3; 2 Chr 13:7). LXX has τῶν ὀρχουμένων ("the dancers").

and his skimpy clothing. To expose oneself—that is, not to give proper attention to one's dress—is unbecoming for a king. David's response, though, "goes for the political and theological jugular," as Campbell puts it,[37] by pointing out that YHWH chose him over Michal's father Saul—David will, therefore, dance before YHWH as he pleases. Furthermore, in direct response to Michal's sarcastic comment, David declares that he will demean himself even more, thus receiving honor (כבד Niph.) from the aforementioned maids.[38] The narrator rounds off the exchange with the statement, "As for Michal daughter of Saul, she had no child to the day of her death."

There are several things going on in this exchange between the king and queen. First, clearly the exchange aims to emphasize the downfall of Saul's line and the rise of David's. As I said above, there is no question about this: the passage has an anti-Saul/pro-David perspective on Israel's kingship. It is David, not Saul, who is king of Israel, who has brought the Ark to its proper resting place in Jerusalem, and whose household will continue. Second, the passage indeed makes a sexual-political statement using clothing, but one that inevitably becomes, within the larger narrative in Samuel-Kings, something of an ironic presaging of David's future troubles with women—his affair with Bathsheba, his impotency with Abishag, and so on.[39] David's reversal of Michal's sarcastic critique stands out as an ironic affirmation of his own failures later in his life. In the immediate context it may appear that David has indeed won the political and theological day, but a bird's-eye view of David's story in the book of Samuel (and 1 Kgs 1–2) reveals a reading that questions David's apparent success in the exchange with Michal.[40] Third, although it is tempting to read the narrator's closing comment as proof that Michal was in the wrong, the comment itself is ambiguous. Being childless is shameful, to be sure (just like being naked), but there is no indication as to the reason for this lifelong shame.[41] Is it a divine punishment brought upon Michal because of her so-called

---

37. Campbell, *2 Samuel*, 67.

38. This is not the only exchange, in the book of Samuel, that includes a reference to David receiving honor. The priest Ahimelech, trying to defend his support of David, tells Saul that David has received more honor than any other servant in the king's household (1 Sam 22:14). Saul, of course, does not buy Ahimelech's defense, and proceeds to have the priest (and all the inhabitants of Nob) executed. Thus, before becoming king, David receives honor from someone that the king (Saul) sees as a threat to his power, and then Saul's own daughter sarcastically honors David, who is now king, for exposing himself to these maids, whom Michal perhaps sees as a threat to her marriage. See also 1 Sam 15:30 and 2 Sam 10:3, which refer to Saul and his *failure* to receive honor.

39. Frank Crüsemann, "Zwei alttestamentliche Witze: I Sam 21:11–15 und II Sam 6:16, 20–23 als Beispiele einer biblischen Gattung," *ZAW* 92 (1980): 223–27; McCarter, *II Samuel*, 188.

40. E.g., John Van Seters, *The Biblical Saga of King David* (Winona Lake, IN: Eisenbrauns, 2009), 279, observes that David's boastful reference to his divine election in 2 Sam 6:21–22 then makes his humble prayer in 7:18–29 seem strongly hypocritical.

41. Auld, *I & II Samuel*, 415.

"theological mistake," her "misconstruing" of David's dancing and self-exposure?[42] Or is it simply because of David's own sexual rejection of her, his personal choice because of his distaste for her criticisms?[43] There is no clear answer.[44] It is certain that the discontinuation of Saul's line is the major issue here—that is what the text wants to emphasize—but precisely how Michal and David's argument over his dancing and revealing attire plays into this remains uncertain.

At this point, it is worth emphasizing the multivocality of Michal throughout her story in the book of Samuel, as well as the multivocality of David throughout the entire corpus of Judean literature.[45] In other words, the literature has no single way of speaking about these figures and their import in Israel's remembered past. The figures of Michal and David, and their roles in the narrative's plot, are irreducible to any one potential statement in the discourse. Michal is partly responsible for David's kingship (she saves David's life, and her marriage to David helps justify his claim to Israel's throne), and yet she is also a potential threat to it (since she is Saul's daughter).[46] The literature's opinion of David and the import of Davidic kingship in Judah's/Israel's ongoing history are unclear, too. Some prophetic texts, for example, envision a future in which a kind of superhuman Davidic kingship is central (e.g., Isa 11:1–5), while others transfer Davidic glory to the people as a collective (e.g., Isa 55:3–5; Zech 12:7–8) or fail to mention anything about David at all (Isa 2:2–4; Mic 4:1–5; Ezek 44–48). Moreover, as I mentioned above, in the book of Samuel itself (and in 1 Kgs 1–2) David's house takes a turn for the worse as David struggles to control his family and his kingdom.[47] Many scholars comment on a marked change in David's fortune after his affair with Bathsheba and the

---

42. E.g., Baden, *Historical David*, 190, states, "The Bible implies that this was divine punishment for Michal's behavior," before going on to argue that what *really* happened (note the subtitle of Baden's book) was that David refused to have children with her for political reasons to ensure the discontinuation of Saul's line.

43. Marti J. Steussy, *David: Biblical Portraits of Power* (Columbia: University of South Carolina Press, 1999), 74, points out that MT 2 Sam 21:8–9 states that Michal did have sons from another marriage, five of them, whom David hands over to the Gibeonites to be impaled. Thus, in addition to denying Michal children with himself, David enabled the death of her other offspring.

44. Alter, *Art of Biblical Narrative*, 125–26.

45. Clines, "Michal Observed"; Athalya Brenner, "Michal and David: Love between Enemies?" in *The Fate of King David: The Past and Present of a Biblical Icon*, ed. Tod Linafelt, Claudia V. Camp and Timothy Beal, LHBOTS 500 (New York: T&T Clark, 2010), 260–70.

46. Willi-Plein, "Michal und die Anfänge des Königtums."

47. Of course, this is mitigated in the balance of the book of Kings, where David stands as the righteous benchmark for kingship. Alison L. Joseph, "Who Is like David? Was David like David? Good Kings in the Book of Kings," *CBQ* 77 (2015): 20–41, argues therefore that David himself (as represented in the book of Samuel) does not measure up to the Davidic standard of the book of Kings.

subsequent murder of Uriah. The point at which David's fortunes begin to change, however, is blurry. Jacob Wright, for instance, has recently argued that already in 2 Sam 8, well before the Bathsheba episode, David's megalomania and selfish interests are apparent—the king is concerned with making a name for himself rather than for YHWH.[48] Robert Polzin, too, draws attention to the links between Eli's fall/Samuel's rise and Saul's fall/David's rise in 1 Samuel, which, he argues, establishes a framework for the glorious rise and tragic fall of Davidic kingship in Israel, which ultimately ends in exile.[49] Within this framework, Polzin suggests that Michal's critique of David and her subsequent childlessness are actually representations of ideals—Michal, in Polzin's reading, signifies the position of the Deuteronomist: critical of kingship in general and thus hoping for a non-kingly, non-dynastic future, that is, a future like Michal's. All this to say, in postmonarchic Judah, the jury was probably still out on David and Michal.[50]

Considering this multivocality, then, we should not rush to conclude that Michal's reaction to David's behavior and state of (un)dress in 2 Samuel 6 is necessarily "wrong" or "mistaken," from the perspective of Judean readers in the Persian era and later. We cannot assume that, for the literati, David was "right" about his dancing and related uncovering simply because he was David and his house continued while Saul's did not. I repeat: the absolute end of Saulide kingship

---

48. Jacob L. Wright, *David, King of Israel, and Caleb in Biblical Memory* (New York: Cambridge University Press, 2014), 89–91.

49. Robert Polzin "A Multivoiced Look at the Michal Narratives," in *Telling Queen Michal's Story: An Experiment in Comparative Interpretation*, ed. David J.A. Clines and Tamara C. Eshkenazi, JSOTSup 119 (Sheffield: JSOT), 261–69.

50. The jury was still out on Saul as well. Despite Saul's failed kingship, his obvious loss of YHWH's favor, there would have been some underlying sympathy for him among the Judean literati. The book of Samuel contains different voices concerning Saul, as it does concerning David and Michal, voices which speak to the long and complicated history of the book's composition, but which also speak to the mind-sets of those who received and maintained the book in antiquity (David Jobling, *1 Samuel*, Berit Olam: Studies in Hebrew Narrative and Poetry [Collegeville, MN: Liturgical, 1998], 19). Note, e.g., a trend toward heroicization of Saul in texts like 1 Sam 11 and 2 Sam 21:10–14 (Brian R. Doak, "The Fate and Power of Heroic Bones and the Politics of Bone Transfer in Ancient Israel and Greece," HTR 106 [2013]: 201–16). There is also the book of Esther and its redemption of Saul's failure to eradicate the Amalekites. Later Jewish literature, too, offers a variety of opinions about Israel's failed first king: Rabbinic texts generally praise him, Pseudo-Philo criticizes him, and Josephus, devoting much attention to him, provides something of a middle ground (Louis H. Feldman, "Josephus' View of Saul," in *Saul in Story and Tradition*, ed. Carl S. Ehrlich and Marsha C. White, FAT 47 [Tübingen: Mohr Siebeck, 2006], 214–44; Hanna Liss, "The Innocent King: Saul in Rabbinic Exegesis," in *Saul in Story and Tradition*, 245–60; Joachim Vette, "Samuel's 'Farewell Speech': Theme and Variation in 1 Samuel 12, Josephus, and Pseudo-Philo," in *Literary Constructions of Identity in the Ancient World*, ed. Hanna Liss and Manfred Oeming [Winona Lake, IN: Eisenbrauns, 2010], 325–39).

is certain in the text, but the (in)appropriateness of David's action and his clothing in the narrative are open to debate. Moreover, given the general sociocultural expectation for kingly clothing in an ANE milieu, outlined above, I would even suggest that the discourse in ancient Judah leaned toward *David* being in the "wrong" on this issue, at least when it came to his clothing and his related bodily exposure.

Here it is informative to turn to Chronicles and its contribution to the discussion. As I mentioned at the outset, Chronicles' version of the narrative differs in its recounting of David's clothing. First Chronicles 15:27 states that during the procession, David was "wrapped in a robe of fine linen," as were all the other cultic functionaries, and it adds, seemingly as an afterthought, that also "upon David was a linen ephod." Chronicles' version differs, too, in its recounting of Michal. First Chronicles 15:29, just like 2 Sam 6:16, relates how Michal was watching out the window, how she saw David's dancing and playing about, and how she despised him for it.[51] The account in Chronicles, however, does not relate anything about the sardonic exchange between the king and queen. Instead, it recounts his appointing of Levitical servants and the psalms they sang in praise of YHWH (16:4–43), saying nothing more about Michal.

Much could be, and has been, said about the similarities and differences between the book of Samuel's and Chronicles' versions of the Ark procession.[52] But here I want to focus only on the issue of David's clothing and Michal. The fact that Chronicles makes a point of mentioning David's "robe of fine linen," a point not made in Samuel, and that Samuel, unlike Chronicles, includes a tension-filled exchange between David and Michal concerning indecent exposure, is a conspicuous difference in the versions. What, though, might this tell us about Judean understandings of kingly clothing?

It is possible, even probable, that Chronicles' version attempts to cover up David's wardrobe mishap, so to speak. In this way, it lends sympathy to Michal's own understanding of the situation in 2 Samuel 6. Chronicles' perspective seems to be in line with Michal's in 2 Samuel 6, that is, a king should be properly clothed at such an event.[53] However, Chronicles also shows no favor toward Michal—she

---

51. On Michal "at the window," see Nehama Aschkenasy, *Woman at the Window: Biblical Tales of Oppression and Escape* (Detroit: Wayne State University Press, 1998), 35–41, who comments that Michal's "two window scenes [1 Sam 19:11–12 and 2 Sam 6:16] ... mark her transformation from power to powerlessness" (35).

52. See, e.g., Knoppers' extensive discussion (*I Chronicles 10–29*, 578–661).

53. See Clines, "Michal Observed," 59, who argues that Michal believes David is not acting like a proper king; also Ora Horn Prouser, "Suited to the Throne: The Symbolic Use of Clothing in the David and Saul Narratives," *JSOT* 71 (1996): 27–37, who shows how, in the narrative of Saul's fall and David's rise, Saul continually loses clothing (or pieces of clothing) while David gains it, thus symbolizing David's accession to the throne. In 2 Sam 6, then, David's self-exposure, his lack of proper clothing, might symbolize his lack of kingliness in this situation.

appears only once in the book, and in this instance she is represented as despising David for his celebratory dancing. In Chronicles' account of the Ark's procession, there is no hint that David's behavior is questionable. It is, to the contrary, exceptionally remarkable. He conducts extensive preparations to prepare the people and Jerusalem for the Ark's arrival, he appoints proper cultic personnel to tend to it after its installation, and he thus paves the way for the completion of cultic centralization in Jerusalem under Solomon.[54] Michal, then, stands out as the lone critic, unduly despising the king and his (fully clothed) celebrations. It seems that Chronicles wants its readers to forget David's skimpily clothed display, which Michal points out in 2 Samuel 6 and which apparently does not follow kingly conventions, but also wants the readership to remember Michal as misguided in her disgust with David. In Chronicles, the king's dancing, in and of itself, is acceptable and even preferable, especially since Saul, and obviously his daughter too, had little regard for the Ark (1 Chr 13:3).[55]

At the same time, the book of Samuel, which Judean literati also undoubtedly read and reread and contemplated (Chronicles did not replace or override it), presents Michal's critique ambiguously, perhaps even sympathetically, as part of a narrative that is more expressly critical of David and his kingship. Did the postmonarchic readership—those responsible for the maintenance and promulgation of this literature, including the books of Samuel and Chronicles—want to have its cake and eat it too?

Recent developments in cognitive psychology research offer some insights that may help us address this question. According to the work of Charles Stone and William Hirst, a particular narrative detail is more likely to be forgotten if only the detail itself is bracketed, and not its immediate narrative context; the detail is less likely to be forgotten, however, if its immediate narrative context is bracketed too.[56] For example, when I assign ancient texts to my students, I ask them to read the texts closely before class, and then I often review and paraphrase the narratives in class before we discuss them. If I were to assign the standard version of *Gilgamesh*, for instance, and then, while paraphrasing it in class, if I were to omit Gilgamesh and Enkidu's battle with Humbaba from my paraphrase, the students would, in our subsequent discussion, be more likely to *forget* that portion of the narrative, according to Stone and Hirst's research. However, if I were not to paraphrase the story at all, and simply let the students recall the text themselves, they would be more likely to *remember* the battle with Humbaba (i.e., assuming they had actually done their homework!).

---

54. Knoppers, *I Chronicles 10–29*, 659; Sara Japhet, *The Ideology of the Book of Chronicles and Its Place in Biblical Thought*, trans. Anna Barber (Winona Lake, IN: Eisenbrauns, 2009), 367–68.

55. Sara Japhet, *I & II Chronicles: A Commentary*, OTL (Louisville, KY: Westminster John Knox, 1993), 308.

56. Charles B. Stone and William Hirst, "(Induced) Forgetting to Form a Collective Memory," *Memory Studies* 7 (2014): 314–27.

This sort of research raises interesting questions about what details an ancient reader might have bracketed or forgotten while reading or discussing the book of Samuel or Chronicles. We know, for example, that reading Chronicles would certainly not induce "forgetting" of Michal. She is clearly present in the account, as is her disgust at David's dancing, amid many of the same details that appear also in Samuel. This case is unlike, say, the case of Bathsheba, who does not show up at all in Chronicles' account of the David and Solomon narrative. In the case of Chronicles' bracketing of the Bathsheba affair, reading the book's historiography might actually induce forgetting of Bathsheba all together: Chronicles tells of Uriah, Nathan, Joab and the siege of Rabbah, and of course David and Solomon—most of the major elements surrounding the Bathsheba episode—but Bathsheba herself goes unmentioned.[57] Stone and Hirst's work suggests that in this case, Bathsheba would indeed be forgotten.[58]

With Michal, Chronicles would certainly contribute to the remembering of the queen herself and her critical stance toward David, but it would perhaps, at the same time, induce the forgetting of specific details of her criticism. It would, thus, encourage its readership to forget that Michal herself had possibly been correct about David's lack of clothing and his bodily exposure. But the book simultaneously would have reinforced her position that a king should indeed be fully clothed, in a robe of fine linen no less, in the context of a civic celebration such as the Ark's procession. In this way, the book effectively supported Michal's conclusion

---

57. She does, however, show up in Chronicles' genealogies, but with a different name: Bathshua, "daughter of error" (1 Chr 3:5). While the historiographical narrative in Chronicles perhaps induced forgetting of Bathsheba, the genealogies perhaps "subtly denigrated" her (Sara M. Koenig, *Isn't This Bathsheba? A Study in Characterization*, PTMS 177 [Eugene, OR: Pickwick, 2011], 43–44).

58. Of course, the problem is, Stone and Hirst's research involves single conversations between individuals and how groups remember details from single occurrences of news reports and public events—instances in which someone/thing did not and could not provide a reminder of forgotten details. Their research does not address the ongoing rereading and comparison of written texts. The literati in Judah must have had constant access to a library of these texts, which enabled them to read, reread, repeatedly compare and consider similarities and differences in the various narratives, in ways that are not analogue to the situations and contexts that present-day social psychologists have analyzed thus far. The literati would have read Samuel and Chronicles time and again, thus limiting the possibility of ever really "forgetting" Bathsheba and her import in David's story in that social context—instead, reading Chronicles gave the literati license to deemphasize the import of Bathsheba in the monarchic past. Perspectives from cognitive psychology are nonetheless beginning to offer some helpful heuristics for approaching these questions, providing new ways to think about the socio-mnemonic relationship between these ancient books. And in the case of Bathsheba, for instance, the work of Stone and Hirst provides one way of understanding how the Judeans might have successfully bracketed or "forgotten" her during the act of reading Chronicles.

about David's inappropriate clothing but, by removing her actual comments about bodily exposure from the equation, it encouraged a negative memory of the queen in general. Related to this issue, of course, is David's behavior in the first place. By bracketing any mention of David's revealing display, his scant clothing and the "glory" it provided him—in addition to bracketing Bathsheba and the fallout from that episode—reading Chronicles would have successfully induced forgetting of the entire sexual-politic that features so prominently in the book of Samuel.

We may apply the same sort of thinking in the other direction to the book of Samuel's account. The version in Samuel does not mention anything about a "robe of fine linen" and of course the discourse there prominently features the sexual-politic and David's struggles in the latter part of his reign. Thus, the act of reading this account would have induced "forgetting" of knowledge concerning these matters known from Chronicles' version. The Chronicles account, then, did not necessarily "whitewash" David or excuse him, as it were, from what appears to have been a kingly impropriety. It made one statement—Samuel made another—in a multivocal discourse about the king, his actions, and his clothing in the past. When it came to kingship, Judean discourse was thoroughly multivocal: it presented a variety of claims about kingship in the past, about kingship's ongoing viability as a concept for thinking about the postmonarchic present, and about the potential for a return of Israelite kingship in the future.[59] The Judean literati of the early Second Temple era had Chronicles but they had Samuel too. Each text contributed to the Judean remembering of kingship, and the various voices in each text balanced each other and played off each other. Moreover, as in this particular case, the texts induced the "forgetting" of details in support of particular ideological and historiographical statements about the successes and failures of the Israelite/Judahite monarchy.

At stake here, then, is an ideology of kingly and divine glory, as Rosenstock argues, and clothing appears to be a foundational element of that ideology. The ideological debate, however, did not center itself on the effectiveness of phallic power or the appropriateness of David's lack of clothing and his bodily display—in fact, there seems to be little question that, for the Judeans, it was inappropriate for a king to march into a city, his deity in tow, wearing nothing but a skimpy undergarment. The question of clothing, then, in 2 Samuel 6 and 1 Chronicles 15, would have been, simply: What exactly was David wearing?[60]

---

59. Ian D. Wilson, *Kingship and Memory in Ancient Judah* (New York: Oxford University Press, 2017).

60. My thanks go to everyone who participated in the PNWSBL Hebrew Bible Research Group on Clothing. It was an outstanding group that produced keen research and fruitful discussions. Special thanks go to Sara Koenig and Tony Finitsis for their detailed and constructive feedback on earlier versions of this particular chapter and to my research assistant Dariya Veenstra, who helped prepare the manuscript for publication.

7

DISROBING AN ISAIANIC METAPHOR מְעִיל צְדָקָה (MĔ'ÎL ṢĔDĀQÂ "ROBE OF RIGHTEOUSNESS") AS POWER TRANSFER IN ISAIAH 61:10

Scott R.A. Starbuck

Dress in the HB, whether physical or metaphorically suggestive, functioned "to construct and communicate identity, as a means to conform or distinguish, as a locus of dispute and resistance, or as a path to or expression of holiness."[1] Metaphorically and physically, dress signified position, status, inclusion, exclusion, and confidence. The lack of it, conversely, often conveyed shame, need, and want. In a literary text, the mention and description of dress lend to characterization and embodied performance. As such, dress references should awaken the attention of the exegete. However, often the opposite is the case and references to clothing receive only cursory treatment. Consequently, much that would meet the eye is simply missed.

This is the case for the book of Isaiah, where at least ten references are made to robe-like clothing.[2] Of particular interest is the use of מְעִיל (mĕ'îl "robe" *of righteousness*) in Isaiah 61:10:

שׂוֹשׂ אָשִׂישׂ בַּיהוָה תָּגֵל נַפְשִׁי בֵּאלֹהַי כִּי הִלְבִּישַׁנִי בִּגְדֵי־יֶשַׁע מְעִיל צְדָקָה יְעָטָנִי כֶּחָתָן יְכַהֵן פְּאֵר וְכַכַּלָּה תַּעְדֶּה כֵלֶיהָ׃

I will greatly rejoice in the LORD, my whole being shall exult in my God; for he has clothed me with the garments of salvation, he has covered me with <u>the robe of righteousness</u>, *as a bridegroom decks himself with a garland, and as a bride adorns herself with her jewels.*[3]

---

1. Kristi Upson-Saia, Carly Daniel-Hughes, and Alicia J. Batten, *Dressing Judeans and Christians in Antiquity* (Farnham: Ashgate, 2014), 1.

2. In English translations, various Hebrew words in Isaiah are often, but not always, translated by the term "robe": מְעִיל (mĕ'îl), בֶּגֶד (bĕgĕd), כֻּתֹּנֶת (kuttōnĕt), מַחֲלָצוֹת (mahălāṣôt), פְּתִיגִיל (pĕtîgîl), לְבוּשׁ (lĕbûš), and מַלְבּוּשׁ (malĕbûš).

3. NRSV.

On the face of it, this appears to be a text of singular significance, particularly because it claims that the deity has "clothed" his servants in a very specific way. Ehud Ben Zvi demonstrates that mention of YHWH's act of clothing of others received significant attention among the literati of Yehud.[4] The fact that YHWH covers the speaker(s) in this text with the robe of righteousness should, likewise, give rise to significant exegetical discussion. However, even a cursory reading of available commentaries demonstrates that the opposite is the case. Watts,[5] McKenzie,[6] and Childs[7] omit meaningful commentary on the metaphor. Brueggemann[8] simply notes that liturgical dress is metaphorically pictured in contrast to military imagery in Isa 59:17. Paul[9] provides more commentary and unpacks the lexemic parallelism of the verse, but draws no conclusion of its cultural claim within the overall text. The commentary of Blenkinsopp[10] addresses by seeking to decode "the symbolism of investiture … which combines the images of royalty … and the bridal couple." He incisively notes that the ancient royal rite of priestly investiture is invoked by the text but refrains from interpreting the force of the metaphor for the intended audience(s).

Whereas it is understandable that commentators who are assigned the entirety of the text might pass over or leave underexplored the cultural force of מְעִיל צְדָקָה (mĕ'îl ṣĕdāqâ "robe of righteousness"), one suspects that the cultural and political significance of the reference remains to be revealed, and if I'm allowed the pun: disrobed. It should be noted as well that the lack of attention given to the idiom by exegetes is also due to the challenges of working with clothing references in general.

The referencing of dress in the biblical text raises a number of challenges for the interpreter. In *A Cultural History of Jewish Dress*, Eric Silverman advances the often

---

4. E. Ben Zvi, "Were YHWH's Clothes Worth Remembering and Thinking about among the Literati of the Late Persian/Early Hellenistic Judah/Yehud? Observations and Considerations," in this volume, 177.

5. John D.W. Watts, *Isaiah 34–66* (vol. 25, Revised Edition; Word Biblical Commentary; Nashville, TN: Thomas Nelson, Inc, 2005), 871.

6. John L. McKenzie, *Second Isaiah: Introduction, Translation, and Notes* (vol. 20; Anchor Yale Bible; New Haven; London: Yale University Press, 2008), 182.

7. Brevard S. Childs, *Isaiah: A Commentary*, ed. William P. Brown, Carol A. Newsom, and Brent A. Strawn, 1st edn.; The Old Testament Library (Louisville, KY: Westminster John Knox, 2001), 506.

8. Walter Brueggemann, *Isaiah 40–66*, ed. Patrick D. Miller and David L. Bartlett; Westminster Bible Companion (Louisville, KY: Westminster John Knox, 1998), 218.

9. Shalom M. Paul, *Isaiah 40–66: Translation and Commentary* (Eerdmans Critical Commentary; Grand Rapids, MI; Cambridge, UK: William B. Eerdmans Publishing Company, 2012), 547–48.

10. Joseph Blenkinsopp, *Isaiah 56–66: A New Translation with Introduction and Commentary* (vol. 19B; Anchor Yale Bible; New Haven; London: Yale University Press, 2008), 231.

unstated obvious, which is that dress "resists any unitary or simple meaning."[11] Batten, Daniel-Hughs, and Upson-Saia further this observation in their analysis of Judean fashion:

> Dress ... figured significantly in daily life, in texts, and in ritual practices. It functioned in a range of ways: as a way to construct and communicate identity, as a means to conform or distinguish, as a locus of dispute and resistance, or as a path to or expression of holiness.[12]

Dress, in Hebrew terminology, comprises a relatively small lexicon "to refer to a broad range of indeterminate garments."[13] Even when the translator is relatively sure of what a particular Hebrew lexeme generally means, it means what it means and it then, potentially, means even more: "biblical garb, both real and metaphoric, conveyed symbolic messages concerning power, gender, and identity."[14] In other words, references to the garment itself may not, standing alone, provide interpretive precision and because of this are treated practically as passing references. When working with references to clothing, especially if metaphorically intended, a wider interpretive context of modifiers and parallel terms can prove productive, if not necessary.

Thankfully, such is the case for the reference to מְעִיל צְדָקָה in Isa 61:10. If its clothing metaphor is thoroughly explored as a major multivalent trope, it becomes evident that the phrase מְעִיל צְדָקָה visions an emotionally positive reversal of social status likely contributing to communalized (democratized) attempts to reorganize the postexilic community. As such, it illustrates the power of imagined clothing for political and sacerdotal agendas.

Visualizing מְעִיל

The first step in comprehending the complex metaphor is to understand the term מְעִיל (*měʻîl* "robe") in its simple-referential sense. On the one hand, this task is complicated by the fact that the clothing term parallel to מְעִיל in Isa 61:10, בֶּגֶד (*běḡěḏ* "garment"), is quite general and, because of its wide use within the HB, unable to help pinpoint a precise meaning of מְעִיל. On the other hand, when one seeks to precisely translate the lexeme מְעִיל, one is stymied by lack of lexical cognates and a dearth of Israelite iconography.

---

11. E.K. Silverman, *A Cultural History of Jewish Dress* (New York: Bloomsbury Academic, 2013), 1.

12. Upson-Saia, Daniel-Hughes, and Batten, *Dressing Judeans and Christians in Antiquity*, 1.

13. Silverman, *A Cultural History of Jewish Dress*, 5.

14. Ibid., 1.

It is not uncommon, then, to use a generalized English term, such as "robe," to point the reader in an approximate direction. When translators opt for "robe," they seem to have in mind the garment depicted in numerous pictorial representations of royalty found in the ANE. It is a garment *with sleeves* and a hem at ankle length, often pictured adorned by an overlaying tunic, apron, or scarf. In the representation of King Sargon II and his vizier, both wear this type of garment, although they are accessorized differently.[15] In fact, members of the king's court wear similar ankle-length robes.[16] Even when depicted as a "common" worker, Ashurbanipal still wears the "robe," but it is no longer accented with ceremonial outergarments.[17] Military, however, are often pictured as wearing something more akin to a kilt, long archers are represented as wearing the ankle-length robe even in battle.[18] Assyrian and Aramaic scribes wear similar ankle-length robes what are then adorned with a decorative sash.[19]

The same type of garment is displayed on the bilingually inscribed figure (Governor of Gozan)[20] at Tell Fakhariyeh.[21] This garment clearly has a hem, is sleeved, and is wrapped by some sort of cross-body sash that is then fastened around the waist. Interestingly, the back of the robe is best described as "v-necked," while the front of the robe is not. As in the case of the Ashurbanipal inscription,[22] text is written on the robe of the figure suggesting, perhaps, the "messaging" import of the garment itself, which is to say the garment's unspoken symbolic messaging was focused and made explicit through accompanying text.

Israelites are portrayed wearing a similar garment on the Black Obelisk of Shalmaneser III. The Israelite king Jehu does obeisance before the Assyrian king. Jehu wears a long ankle-length garment with a fringed hem.[23] Likewise, Israelite captives, perhaps nobility, are pictured bearing tribute in ankle-length robes with fringed hems. However, their garments may be simply thrown over the shoulder

---

15. See https://en.wikipedia.org/wiki/Sargon_II#mediaviewer/File:Sargon_II_and_dignitary.jpg.
16. See https://www.ancient.eu/uploads/images/2745.jpg?v=1485680737.
17. See https://www.britannica.com/biography/Ashurbanipal.
18. See https://commons.wikimedia.org/wiki/User:Ealdgyth#/media/File:Britishmuseumassyrianreliefarchersnimrud.jpg.
19. See http://classes.bnf.fr/ecritures/grand/AL07_0009.htm.
20. D.J. Green, *"I Undertook Great Works": The Ideology of Domestic Achievements in West Semitic Royal Inscriptions* (Tübingen: Mohr Siebeck, 2010), 234n. 11, and W.R. Garr, "'Image' and 'Likeness' in the Inscription from Tell Fakhariyeh," *IEJ* 50, 3-4 (2000): 227.
21. See http://www.oocities.org/encyclopedia_damascena/ancientsyria/images/mus021.jpg. See also the plates in A. Assaf, P. Bordreuil, and A.R. Millard, *La statue de Tell Fekherye et son inscription bilingue assyro-araméenne* (Etudes Assyriologiques; Paris: A.D.P.F., 1982), especially plates I-IV.
22. See https://www.britannica.com/biography/Ashurbanipal.
23. See https://en.wikipedia.org/wiki/Jehu#/media/File:Jehu-Obelisk-cropped.jpg.

rather than worn poncho-like.²⁴ The depiction of Israelite prisoners in the ninth-century Black Obelisk is almost identical to the depiction of prisoners captured at Astartu, which is south of Damascus, displayed in the palace of Tiglath-pileser III.²⁵ This begs the question as to if this is reflective of Assyrian visual propaganda rather than a realistic cultural representation. They figuratively "disrobed," that is, with their garments thrown over their shoulders, because they are in fact prisoners.²⁶

HB literary usages of מְעִיל

Occurring twenty-eight times in the HB, מְעִיל is often used as a *Terminus technicus* for either a royal or sacerdotal garment. Jonathan, a prince, and Saul, a king, both wear a מְעִיל.²⁷ The princess Tamar wears מְעִילִים (*mĕʿilim* "robes").²⁸ According to the Chronicler, David himself was officially clothed in a מְעִיל.²⁹ The prophet Ezekiel uses the term to describe that which will be stripped off from foreign rulers.³⁰ Job, in the narrative prologue describing his legendary standing, wears a מְעִיל.³¹ These passages suggest a garment signifying rank, dignity, and elite status.³² Perhaps the elite marker was expressed through complex embroidery, particularly at the hem.³³

In Exodus, מְעִיל is expressly connected with the professional priesthood.³⁴ Specifically, for the Priestly Source the מְעִיל is the blue garment that is worn by the high priest under the ephod.³⁵ William Propp suggests it was akin to a poncho

---

24. See http://www.britishmuseum.org/research/collection_online/collection_object_details/collection_image_gallery.aspx?partid=1&assetid=327360001&objectid=367012.

25. See http://www.britishmuseum.org/research/collection_online/collection_object_details/collection_image_gallery.aspx?partid=1&assetid=326418001&objectid=369627.

26. Disrobing as shaming continues in artistic representation into the first century CE on the Judaea Capta coinage. One particularly striking example is of a priest stripped of his upper garment and appearing semi-naked shamed and bound. See J.E. Taylor, "Imagining Judean Priestly Dress: The Berne Josephos and *Judaea Capta* Coinage," in *Dressing Judeans*, 201–11.

27. 1 Sam 18:4; 1 Sam 24:5, 12.

28. 2 Sam 13:18.

29. 1 Chron 15:27.

30. Ezek 26:16.

31. Job 1:20; 2:12. See Job 24:19 for a clearly metaphorical usage.

32. P.J. King and L.E. Stager, *Life in biblical Israel* (Louisville: Westminster John Knox, 2001), 269.

33. See M.G. Houston, *Ancient Egyptian, Mesopotamian & Persian Costume* (Mineola, N.Y.: Dover Publications, 2002), 135, fig. 130, for a drawing in the ornate fringed robe of Ashur-nasir-pal.

34. Exod 28:4, 31, 34, 29:5, 39:22–26.

35. Exod 28:4, 31, 34; 29:5; 39:22, 23, 24, 25, 26. See also Lev 8:7.

since "it has a single hole for the head (Exod 28:32) with no special provision for the arms."[36] Although there are no secure cognates for the term, it is likely that the מְעִיל started as a term within the royal lexicon. John Durham's cautions seem wise:

> The composite set forth in this chapter no doubt reflects an evolution of vestments, and perhaps also *an adaptation of royal sacral vestments to priestly sacral use following the demise of Israel's sacral monarchy with and beyond the Babylonian exile*. There can be little doubt that in pre-exilic Israel, certainly in the united monarchy of David and Solomon, and probably in the monarchies of Judah and Israel, the ruling king was always in title and frequently in practice the head or chief priest, in the terminology of this chapter, "Aaron." Thus at least some of the ornate vestments described here probably began as vestments for the sacral king, performing his duties as YHWH's own anointed one. As time passed, the kings turned over some of these duties to the priests; then with the successive Assyrian and Babylonian destructions of the two monarchies, the priests took over the royal vestments, and by the postexilic period, many of the royal functions as well (emphasis mine).[37]

This being the case, the term מְעִיל contains an intrinsic multivalence in P. As a sacerdotal vestment, it is also a royal-substitute signifier. Either way, it is an *elite leadership signifier.* W. Randall Garr suggests a similar symbolic denotation of the robe worn by Governor Had-yiṯʿî in the Tell Fakhariyeh bilingual inscription.[38] The statue represents a bearded male wearing a long robe. His hands are clasped at his waist indicating a pious posture before the gods.[39] Although the figure is referred to as "governor of Gozan" in line 8 of the Akkadian inscription, he is named "king of Gozan" in line 6 in the Aramaic inscription. Garr posits that "the royal title may intentionally convey and reinforce the two royal roles depicted of Had-yiṯʿî—that of exemplary cultic attendant (L.6) and that of singular executive power (L.13)."[40] There is, then, a convergence of both terms which is actually inscribed *on* the robed statue evoking embodying a broader symbolism beyond

---

36. W.H.C. Propp, *Exodus 19–40: A New Translation with Introduction and Commentary* (vol. 2A; Anchor Yale Bible; New Haven; London: Yale University Press, 2008), 433. It should be noted that "no provision for the arms" may be a priestly adaptation of the otherwise sleeved royal garment.

37. J.I. Durham, *Exodus* (vol. 3; Word Biblical Commentary; Dallas: Word, Incorporated, 1998), 385.

38. See figures 10 and 11.

39. Garr, "'Image' and 'Likeness' in the Inscription from Tell Fakhariyeh," *IEJ* (2000) vol. 50 n. 1.4, 227.

40. Ibid., 233 n. 39.

the "literal and referential."[41] The confluence of royal and sacerdotal connotation is important to note, as it informs a similar confluence in Isa 61:4–11.[42]

Such multivalence and overlapping of lexical fields make the use of מְעִיל in the Samuel story quite intriguing. Significantly, Hannah brings a מְעִיל to the boy Samuel each year. This term first appears in the Samuel cycle after Hannah's song, which concludes with "The LORD will judge the ends of the earth; he will give strength to his king and exalt the power of his anointed (1 Sam 2:28),"[43] a propoleptic anticipation of the rise of kingship within Israel. Ten verses earlier, a dual notice is made that Samuel was ministering before YHWH dressed in a linen ephod, and each year, his mother would bring him a small מְעִיל (1 Sam 2:18–19). The reference to the ephod carries sacerdotal connotations.[44] Hannah, by contrast, brings him an article of clothing yearly that also is associated with royal status. It is likely that the מְעִיל is a symbolic indicator that Samuel is going to play the role of king maker and king breaker. The clothing of Samuel also anticipates a significant political shift in the priesthood. McCarter illustrates this in his commentary:

> By a deliberate selection of terminology Samuel is implicitly characterized as a priest, ministering to YHWH and clad in sacerdotal garments ... The impact of such a characterization in such a context is unavoidable: the good and the wicked, the chosen and the rejected are set before us in an almost simplistic juxtaposition. We are prepared for the fall of the house of Eli and, with equal certainty, for a corresponding rise in the fortunes of Samuel.[45]

The religio-historical situation behind the texts suggests political struggle, displacement, and transfer.[46] As is often noted, these are texts that seek to

---

41. Ibid., 232 n. 39.

42. See Ian Wilson, "Indeed, for the Hittite king, there was no real distinction between political and cultic concerns. More often than not, this was the case throughout the ancient Near Eastern world." "The Emperor and His Clothing: David Robed and Unrobed in front of the Ark and Michal," in this volume, 127.

43. NRSV.

44. KB: אֵפוֹד בַּד ('ēpōḏ baḏ "a cultic garb made of linen").

45. P.K. McCarter Jr., *I Samuel: A New Translation with Introduction, Notes and Commentary* (vol. 8; Anchor Yale Bible; New Haven; London: Yale University Press, 2008), 85.

46. For example, Breuggemann draws out this likelihood in his commentary: "From a historical perspective, this peculiar text reflects a change in the arrangement of priestly power and authority. The divine decree is probably an intrusion in the text and demonstrates how narrative can be used for purposes of propaganda and establishing legitimacy. The rise of the house of Zadok as such, however, has no bearing on the narrative of Samuel. It is of interest only to a later political force that has made good and partisan use of the narrative." W. Brueggemann, *First and Second Samuel* (Interpretation, a Bible Commentary for Teaching and Preaching; Louisville, KY: John Knox, 1990), 24.

aggrandize the legitimacy of Samuel over and against Saul, perhaps at the later service of David.[47]

In the same vein, later in the Samuel narrative, when Saul is rejected as king, Saul takes hold of the hem of Samuel's מְעִיל so that it rips in two.[48] In tearing Samuel's מְעִיל, Saul has mirrored the tearing of the kingdom away from Saul as well ripping executive authority from Samuel who up until this point has been the uncontested leader of Israel in his roles of prophet, priest, judge. From this connection, it is difficult to deny the royal, and perhaps also priestly, connotations attendant with Samuel's מְעִיל. So symbolic of Samuel's "king making and king breaking" position was Samuel's מְעִיל that Saul is able to recognize the phantomized Samuel when the medium of Endor conjures him.[49]

In sum, the use of מְעִיל in the HB generally and in the story of Samuel specifically support the conclusion that מְעִיל often functioned as an elite leadership signifier with royal and/or sacerdotal force. With this in mind, the uses of מְעִיל in Third Isaiah can be better understood.

Third Isaiah literary usages of מְעִיל

There are two attestations of מְעִיל in Third Isaiah: Isa 59:17 and the text in question, Isa 61:10. The first case uses מְעִיל tropologically. In Isa 59:17b YHWH appears as the Divine Warrior "wrapped in zeal *as* in a robe,"[50] (וַיַּעַט כַּמְעִיל קִנְאָה). Isa 59:17:

וַיִּלְבַּשׁ צְדָקָה כַּשִּׁרְיָן
וְכוֹבַע יְשׁוּעָה בְּרֹאשׁוֹ
וַיִּלְבַּשׁ בִּגְדֵי נָקָם[51]
וַיַּעַט כַּמְעִיל קִנְאָה׃

He clothed *himself* with righteousness (legitimacy) like a coat of mail,
With a helmet of victory on his head;
He clothed *Himself* with garments of retribution,
Wrapped *himself* in zeal as in a robe.

Here מְעִיל is invoked technically through a simile, which is to say that YHWH is not wrapped in a robe but is wrapped in zeal likened to one wrapped in a robe. Standing parallel to וַיִּלְבַּשׁ בִּגְדֵי נָקָם, "He clothed Himself with garments of

---

47. See, for example, Antony F. Campbell, *1 Samuel* (vol. 7; The Forms of the Old Testament Literature; Grand Rapids, MI: William B. Eerdmans Publishing Company, 2003), 3.
48. 1 Sam 15:27.
49. 1 Sam 28:14.
50. JPS.
51. תִּלְבֹּשֶׁת (tilĕbōšet "garment") in the MT is likely a later gloss as it is missing in LXX and Syr.

retribution,"[52] the simile modifies the more general מְעִיל militarily by adding connotations of juridical power (since in the ANE warfare was viewed as the implementation of divine justice) and legitimacy.

Isa 61:10 is located within a "self-contained message"[53] in Isa 60–62 that scholars generally consider to be the earliest unit of Third Isaiah. As the earliest unit, it provided a foundational center around which the larger redaction of Third Isaiah formed. Isa 60–62 itself is comprised of four separate form-critical sections: Isa 60:1–22, Isa 61:1–3, Isa 61:4–11, and Isa 62:1–12. Logically then, the primary sense-unit in which to understand the use of מְעִיל in Isa 61:10 is Isa 61:4–11:

v. 4   And they shall build the ancient ruins,
     Raise up the desolations of old,
     And renew the ruined cities,
     The desolations of many ages.

v. 5   Strangers shall stand and pasture your flocks,
     Aliens shall be your plowmen and vine-trimmers;

v. 6   While you shall be called "Priests of the LORD" (כֹּהֲנֵי יהוה),
     And termed "Servants of our God" (מְשָׁרְתֵי אֱלֹהֵינוּ).
     You shall enjoy the wealth of nations
     And revel in their riches.

v. 7   Because your shame was double—
     Men cried, "Disgrace is their portion"—Assuredly,
     They shall have a double share in their land,
     Joy shall be theirs for all time.
     For I the LORD love justice (מִשְׁפָּט),

v. 8   I hate robbery with a burnt offering.
     I will pay them their wages faithfully,
     And make a covenant with them for all time (וּבְרִית עוֹלָם).
     Their offspring shall be known among the nations,

v. 9   Their descendants in the midst of the peoples.
     All who see them shall recognize
     That they are a stock the LORD has blessed.[54]

v. 10 I will greatly rejoice in the LORD,
     My whole being shall exult in my God.
     For he has clothed me with garments of salvation (בִּגְדֵי־יֶשַׁע),
     He has covered me with the robe of righteousness (מְעִיל צְדָקָה),[55]

---

52. JPS.
53. C. Westermann, *Isaiah 40–66: A Commentary* (OTL; Philadelphia: Westminster, 1969), 352.
54. JPS.
55. NRSV.

> Like a bridegroom adorned with a turban (פְּאֵר),
> Like a bride bedecked with her finery.

v. 11 For as the earth brings forth her growth
And a garden makes the seed shoot up,
So the Lord GOD will make
Victory and renown (צְדָקָה וּתְהִלָּה) shoot up[56]
In the presence of all the nations.

In this passage, the prophetic persona enjoins an audience in second- and third-person address. In v. 8, the voice of the prophetic persona shifts to the divine voice speaking in first person. This first-person address is then mirrored in Isa 61:10, presumably in some form of antiphonal response, by the community that is initially addressed by the prophetic persona. It is not clear whether the divine voice continues speaking in Isa 61:9 or whether the prophetic persona resumes in third-person address, nor is it beyond dispute as to whom is speaking in v. 11.

Given this, it is clear that Isa 61:10 is the first-person collective response of the community referred to in third person in vv. 4, 7, 8, and 9 and in second person in v. 6.

This means the community that is metaphorically clothed with the garments of salvation and with the robe of righteousness (v. 10) is also promised an *everlasting covenant* (v. 8) as well as to be called or renamed *priests of YHWH* and *ministers of our God* (v. 6). Additionally, this community will be actively engaged in the reconstruction of Yehud (v. 4) while foreigners provide tangible support through labor (v. 5) and financing (v. 6b). Emotionally, the status of the community addressed will be transformed from shame into joy (v. 7), renown (v. 9a), and blessing (v. 9b). Working together, these terms suggest a significant change of social and political status.

Communalized (democratized) מְעִיל

There is ample reason to read the two references of מְעִיל in Third Isaiah, Isa 59:17 and 61:10, as serving complementary theological aims. Specifically, parallelism between terms in the full verse of Isa 59:17 overlaps with verbal clusters in Isaiah 61. In the four bicola of Isa 61:4–11, three verbs occur and one is assumed. The verb לבש (*lābaš* "to clothe") is used twice in parallel as the first element of the A cola. This same verb occurs in Isa 61:10 "he clothed me" (הִלְבִּישַׁנִי *hilĕbîšanî*) to describe the metaphorical clothing of the community experiencing reversal. The other verb used to indicate YHWH's dressing for battle in Isa 59:17, עָטָה (`āṭâ "to wrap oneself"), also occurs in Isa 61:10. Other significant word clusters are shared between Isa 59:16–17 and Isa 61:10. Whereas the phrases בִּגְדֵי־יֶשַׁע (*biḡĕdê-yeša*` "garments of salvation") and מְעִיל צְדָקָה (*mĕ*`*îl ṣĕḏāqâ* "robe of righteousness") in Isa 61:10 are unique in the HB, it is the exact same nominal parallelism used in

---

56. JPS.

Isa 59:17, בְּגְדֵי // מְעִיל (mĕ'îl//biḡĕḏê). In Isa 59:16, "He saw that there was no one, and was appalled that there was no one to intervene; so his own arm brought him *victory*, and his *righteousness* upheld him," the nominal paring of צְדָקָה //יֵשַׁע (ṣĕḏāqâ//yēša') occurs as in Isa 61:10 otherwise only found in so paired in Isa 45:8, "Shower, O heavens, from above, and let the skies rain down righteousness; let the earth open, that *salvation* may spring up, and let it cause *victory* to sprout up also; I the LORD have created it." Shared clusters between Isa 59:17 and Isa 45 emerge thematically connecting the march of the divine warrior in Isa 59 delivering on the promise in Second Isaiah (Isa 45:8). Following the same word cluster associations, a poetic argument is voiced that the community of Isa 61 is equipped through a metaphorical robing, to serve as the instruments of salvation and righteousness in a redeemed Jerusalem. To the extent that the community is "robed" in this way, it would seem that they participate in the royal office of deliverance and justice based on the manifold connections we have seen lexically and contextually between the term מְעִיל and kingship, human or divine.

Significantly, the community's rejoicing and attendant clothing in Isa 61:10 hinge on the divine declaration in 61:8 that YHWH is a אֹהֵב מִשְׁפָּט (ʾōhēḇ mišĕpāṭ "lover of justice") and שֹׂנֵא גָזֵל בְּעוֹלָה (śōnēʾ gāzēl ba'ôlâ "a hater of robbery by burnt offering") and, because of this he will make an eternal covenant (וּבְרִית עוֹלָם אֶכְרוֹת לָהֶם:/ûḇĕrît 'ôlām 'eḵĕrwôṯ lāhem) with those who are metaphorically decked in garments of salvation and the robe of righteousness in v. 10. As Beuken points out, this promise echoes the communalization or democratization[57] of the royal covenant in Isa 55:3: "I will make with you an eternal covenant, my steadfast sure love for David" (וְאֶכְרְתָה לָכֶם בְּרִית עוֹלָם חַסְדֵי דָוִד הַנֶּאֱמָנִים/wĕʾeḵĕrĕṯâ lāḵem bĕrît 'ôlām ḥasĕḏê ḏāwiḏ hanneʾĕmānîm). Whereas Isa 55:1–5 uses the type scene of the royal banquet to convey an anticipated change in status of the faithful community that is bequeathed the royal office, the community of Isa 61 receives its eternal covenant through the motif of reclothing.

The literati of Yehud would make clear connections between communalized covenants in Isa 55 and 61. Contemporary scholarship underscores these connections in different ways. For example, in his work on the reconceptualization of the Davidic Covenant in Isaianic text, Sweeney draws attention to the fact that Isa 55 is an introduction to the Third Isaiah corpus.[58]

Significantly, prior to Isa 54:17, Second Isaiah invokes a collective "servant" of YHWH. Beuken has identified a primary theme in Third Isaiah shifting to the "servants" of YHWH,[59] whom Sweeny identifies as "the righteous and prosperous

---

57. I prefer the term "communalization" to avoid the anachronistic freighted connotations of "democratization."

58. M.A. Sweeney, "The Reconceptualization of the Davidic Covenant in Isaiah," in *Studies in the Book of Isaiah: Festschrift Willem A.M. Beuken*, ed. J. van Ruiten and M. Vervenne (Leuven: Leuven, 1997), 42.

59. W.A.M. Beuken, "Servant and Herald of Good Tidings: 'The Servants of Yahweh,'" JSOT 47 (1990): 67–87.

offspring that the servant in Isa 53:10 will ultimately see."[60] Isa 55:1–5 begins with an invitational call not to a single collective figure but to a community, perhaps even the community of the servants of Isa 54:17. It is this community, not a collective individual, that is promised an everlasting covenant in Isa 55:3. Reading canonically, the shift from a singular "servant" of YHWH to the "servants of YHWH" has already happened in Isa 55:1–4. Yet, in Isa 55:5, the community receiving the covenant is not pointed to a plural but a singular, given the 2ms verbal forms and pronominal suffixes (גּוֹי לֹא־תֵדַע תִּקְרָא וְגוֹי לֹא־יְדָעוּךָ אֵלֶיךָ/*gôy lōʾ-tēdaʿ tiqĕrāʾ wĕgôy lōʾ-yĕdāʿûkā ʾēlekā*). This shift may be more of a hinge between a collective designation of a singular "servant" and this group's own disciples (or descendants per Isa 54:17). As such, Isa 55:1–5 couples the concerns for restorative justice in both Second Isaiah and Third Isaiah through the transfer of the Davidic Covenant to the "servant" and "servants." This being the case, the reclothing of the community referenced in Isa 61 with the "garments of salvation" and the "robe of righteousness," a community that is also included in likely the same eternal covenant, is a community that is dressed for the cause of justice and righteousness in the stead of a Davidic king.

At the same time, the clothing metaphor reaches beyond the royal office to that of the priesthood. The use of מְעִיל in Isa 61:10 expands word clusters associated with royal prerogatives with word clusters associated with the priesthood. Beuken's translation is instructive:

שׂוֹשׂ אָשִׂישׂ בַּיהוָה
תָּגֵל נַפְשִׁי בֵּאלֹהַי
כִּי הִלְבִּישַׁנִי בִּגְדֵי־יֶשַׁע
מְעִיל צְדָקָה יְעָטָנִי
כֶּחָתָן יְכַהֵן פְּאֵר
וְכַכַּלָּה תַּעְדֶּה כֵלֶיהָ׃

v.10a   I greatly rejoice in YHWH
my soul exults in my God.
Surely, he has clothed me with the garments of salvation,
he has wrapped me in the robe of righteousness.
v. 10b   as a bridegroom priest-like decks himself with a turban
as a bride adorns herself with jewels.[61]

The language of being "clothed in righteousness" echoes to the divine promise in Ps 132:16, וְכֹהֲנֶיהָ אַלְבִּישׁ יֶשַׁע (*wĕkōhăneyhā ʾalĕbîš yešaʿ* "let your priests wear righteousness"). In Isa 61:6a, the community is explicitly called "priests of YHWH"

---

60. Sweeney, "The Reconceptualization of the Davidic Covenant in Isaiah," 42.
61. W.A.M. Beuken, "Servant and Herald of Good Tidings: Isaiah 61 as an Interpretation of Isaiah 40–55," in *The Book of Isaiah = Le livre d'Isaïe: les oracles et leurs relectures unité et complexité de l'ouvrage*, ed. J. Vermeylen (Leuven: Leuven University Press, 1989), 412.

and "ministers of our God."[62] In Isa 61:10b, the community is likened to the bridegroom that acts the part of the priest (יְכַהֵן/yĕkahēn).[63] A further connection is made because the bridegroom puts on a turban,[64] just as priests do in Exod 39:28 and Ezek 44:18. Clearly, the royal metaphor invoked through the מְעִיל צְדָקָה is expanded to intersect and include the sacerdotal. Carmen Imes demonstrates, מְעִיל, itself, is a standard element of the most public display of priestly power, authority, and divine representation.[65] Accordingly, Sweeny observes, "It is clear that the servants of YHWH are to fulfill a priestly or cultic role in relation to the large world order being established by YHWH in Zion."[66] If the servants of YHWH are to be identified with a larger group than the official priesthood, then some sort of significant power transfer is indicated regarding those newly clothed in the מְעִיל צְדָקָה.

Physical and metaphorical reclothing as power transfer

Having established the multivalence of מְעִיל צְדָקָה in Isa 61:10 and how this phrase carried both communalized royal and priestly connotations, the question of the intended extent of the metaphor remains. Isa 61:1–3 closely linked to 61:4–10 and in fact situating the charges of 61:4–10 in the context of dramatic reversal:

> v. 3   To provide for the mourners in Zion—
> 　　　　To give them a turban instead of ashes,
> 　The festive ointment instead of mourning,
> 　　　A garment of splendor instead of a drooping spirit.
> 　They shall be called terebinths of victory,
> 　　　Planted by the LORD for His glory.[67]

Those who mourn will become glad; those who are weak shall praise. The community presumably resonates with the identification that they are oppressed,

---

62. For the use of שרת šrt with or parallel to כהן khn, see Jer 33:21, 22; Ez 45:4, 5; Joel 1:9, 13; 2:17.

63. BDB: II. [כָּהַן] / kāhan] vb. only Pi. denom. act. as priest or *be* or *become priest* Dt 10:6 or *play the priest*.

64. KB: פְּאֵר / pĕ'ēr "head wrap, turban."

65. C. Imes, "Between Two Worlds: The Functional and Symbolic Significance of the High Priestly Regalia," in this volume, 34.

66. Sweeney, "The Reconceptualization of the Davidic Covenant in Isaiah," 59. Note also, "Insofar as earlier materials in Isaiah anticipate the emergence of a remnant of Israel that will continue (e.g., Isa 6:13), the 'servants of YHWH' in Isaiah 74,17b constitute that remnant," Sweeney, "The Reconceptualization of the Davidic Covenant in Isaiah," 46.

67. JPS.

broken-hearted, and even captive. Most importantly, they will be *reclothed*, metaphorically, in a garment of splendor, in the festive ointment, and with turban instead of ashes. The term used for turban in v. 3 is identical to that in v. 10 (פְּאֵר/*pĕʾēr*). Shalom M. Paul identifies the artistic prowess used to communicate the reversal: "a transposition of the letters פְּאֵר-אֵפֶר/*pʾr-ʾpr* accentuates their reversal of fortune. Instead of the 'ashes' (אֵפֶר/*ʾēper*) of mourning, the Lord shall place a turban (פְּאֵר) on their heads."[68] The phrase שֶׁמֶן שָׂשׂוֹן (*šemen śāśôn* "festive ointment") or "oil of gladness" also occurs in the context of a royal wedding scene in Psalm 45:8, detailing what *the king wears*. There are no exact parallels for the "garment of splendor" (מַעֲטֵה תְהִלָּה/*maʿăṭēh tĕhillâ*),[69] but it is important to note that the "splendor" that the garment would presumably be to one's eyes will be voiced by the nations according to Isa 61:11, "For as the earth brings forth its shoots, and as a garden causes what is sown in it to spring up, so the Lord GOD will cause righteousness and praise (וּתְהִלָּה/*ûtĕhillâ*) to spring up before all the nations."[70] The presence of these verbal clusters in both Isa 61:1–3 and Isa 61:4–11 demonstrates their intricate linkages as well as the logical development from the first unit to the second. The means it is appropriate to understand the reclothing in Isa 61:10 to be consistent with the reclothing in Isa 61:3, a reclothing indicating the reversal of fortunes or power transfer.

The power transfer visioned in Isa 61:4–11 is also related to the announcement of the restoration of Zion/people of Zion in Isa 62:1–5. This passage expresses the reversal of the community's status from being forsaken and abandoned in v. 4 through an extended marriage metaphor in v. 5. Starting with v. 3, Blenkinsopp's translation is instructive:

> … you will be a splendid crown in YHVH's hand,
> a royal diadem in the palm of God's hand.
> Nevermore will you be called "the Forsaken One,"
> never more will your land be called "the Desolate One";
> but you will be called "I delight in her,"
> and your land will be called "Espoused,"
> for YHVH will take delight in you,
> and your land will indeed be espoused.
> ⁵ As a young man weds a young woman,
> so will your children be united with you;

---

68. S.M. Paul, *Isaiah 40–66: Translation and Commentary* (Eerdmans Critical Commentary; Grand Rapids, MI; Cambridge, UK: William B. Eerdmans Publishing Company, 2012), 540–41.

69. Note the association with the garments of Aaron: "The instructions at Sinai identify these as 'sacred vestments' (בִּגְדֵי־קֹדֶשׁ/ *bigdê-qōdeš*; Exod 28:2), crafted 'for dignity and for splendor' (לְכָבוֹד וּלְתִפְאָרֶת/ *lĕkābôd ûlĕtipʾāret*; Exod 28:2, 40)," Imes, in this volume, 30–31.

70. JPS.

as the bridegroom rejoices over the bride,
so will your God rejoice over you.[71]

This passage clusters the same metaphoric semantic fields (marriage, royalty, joy) that occur in Isa 61:4–11. Combined polyphonically, the resulting metaphoric complex suggests not only power transfer but, more to the point, power transfer through new covenantal agreement. In Isa 62:1–5 this covenant is implicit through the claiming, renaming, and espousing of the remnant community. In Isa 61:8, the covenant is explicitly named as eternal (וּבְרִית עוֹלָם/*ûberît 'ôlām*). Whereas covenant is not necessary for the reversal of fortunes nor even that of a power transfer, the invocation of covenant making by the deity claims a profound and unassailable legitimacy for the community's newly robed status.

It is worth noting that earlier in the Isaianic corpus, the transfer of power is symbolized by reclothing. In Isa 22:20–25, Eliakim son of Hilkiah assumes the position of royal treasurer vacated by Shebna. In assuming this position, YHWH promises to clothe him with (Shebna's) tunic and sash (וְהִלְבַּשְׁתִּיו כֻּתָּנְתֶּךָ וְאַבְנֵטְךָ/*wehilebašetîw kutānēteḵā we'abenēṭeḵā*) in Isa 22:21. The authenticity of this passage stands in question,[72] but the official positional transference signified by the clothing mentioned does not. Outside the Isaianic corpus, the transference of Jonathan's מְעִיל to David in the context of covenant making clearly signifies a propoleptic power transfer from the house of Saul to that of David.[73]

As such, the term מְעִיל holds royal connotations on a fundamental level. Standing in bound form with the absolute צְדָקָה parallel to יֵשַׁע strengthens this association. These are terms associated with victory and justice primary to the royal sphere. At the same time, there is a significant semantic overlap with the priestly sphere in tradition as well as overtly signified in the text. The community will be called priests and ministers (Isa 61:6), they will appear priest-like (Isa 61:10b), and they will be contrary to those who rob through offering burnt offerings (Isa 61:8a). Given that Isa 61:8 וּבְרִית עוֹלָם אֶכְרוֹת לָהֶם (*ûberît 'ôlām 'ekerwôt lāhem* " ... I will make an everlasting covenant with them") picks up the language of covenantal transference from Isa 55:3 " ... I will make an everlasting covenant with them" (וְאֶכְרְתָה לָכֶם בְּרִית עוֹלָם/*we'ekeretâ lākem berît 'wôlām*), it is likely the text supports and then furthers the import of Isa 55:1–5 by extending the transfer of office from

---

71. Blenkinsopp, *Isaiah 56–66*, 232.

72. To summarize: vv. 20–23 do not come from the prophet Isaiah. If Isa 36:3–13 is correct when it speaks of a certain Eliakim who was in charge of the palace in Jerusalem in 701, the conclusion seems unavoidable that a prophetic contemporary of Isaiah is speaking these words, one who might have suggested to the king that Eliakim be appointed and who wanted to bolster his claim that this was the right person for the job by quoting religious statements. See H. Wildberger, *A Continental Commentary: Isaiah 13–27* (Minneapolis, MN: Fortress, 1997), 395.

73. 1 Sam 18:4.

that of king to righteous remnant to also that of priest and righteous remnant.[74] Isa 61:4–11, then, witnesses the communalization of the priestly office in ways parallel to the communalization of the royal office in Isa 55:1–5, and yet, in doing so, it envisions the two offices being merged as one into one remnant people. This means royal and priestly connotations merge through common people into one new covenantal reformulation.

The societal force of מְעִיל צְדָקָה

The force of the symbolic transference is indicated by being clothed in "garments of salvation" and in "a robe of righteousness" in Isa 61:10. Such variation "in dress and adornment were used not only to distinguish insiders from outsiders and solidify community, but also to create intra-group divisions and hierarchies."[75] With perceptions of professional holiness came privilege. Saul Olyan explains:

> Various traditions bear witness to the privileged position of the priest in the cultic life of Israel … Materials of the Priestly Writing, providing some of the most detailed surviving prescriptions for and descriptions of cultic practice, speak of the holiness of the Aaronid priesthood, and Ezekiel 40–48 says as much about the Zadokites. In addition, Numbers 16:1–17:5 (Eng., 16 1:-40) and Ezekiel 44 bear witness to the separation of priests not only from common Israelites but from the Levites as well. According to these texts, only priests of cultic servants are holy; they alone are privileged to wear holy garments.[76]

With this in mind, the fairly generalized metaphor of the מְעִיל צְדָקָה reclothing could be intended to empower, unite, distinguish, and/or divide. Multiple combinations of possibilities exist. Regardless, Isa 61:10 leverages the symbolism of the מְעִיל צְדָקָה to claim a new authority, position, and access in the midst of a struggle for the Restoration community to organize itself without a Davidic king and among any number of priestly voices. One suspects that the symbolic of reclothing of the entire people with sacral garments would present a number of ideological quandaries since, at least in the Priestly Writings and Ezekiel 40–48, great care is taken to keep sacral clothing from the general population.[77]

---

74. See S.R.A. Starbuck, "Theological Anthropology at the Fulcrum: Isaiah 55:1–5, Psalm 89, and Second Stage Tradition in the Royal Psalms," in *David and Zion: Biblical Studies in Honor of J.J.M. Roberts*, ed. B.F. Batto and K.L. Roberts (Winona Lake: Eisenbrauns, 2004), 247–65.

75. Upson-Saia, Daniel-Hughes, and Batten, *Dressing Judeans and Christians in Antiquity*, 4.

76. S.M. Olyan, *Rites and Rank Hierarchy in Biblical Representations of Cult* (Princeton, N.J.: Princeton University Press, 2000), 27.

77. Ibid., 28.

At the same time, it must be admitted from the standpoint of Isa 61, itself, the argument is not settled as to whether the power transfer indicated by the מְעִיל צְדָקָה is intended more to communalize by transferring the royal and priestly charges for justice and right worship to the entire people or even to a righteous remnant of the people, thus eventuating significant conflict with the official priesthood of Yehud,[78] or whether the power transfer intended to realign the Sabbath keeping people of the covenant with the faithful official priesthood to become a nation of priests on behalf of other nations.[79] However, it can be asserted with confidence that a significant power transfer is indicated. The reclothing of the community represented reversal, change, and reformulation to conceptualizations of the royal office as well as the priesthood. Isa 61 purports the communalization of both offices. Because of this, the symbolic use of clothing helped to dynamically envision an embodied performance of the prophetic word by dressing unusual characters in privileged garments of royalty and cult. This embodied performance embraced a significant reversal of social status and emotional condition that has at its deepest motivation empowerment for justice and right relationship, even and especially in an otherwise chaotic, disappointing, and politically divisive historical context. Most significantly, the metaphoric "robing" of the servant community would be felt in the communalization of liturgy—a performative priesthood, rather than through sacrifice (Isa 61:8). The legitimacy of this dramatic political shift is predicated, according to Isa 61:1–10, on YHWH's metaphoric act of robing unusual characters. As such, Isaiah 61:1–10 illustrates how clothing could signify the transfer of power, legitimacy, divine approval, and social authority, supporting a revolutionary mandate for dramatic social change and religious reform. It is a poignant example of clothing visualizing a locus of dispute and resistance as well as an alternate path to holiness.

In sum, the reference to מְעִיל צְדָקָה in Isa 61:10, combined with supporting parallel terms, verbal cluster allusions, and liturgical background, opens up a trove of interpretive possibilities with cultural and political significance when pursued exegetically beyond that of a passing reference. It is reasonable to assume that the literati of Yehud would have heard the text in its fullness, as well, as visioned in its metaphorical social-political claims. The מְעִיל צְדָקָה would have been recognized as a locus of societal dispute, political resistance, covenantal election, and the concomitant power investiture.

---

78. P.D. Hanson, *The Dawn of Apocalyptic* (Philadelphia: Fortress, 1975); L.-S. Tiemeyer, "The Haughtiness of the Priesthood (Isa 65,5)," *Biblica* 85 (2004): 237–44; C. Nihan, "Ethnicity and Identity in Isaiah 56–66," in *Judah and the Judeans in the Achaemenid Period: Negotiating Identity in an International Context*, ed. O. Lipschits, G.H. Knoppers, and M. Oeming (Winona Lake, Eisenbrauns, 2011), 87–97.

79. J. Blenkinsopp, "The 'Servants of the Lord' in Third Isaiah; Profile of a Pietistic Group in the Persian Epoch," *Proceedings of the Irish Biblical Association* 7 (1983): 1–23; B. Schramm, *The Opponents of Third Isaiah Reconstructing the Cultic History of the Restoration* (Sheffield, England: Sheffield Academic Press, 1995).

8

WERE YHWH'S CLOTHES WORTH REMEMBERING AND THINKING ABOUT AMONG THE LITERATI OF LATE PERSIAN/EARLY HELLENISTIC JUDAH/YEHUD? OBSERVATIONS AND CONSIDERATIONS

Ehud Ben Zvi

The starting point of this exploration consists of two basic observations about which there is no significant disagreement in the field. The first is that the core repertoire of the literati of the Late Persian/Early Hellenistic (LPEH) in Yehud/Judah[1] included numerous texts available to them and that asked their readers (i.e., the literati) to imagine (and image) YHWH in anthropomorphic terms.[2] In fact, not only was YHWH imagined in anthropomorphic terms but also references to and images of anthropomorphic, divine body-parts abound. For instance, there are references to YHWH's face, eyes, lips, ears, hand, right hand, back, feet, finger, and so on across the literature of the time (e.g., Exod 14:31, 33:20–33; Deut

---

1. The choice of this textual repertoire is due to the fact that historians may somewhat approximate it from the perspective of another repertoire of texts, namely the collection of books that eventually ended up in the Hebrew Bible (HB) with some notable exceptions such as Daniel and Esther that belong to a later period. The remaining collection consisting of books that at least in some textual form was available to and likely read and reread by the ideologically Jerusalem-centered literati of LPEH Yehud/Judah may be reasonably considered from a pragmatic viewpoint as an approximate representation in broad strokes of their core repertoire.

2. The issue of divine anthropomorphisms in the HB has been studied from a variety of perspectives and needless to say, anthropomorphisms do not represent a uniform category. There is a very substantial, *recent* (i.e., from 2010 on) corpus of research on the question of YHWH's body, see, for example, Esther J. Hamori, *"When Gods Were Men": The Embodied God in Biblical and Near Eastern Literature*, BZAW 384 (Berlin: de Gruyter, 2008); H. Eilberg-Schwartz, "Does God Have a Body? The Problem of Metaphor and Literal Language in Biblical Interpretation," in *Bodies, Embodiment, and Theology of the Hebrew Bible*, ed. S. Tamar Kamionkowski and Wonil Kim, LHBOTS 465 (New York: T&T Clark, 2010), 201–37; Benjamin D. Sommer, *The Bodies of God and the World of Ancient Israel* (Cambridge: Cambridge University Press, 2009); Annette Schellenberg, "More than Spirit:

9:10; Isa 60:13; Zech 14:4; Ps 8:4; 17:1–15; 1 Chr 28:19; *passim*).³ Further, the aforementioned repertoire included multiple texts that communicated and evoked socially acceptable memories of YHWH's human-like behavior (e.g., walking,

---

On the Physical Dimension in the Priestly Understanding of Holiness," *ZAW* 126 (2014): 163–79; Mark S. Smith, "The Three Bodies of God in the Hebrew Bible," *JBL* 134 (2015): 471–88; Deena E. Grant, "Fire and the Body of Yahweh," *JSOT* 40 (2015): 139–61 and the extensive list of works mentioned in these works. (Of course, matters concerning the "body," the "bodylessness" of YHWH, and related topics also have a long research—and centuries of theological debates as well.) Questions such as whether there are taxonomic differences among YHWH's anthropomorphisms or even taxonomic differences in imagined divine bodies, or whether the references to YHWH's body and body-parts were understood in concrete, literal, figurative, metaphorical, analogical, or, for that matter, in multivalent terms have occupied much of this research and demand a separate discussion, which not incidentally should also deal with the question of whether, for example, "literal" and "figurative" constituted true, opposite binaries structuring ways of thinking, imagining, and "feeling" among these literati or, as far more likely in the opinion of this writer, constructed a pragmatic continuum in which shades of one aspect did not preclude the existence of shades of the other among the literati, and the general community. On these matters, see David H. Aaron, *Biblical Ambiguities: Metaphor, Semantics, and Divine Imagery*, BRLAJ 4 (Leiden: Brill, 2001). The argument advanced here, however, does not depend, in any substantial way, on any particular position on these matters. (Even when one states that "time is an arrow," not only does one still conjure the image of a flying arrow, its speed, direction, and so on, but one must also do so as to understand and "feel" the meaning of "time is an arrow.")

3. To be sure, anthropomorphic terms and images used for YHWH often evoked beyond human, and in fact, superhuman body/body-parts. See, for example, Mark S. Smith, *The Origins of Biblical Monotheism: Israel's Polytheistic Background and the Ugaritic Texts* (Oxford: Oxford University Press, 2001), 83–86; cf. Stephen D. Moore, "Gigantic God: Yahweh's Body," *JSOT* 70 (1996): 87–115.

Moreover, in Israel and not only in Israel, anthropomorphic divine imagery may, at times, serve as a tool to "comprehend" that which is by necessity "beyond comprehension" and thus "anthropomorphisms" become "supra-anthropomorphisms" and the mentioned tools both construct and deconstruct at the same time the anthropomorphic character of the relevant deity. On these matters, see, for example, Ronald Hendel, "Aniconism and Anthropomorphism in Ancient Israel," in *The Image and the Book. Iconic Cults, Aniconism and the Rise of Book Religions in Israel and the Ancient Near East*, ed. Karel van der Toorn, CBET 21 (Leuven: Peeters, 1997), 205–28, esp. 205–09 and literature.

On the whole, to some extent anthropomorphism, supra-anthropomorphism, and non- or even anti-anthropomorphism may often be seen, from a systemic perspective, as participating all in a single, dynamic, and self-balancing system that attempts to allow the (socially construed and self-understood) "finite" to imagine/comprehend that which is socially construed as "infinite"—to borrow medieval philosophic terms—while at the same time strongly maintain their (construed) absolutely "finite" and "infinite" respective characters. This involves, by necessity, processes of "bridging" and "unbridging."

sitting, standing, dwelling, seeing, trampling, and *passim*) and social roles (e.g., as a king, warrior, teacher, and so on).[4]

The second observation is that given the general sociocultural contexts in which the literati lived, they neither imaged nor imagined YHWH's human-like body to be naked, nor did memories of a naked YHWH populate their mnemonic landscape.[5] This is certainly true when they imagined YHWH as a superhuman

---

4. It is to be stressed that the fact that anthropomorphic images were included in the discourses, memories, and basic imaginative horizon of the (very much human) community, does not mean at all that there was an absence of non- or even anti-anthropomorphic positions and texts within the very same community, each evoking and at times reshaping and rebalancing other images and memories. The coexistence of various approaches on these matters not only characterizes well the world of the literati discussed here (see, e.g., Deut 4:12), but is also a feature of other discourses, see, for instance, the case of rabbinic Judaism. For anthropomorphism in the rabbinic period, see, above all, *Shiur Qomah*, and, among many others, b. B. Meṣ 86b, GenR 48.1. On these matters, see, for example, Meir Bar-Ilan, "The Hand of God: A Chapter in Rabbinic Anthropomorphism," in *Rashi 1040–1990: Hommage à Ephraim E. Urbach*, ed. Gabrielle Sed-Rajna (Paris: CERF, 1993), 321–35, and available as an open access text at https://faculty.biu.ac.il/~barilm/articles/publications/publications0035.html; and cf. Moore, "Gigantic God." See also Alon G. Gottstein, "The Body as Image of God in Rabbinic Literature," *HTR* 87 (1994): 171–95; David H. Aaron, "Shedding Light on God's Body in Rabbinic Midrashim: Reflections on the Theory of a Luminous Adam," *HTR* 90 (1997): 299–314; recently and particularly on *Shiur Qomah*, Marvin A. Sweeney, "Dimensions of the Shekhinah: The Meaning of the *Shiur Qomah* in Jewish Mysticism and Rabbinic Thought," *HS* 54 (2013): 107–20 and the bibliography cited in all these works.

5. Being stripped naked, showing one's naked body, walking barefoot (see below), and the like were not associated in the discourse of ancient Israel with an increase in or a projection of the honor of the relevant person, but with shame (see, e.g., Gen 3:7, 10). Nakedness, hunger, sickness, and the like were considered chaotic features or lacks to be taken care of by the proper ordering authority (e.g., Gen 3:21; Isa 58:7; 2 Chr 28:15). Nakedness was associated with powerlessness and social indignity. Examples may be multiplied. See, for example, Sharon R. Keller, "Aspects of Nudity In the Old Testament," in *Notes in the History of Art 12. No. 2. Essays on Nudity in Antiquity in Memory of Otto Brendel* (New York: Ars Brevis, 1993), 32–36. Given that YHWH was construed as a victorious heroic king, it is worth noting that in neo-Assyrian visual art, the defeated were associated with nakedness, following a long tradition in Mesopotamia, in which death was also associated with nakedness. See, for example, Zainab Bahrani, "The Iconography of the Nude in Mesopotamia," in *Notes in the History of Art 12. No. 2. Essays on Nudity in Antiquity in Memory of Otto Brendel* (New York: Ars Brevis, 1993), 12–19 (15–16); Julia Asher-Greve and Deborah Sweeney, "On Nakedness, Nudity, and Gender in Egyptian and Mesopotamian Art," in *Images and Gender: Contributions to the Hermeneutics of Reading Ancient Art*, ed. Silvia Schroer, OBO, 220 (Fribourg: Academic Press/Göttingen: Vandenhoeck & Ruprecht, 2006), 125–76 and bibliography. Moreover, the mentioned concept in ancient Israel that being naked along with being hungry and the like are among the states that proper authority is supposed to

king or warrior, as often the case, or as a friendly YHWH who walks about with Enoch (Gen 5:22).[6] Moreover, it is extremely unlikely that they imagined the deity naked, whether the references to the human-like body was taken to be "concrete,"

reverse is certainly not unique to ancient Israel. It is also well attested in neo-Assyrian texts, see, for example "those who were sick for many days have got well … [t]he hungry has been sated, the parched have been anointed with oil, the needy have been covered with garments" (letter from Adad-šumu-uṣur to Assurbanipal; SAA 10.226). There are no representations in neo-Assyrian visual art of Assyrian kings being naked or being stripped naked. Such representations would have been beyond the realm of the possible in this cultural context.

As for gods, there is no lack of literature referring to the garments of the gods in the ANE (e.g., "Bless Sargon, who holds fast the hem of your garment, the shepherd of Assyria, who walks behind you!," Nanaya Hymn of Sargon II; SAA 3, 4 r 2.18; available at the State Archives of Assyria Online (SAAo); http://oracc.museum.upenn.edu/saao/). On garments for deities, other supernatural beings, cultic performers, and other textiles associated with cultic rituals and settings, see Salvatore Gaspa, *Textiles in the Neo-Assyrian Empire: A Study of Terminology*, Studies in Ancient Near Eastern Records 19 (Berlin: de Gruyter, 2018), esp. § 5.5–5.5.2 (130–56) and esp. for "wardrobe of male deities" see § 5.5.1.2 (140–50). The variety within this wardrobe is worth stressing. For earlier studies, see A. Leo Oppenheim, "The Golden Garments of the Gods," *JNES* 8 (1949): 172–93; Paul-Alain Beaulieu, *The Pantheon of Uruk during the Neo-Babylonian Period* (Cuneiform Monographs, 23; Leiden/Boston: Brill/Styx, 2003), 9–25 and *passim*; particularly on Mesopotamian rituals of clothing the divine statue/the deity, see, for example, Eiko Matsushima, "Divine Statues in Ancient Mesopotamia: Their Fashioning and Clothing and Their Interaction with Society," in *Official Cult and Popular Religion in the Ancient Near East*, ed. Eiko Matsushima (Heidelberg: Winter, 1993), 209–19; Eiko Matsushima, "Eleven Neo-Babylonian Texts Relating to the Lubuštu (Clothing Ceremony)," in *Essays on Ancient Anatolia and its Surrounding Civilizations*, ed. Prince Takahito Mikasa (Wiesbaden: Harrassowitz, 1995), 235–43; Beaulieu, *Pantheon*, 36–39, and *passim*. For Sargonid times and the question of overlap between the garments of deities in seals and humans in positions of authority, and probably in a cultic/religious setting, see Benjamin R. Foster, "Clothing in Sargonic Mesopotamia: Visual and Written Evidence," in *Textile Terminologies in the Ancient Near East and Mediterranean from the Third to the First Millennia BC*, ed. C. Michel and M.-L. Nosch, Ancient Textiles Series 8 (Oxford/Oakville: Oxbow Books, 2010), 110–45 (123–24).

6. Neither YHWH nor Enoch was imagined as strolling naked together. "Clothing is one way in which human beings are distinct from animals, but it is also the key qualification that allows human beings to meet God," Michaela Bauks, "Text- and Reception-Historical Reflections on Transmissional and Hermeneutical Techniques in Genesis 2–3," in *The Pentateuch: International Perspectives on Current Research*, ed. Thomas B. Dozeman, Konrad Schmid, and Baruch J. Schwartz, FAT 78 (Tübingen: Mohr Siebeck, 2011), 139–68; citation from p. 166. Particularly relevant to the present issue is that there are no visual representations in which main male gods such as Assur, Marduk, or Ahura Mazda, all of which are deities comparable to YHWH in ancient Israel, appear naked, and for good reason.

"figurative," or in any other way. To read these texts and to conjure a mental visual representation of a naked YHWH would have been "unthinkable" within that cultural context,[7] and so too would have been the associated image of YHWH walking barefoot.[8]

Given that memories and images of a naked YHWH were beyond the realm of possibility within the world of the literati[9] and given that they did image, on numerous occasions, YHWH as having a human-like body, one might have expected multiple references to YHWH's garments (and also to YHWH's sandals). Moreover, given that clothing performs numerous important functions such as communicating status and identity, projecting power or a lack thereof, and serving to mark hierarchies, boundaries, and the like,[10] one would have anticipated a

---

The case of goddesses/supernatural female figures is different and deserves a separate discussion that may be informed by an important distinction between "nakedness" as an absence of "normal" attributes (and their semiotic) markers and thus directly contrasted with "clothed" (*which is the case relevant to our present purposes*) and "nudity" in which the nude body stands not as an absence of "normal" attributes, but as the social/semiotic counterpart of empowering clothes and thus projecting power. Much, though not all, of these differences directly relate, embody and communicate gender constructions. As interesting as these issues are and as hotly debated in general (in relation to the ANE and Egypt in particular) they stand outside the purview of the present contribution. On these matters see Asher-Greve and Sweeney, "On Nakedness, Nudity, and Gender in Egyptian and Mesopotamian Art" and the excellent bibliography there. Also beyond the scope of this contribution is any study of the conceptual field of "practical nudity," in which nudity was "normally" expected as part of the performance of a particular social role (e.g., servants, dancers, children, or for that matter, certain Old Babylonian priests) which to a large extent might be seen as grounded in the intersectionality of the "nudity" mentioned above and constructions of social class, roles, and the like.

7. To be sure, this attitude is certainly not unique to the YHWH construed by and vicariously encountered by the literati of the LPEH period as they read their core textual repertoire. As mentioned above, there are no visual art representations of a naked Assur, Marduk, or Ahura Mazda.

8. Cf. 2 Sam 15:30; Isa 20:2–4; Ezek 24:17, 23; Mic 1:8; 2 Chr 28:15. Cf. Christine Palmer, "Unshod on Holy Ground: Ancient Israel's 'Disinherited' Priesthood," in *Fashioning Jews: Clothing, Culture and Commerce*, ed. Leonard J. Greenspoon (Studies in Jewish Civilization, 24; West Lafayette, IN: Purdue University Press, 2013), 1–18.

9. Given the focus of this contribution and the main characters discussed here, there is no need to address the constructions of the naked female in contradistinction with the male body among the mentioned literati in this contribution.

10. These matters have been attested time and again and across different cultures. The literature on these and cognate matters is immense. See, for example, and from different perspectives and discussing various different cultures, Dick Hebdige, *Subculture: The Meaning of Style* (New York: Methuen, 1979); Mary Ellen Roach-Higgings, Joanne B. Eicher and Kim K.P. Johnson, eds., *Dress and Identity* (New York: Fairchild, 1995); Robert J. Ross,

sustained set of images about YHWH's garments that would be commensurate with YHWH's incomparable power and status within the ideological world of these literati. In fact, YHWH's garments would have been impressive to the utmost degree and very much worth remembering. One might have expected feverish imagination in terms of, for instance, the color and general visual effects, the texture and rare properties of the materials being used, and even the aroma spread by them[11]; for these were garments meant both to communicate YHWH's majesty and power and to be imagined as worthy of being in direct contact with the divine holy body and creating boundaries around it.

Yet, the fact is that the texts that existed within the core repertoire of these literati included very little regarding any of these matters. In fact, one can find

---

Clothing: A Global History: Or the Imperialists' New Clothes (Cambridge: Polity, 2008); S.J. Lennon, "Clothing and Adornment: Social Psychology Perspectives," in *Encyclopedia of Body Image and Human Appearance*, ed. Thomas Cash, vol. 1, 2 vols. (London: Elsevier, 2012), 320–26; Emily J. Rozier, "Fashion," in *Handbook of Medieval Culture: Fundamental Aspects and Conditions of the European Middle Ages*, ed. Albrecht Classen, vol. 1, 3 vols. (Berlin: de Gruyter, 2015), 415–30 and cited works.

On the conceptual importance in the LPEH period of clothing in the construction of the priests in general and the high priest in particular, see Christophe Nihan and Julia Rhyder, "Aaron's Vestments in Exodus 28 and Priestly Leadership," in *Debating Authority. Concepts of Leadership in the Pentateuch and the Former Prophets*, ed. Katharina Pyschny and Sarah Schulz (BZAW 507; Berlin/New York: de Gruyter, 2018), 45–67 and Christophe Nihan, "Le pectoral d'Aaron et la figure du grand prêtre dans les traditions sacerdotales du Pentateuque," in *Congress Volume Stellenbosch 2016*, ed. Louis Jonker, Gideon Kotzé and Christl M. Maier VTSup 177 (Leiden: Brill, 2017), 23–55. It is worth noting that in this period, the figure of the high priest takes over some of the symbolic roles associated with kings and as demonstrated in the works mentioned above, this is reflected also in matters of clothing.

From a more general perspective, garments are a medium, and as in all media, the main issue is not their explicit contents (color, shape, materials, and so on), but the multiple ways in which these garments influence society at large and impact those seeing them—whether in the "real" world or in worlds of memory.

For a recent work on clothing in the HB as seen through midrashic lenses, and addressed to the general public, see Norman J. Cohen, *Masking and Unmasking Ourselves. Interpreting Biblical Texts on Clothing and Identity* (Woodstock, VT: Jewish Lights Publishing/Skylights Publishing, 2012).

11. Cf. with the description of the garments of the human king in Ps 45:9. Perhaps one might have even expected an aural element too, for example, references to the sound or complete silence made by YHWH's garments and sandals when YHWH walks, enters, or sits in the divine council, comes to battle, or when walking peacefully in the garden (see Gen 3:8, 10; 2 Sam 5:24 / 1 Chr 14:15; of course, there are other sounds associated with YHWH, e.g., thunder, see e.g., Ps 29: 3–9; on explicit, sound-making priestly garments, see Exod 28:33–35; 39: 25–26; Sir 45:9).

only two or potentially three relevant texts and none of them says too much about the divine clothes.[12] The literati who read and reread Isa 6:1–4 involved themselves in imagining and vicariously partaking in the multi-sensorial world experienced by the prophetic character Isaiah as reported by the relevant account in the book. They (over)see, as it were, YHWH sitting on an incredibly large throne. They see flying seraphs. They (over)hear their voices and understand their language. They feel the threshold shaking. They smell, see, and breathe the smoke that pervades the house. But what about YHWH's garment? It is only briefly and somewhat "accidentally" mentioned to make the point that the entire temple was filled with YHWH's "lower hem" (שׁוּלָיו šûlāyw; i.e., the lower hem of YHWH's robe).[13] The

---

12. Isa 6:1–3, Isa 63:1–3; Ezek 16:8. Dan 7:9 is the fourth text that explicitly mentions YHWH's garment, but Dan 7:9 or the book of Daniel in general was not available to these literati, since it postdates the period discussed here. Significantly, the same pattern is noticeable in terms of references to YHWH's footwear. The only references to YHWH's sandals are in Ps 60:10; 108:10 (see below).

Incidentally, Ps 104:2 refers to the luminescent aspect of the presence of YHWH, not to anthropomorphic garments. Moreover, note also that the precise phrasing of the text, namely "YHWH wrapped in light *as with* a garment" (emphasis mine) and cf. with very similar phrasing in v. 6 in which תהום is clearly not a reference to a garment. Associations between YHWH and luminescence appear elsewhere in the HB (e.g., Isa 10:17; 60:1; Mic 7:8–9; Ps 27:1; 97:11; 112:4). One has to grant, however, that given the immediate literary context of the reference to light in Ps 104:2 in which YHWH is constructed as a storm god, it may well be that אור here points to lightning (cf. Hab 3:4; Job 36:30; 37:11) and see John Day, "Ps 104 and Akhenaten's Hymn to the Sun," in *Jewish and Christian Approaches to the Psalms: Conflict and Convergence*, ed. Susan Gillingham (Oxford: Oxford University Press, 2013), 211–28 (219). There has been much debate on Ps 104 and its background, but these matters have no bearing on the matters discussed here (that said, see bibliography in Day, "Ps 104"). On a development much later than the LPEH period that might have been influenced by the language of Ps 104, see below.

13. The relevant text reads, וְשׁוּלָיו מְלֵאִים אֶת־הַהֵיכָל. I follow here a widespread understanding of the Hebrew term שׁוּל (šûl) as meaning "(lower) hem" and cf. Exod 28:33–34; 39:24–26, in which there is a reference to the שׁוּל present in the priestly vestments. Lyle Eslinger has proposed that שׁוּל refers to YHWH's penis. See his "The Infinite in a Finite Organical Perception (Isaiah VI 1–5)," *VT* 45 (1995): 145–73. For a response to Eslinger, see, for example, Smith, *Origins of Biblical Monotheism*, 246–47 n. 37. One may notice also that the term שׁוּל appears in Jer 13:22, 26; Nah 3:5; Lam 1:9 in reference either to the hem of a garment used by women as a *pars pro toto* or metaphorically for the hem/lower part of the body and thus referring to the pubic area of women (cf. HAL). In neither case, שׁוּל may be understood as "penis." Another, and very different proposal for שׁוּל has been suggested. Hurowitz, although he agrees that שׁוּל may mean "hem," entertains the possibility that the term stood for a relatively lower level heavenly beings or assistants. See Victor (Avigdor) Hurowitz, "Isaiah's Impure Lips and Their Purification in Light of Akkadian Sources," *HUCA* 60 (1989): 39–89 (42 n. 3) and cf. later midrashim in which the term is understood

robe is actually not mentioned explicitly and nothing is said about its hem even, except that it is so large. The gazing, hearing, smelling, the entire gamut of sensorial inputs that the character in the text and that the readers experience does not include any substantive interaction with the garment itself.[14] The reference to the garment is of much secondary importance and primarily functions to characterize YHWH's temple as a space.

The text of Isa 63:1–3 encoded and communicated an image of YHWH's בגדים *bəgādîm*, that is, garments as soaked in blood. The reference to the bloody garments here served to underscore the characterization of YHWH as a bloody, victorious superhero who has just trampled his enemies in his wrath and as a result their "juice" spattered his garments.[15] There is a stressed emphasis on the redness of the

---

as referring to nothing else but priests and in the very case of Isa 6:1 to "the eighty priests who were with Uzziah" (*Yalkut Shimoni*, Prophets and Writings, Isaiah, 404 and which is reflected later in *Ze'enah u-Re'enah*; see Morris M. Faierstein, *Ze'enah u-Re'enah: A Critical Translation into English* [Studia Judaica 96; Berlin: de Gruyter, 2017], 480). For a recent summary of positions leading again to the choice of "hem" as the most likely understanding of the term שׁוּל see Torsten Uhlig, *The Theme of Hardening in the Book of Isaiah: An Analysis of Communicative Action* (FAT 2, 39; Tübingen: Mohr Siebeck, 2009), 84–86. Shawn W. Flynn, argues that שׁוּל in Isa 6:1 refers to something like the Mesopotamian flounced *pala* and its use was restricted to cultic and royal contexts, in this volume, 25–26.

14. Comparative data are particularly relevant in this context. See "Assyrian kings tell us that they took hold of the hem of the garments that covered the cult statues … [t]he mention of this act—a prerogative of kings—is illustrative of the proximity existing between Assyrian kings and gods … [m]ore importantly, the function of the hem as *pars pro toto* of the garment of a person—and as an expression of personal identity—is transferred to the realm of god-human interaction: the hem represents the specific deity's identity and holding fast of the hem of the god's garment illustrates the exceptional bodily experience of the king's contact with his god" (Gaspa, *Textiles*, 150).

Gaspa refers, for example, to texts such as "Bless Sargon, who holds fast the hem of your [Nanāya's] garment, the shepherd of Assyria, who walks behind you!" (SAA 3, 4 4 ii 18; available at oracc.museum.upenn.edu/saao/knpp/saa_03).

One can easily notice: (a) instead of a king of Judah, the main human character populating the scene in Isa 6:1 is a prophet (not even a priest) and (b) there is an act of seeing, but certainly not an act of touching, never mind, holding the hem. The Judahite king envisaged in Isa 6 and remembered by the group is nothing like an Assyrian king, and nor is the prophet, who is the only present at the reported event. YHWH's robes are not worth mentioning in any detail and certainly do not empower the prophet. It is even debatable whether the hem here stands as *pars pro toto* of the robes, or to the contrary, that the text makes a pun based on that (mis)reading, by advancing a "hem" that actually means "hem" and as such conveys even a larger sense of majesty. For a partially different approach to the imagery in Isa 6:1 the contribution of Shawn W. Flynn in this volume, 37–38.

15. The reference to the winepress (גַּת in v 2) and the related imagery plays on and shapes a *nomen-omen* message associating the main city of Edom, בָּצְרָה (*boṣrâ*) Bosra, with the

garments which functions to characterize YHWH as a powerful warrior soaked in blood, but nothing else is said about them.¹⁶

To these two texts, one may add a very different one, Ezek 16:8, which reads, "I spread כְּנָפִי (my skirt) over you [Jerusalem], and covered your nakedness: I pledged myself to you and entered into a covenant with you." Although the text goes on and draws attention to the clothes and adornments that husband YHWH provided her (vv 10–13), nothing is said of the garment of groom YHWH.

Finally, although sandals are not garments, it is worth noting that the pattern discerned above concerning YHWH's garments is attested in relation to YHWH's sandals.¹⁷ They are mentioned twice, in Ps 60:10 (some ET, 60:8) and Ps 108:10 (most ET, 108:9), but only for the sake of being thrown over/hurled upon enemies. No attention is drawn to the divine sandals themselves, nor to any of their potential features, but only to them as (culturally coded) objects to be hurled at some enemy.¹⁸

---

word בָּצִיר *bāṣîr* vintage (e.g., Lev 26:5; Judg 8:2; Mic 7:1), both of which share the same consonants and in the same order and thus may be construed conjuring a similar sonorous and visual "experience," which becomes particularly relevant if, is most likely the case, the literati held a philosophy of language that assumed that the link between signifier (i.e., the word) and signified was not arbitrary at all. The particular shade of red conveyed by the color term חָמוּץ *ḥāmûṣ* in Isa 63:1, beyond being "bloody" is probably carmine or crimson. On the color חָמוּץ (and the general semiotics of the red range); see Scott B. Noegel, "Scarlet and Harlots: Seeing Red in the Hebrew Bible," *HUCA* 87 (2016): 1–47 (20) and bibliography.

16. It is worth noting that whereas there was room for memories of YHWH actively participating in battle supporting Israel (see, e.g., Josh 10:10–11), there was none for detailed images and memories of YHWH's warrior apparel. For vivid and memorable images of a terrifying warrior conveyed by means of his apparel, see the case of Goliath in 1 Sam 17:4–7. There were reasons for their presence within the literati's mnemonic landscape and it is easy to understand their function/s in this context, but the consistent pattern of their absence in the case of warrior YHWH must also be rooted on some reasons, including the existence of alternative options for the fulfillment of the communicative messages that would have been communicated by them, had they existed.

It is worth noting that minor references to clothing meant to evoke a particular characterization occur also in the case of divine messengers/servants such as those in Ezek 9:2–3, 11; 10:2. The references to האיש הלבש הבדים "the man clothed in linen" there serve to associate the character with priestly imagery, but add nothing else about the clothes themselves. The clothes are not memorable, the priestly association is.

17. The Hebrew term is נַעַל *naʿal*. It may be translated in English as "shoe" as well; see NRSV, NJPSV and contrast with NAB. The direct object of the divine action is referred to as Edom, but Edom is part and parcel of a triad of closely related peoples which are all defeated by YHWH, namely Moab, Edom, and Philistines.

18. Although the general pragmatic meaning conveyed by the reference is clear, both what is exactly portrayed at the literal level and the precise symbolic value, or even performative value of YHWH's throwing his sandals/shoes upon Edom is not clear and

One cannot complete this set of observations without pointing out the obvious: there were plenty of occasions in which the garments could have been depicted within the core repertoire of the community. For instance, as Brettler correctly comments, there is "a complete lack of interest in the issue" in Ezek 1 (esp. vv. 26-27).[19] There is plenty of imagination and vivid imagery in Ezek 1, but nothing about YHWH's garments.

Similarly, Micaiah reports via YHWH's word that he has seen YHWH sitting on his throne, as head of a divine council (see 1 Kgs 22:19; 2 Chr 18:18). Not a word is said about YHWH's royal garments. The setting of the reported event, what transpires at the council, and the implication of all the above for the didactic and

---

was not clear already at the time of the ancient versions. The most common position is that "'throwing the shoe' is a symbolic expression for taking possession" (citation from Hans-Joachim Kraus, *Psalms 60-150* [Continental Commentary; Minneapolis, MN: Fortress, 1993], 5). According to this currently prevalent position, the portrayed action at the literal level is to throw/hurl a sandal/shoe. This position is well grounded on the widely attested meaning of the verbal form שׁלך *šlk* in the *hiphil* (see, e.g., HAL and bibliography; at times Ruth 4:7 is brought into consideration, though the relevance of this text to the matter at stake is debatable). This said, the LXX Ps 59 (//MT Ps 60): 10 reads "on Idumea I will put my sandal" (NETS) and the Targum of Psalms, which makes explicit an implicit understanding of the Hebrew text within a particular group, reads "upon the broken neck of the mighty ones of Edom I have cast my shoe" (translation from David M. Stec, *The Targum of Psalms Translated, with a Critical Introduction, Apparatus, and Notes* [The Aramaic Bible, 16; Collegeville, MN: Liturgical, 2004]). Although LXX Ps 107 (//MT 108): 9 reads "on Idumea I will hurl my sandal" (NETS), the Ralph's edition is consistent with "put" instead of "hurl." The Targum here, however, reads "upon the kingdom of Edom I have cast my sandal" (Stec's translation). The Vulgate has *extendam calciamentum* (i.e., stretch out the shoe) in both occasions. The position that instead of "throwing the shoe/sandal" the text might have primarily communicated something akin to "placing the shoe/sandal upon" (even if due to a forceful action, like "throwing"; cf. 2 Sam 20:12) would be consistent with a visual art gesture well known from ancient iconographic sources. See, for example, the central image in Behistun, in which "with his left foot Darius steps on the chest of the figure prostate before him," who is, of course identified as Gaumata (on Behistun's visual art and its messages, see Margaret Cool Root, *The King and Kingship in Achaemenid Art. Essays on the Creation of an Iconography of Empire* [Leiden: Brill, 1979], 59-61; 182-226; citation from p. 185). The point of this gesture is to communicate the total vanquishment and humiliation of the enemy. For perspective based on a proposed Hebrew root II שׁלך on the basis of comparative Northwest Semitics, see Mitchell Dahood, *Psalms II: 51-100: Introduction, Translation, and Notes* (AB, 17, New Haven, CT: Yale University Press, 2008; orig. pub. 1966), 80-81 and 37-38.

19. Marc Z. Brettler, *God Is King: Understanding an Israelite Metaphor*, JSOTSup 76 (Sheffield: Sheffield Academic Press, 1989), 79.

multivalent story of Micaiah are all very much worth remembering.[20] In contrast, YHWH's royal attire is not worth remembering, despite the fact that the literati reading the text did not imagine that the divine king presided over his court naked.

In sum, one can safely conclude that the cumulative weight of these observations strongly suggests the existence of an underlying, but strong tendency to dis-prefer depictions and imaginative exercises involving YHWH's clothes, even if he had to be remembered as not naked. In other words, YHWH's clothes were not much worth remembering or thinking about in Judah/Yehud during the LPEH period, if at all.[21]

But if so, why would such a strong, systemic dis-preference[22] be so dominant? Why would it be acceptable in terms of the generative grammar that characterized

---

20. On the story of Micaiah, see my "A Contribution to the Intellectual History of Yehud: The Story of Micaiah and Its Function within the Discourse of Persian-Period Literati," in *The Historian and the Bible: Essays in Honour of Lester L. Grabbe*, ed. Philip R. Davies and Diana V. Edelman, LHBOTS 530 (London and New York: T&T Clark, 2010), 89–102.

21. Since not all of the texts within the core repertoire of these literati were written in this period, this dis-preference may have existed in slightly earlier periods as well, but the issue goes beyond the scope of this chapter. It is worth stressing that in this chapter the focus is not on particular texts per se *and as separate units*, but on the repertoire as such and subsequently the implied grammars communicated by the core repertoire and internalized by the literati through their reading and rereading of these texts. The reason for this focus is that texts are never read in a vacuum, but within a "universe" of other texts (i.e., within a repertoire) and in a particular social and historical setting (in this case that of the literati of the LPEH period). Further, the literati were socialized into this underlying grammar, whether in ways known or even better unbeknownst to them. They then generated texts, according this grammar, either through their understanding of existing texts, the textual editing of previous texts, or the composition of new texts. The mnemonic narratives as well as imaginative worlds that they shaped and socially shared through their readings were also strongly influenced by this grammar.

The underlying assumption here is that most of the books included today in the HB (but, and relevant to this contribution, excluding Daniel and Esther) in more or less their compositional forms are representative, at least to a significant degree, of the general authoritative repertoire of the Yehudite literati of the LPEH period. This is a reasonable assumption, at least concerning the Pentateuchal collection, the Deuteronomistic Historical collection, the Prophetic books collection, Chronicles, and most of the Psalms and Proverbs.

22. This dis-preference is at work in numerous texts, across literary genres and significantly, independently of viewpoints on or tendencies about anthropomorphism reflected in the text. It might be worth noting that the concept of "dis-preference" I am using here (and elsewhere in my research on social memory in ancient Israel) should not be confused with that of "censorship." The latter conjures images of bureaucratic power exerted upon others and of conscious intentionality. In contrast, the systemic generative grammars mentioned here have such a strong influence in shaping social mindshare within a group (and regulating the emergence and social reproductive success of texts and memories

the social mindscape of the literati to imagine, draw attention to, and remember images such as those showing "the appearance of the likeness of YHWH's glory" (Ezek 1:28) through a wealth of sensory reported experience? Similarly, why would it be acceptable to describe YHWH as riding clouds (e.g., Isa 19:1; Ps 68:5), standing on the Mount of Olives like a giant and splitting it entirely (e.g., Zech 14:4), and so on, but on the other hand, not acceptable (or worthwhile) to draw attention to YHWH's clothes? Why were they not worth remembering (or even imagining)?

Obviously, the response cannot be that there was a "failure of (social) imagination" (i.e., to argue that the clothes of the deity are so majestic that stand beyond human imagination). Lack of imagination is certainly not what characterized the literati's core repertoire nor, for that matter, their discourse (see, e.g., Ezek 1 and notice the lack of references to YHWH's clothing or something looking like the "likeness" of YHWH's garments for that matter in such a text).

A good starting point for exploring the potential, systemic reasons for the existence of the mentioned grammar of dis-preference is to note that it is at work not only in relation to YHWH but also, at least to a substantial extent, in relation to the human Israelite/Judahite king.
As Brettler noticed long ago:

> Almost nothing is known about the clothing that the king wore. The only descriptions of royal garments in the Bible are post-exilic or describe foreign kings. Esth. 8:15 describes, לבוש מלכות תכלת וחור ועטרת זהב גדולה ותכריך בוץ וארגמן, 'royal robes of blue and white, with a magnificent crown of gold and a mantle of fine linen and purple wool'. According to Jon 3:6, the king of Assyria wore an אדרת, a type of overgarment ... According to Judg. 8:26, the Midianite kings wore ארגמן, 'purple' and had jewelry called נטפות, 'crescents' and שהרנים, 'pendants'. It is unclear whether these descriptions of foreign royal attire are accurate or reflect Israelite royal garb ... Ps. 45:9 implies that the royal garb was perfumed, but it is uncertain if this was generally true or is specific to the royal wedding which this psalm describes.[23]

within it) in the long term particularly because neither conscious intentionality nor bare exercise of power by those able to do so over those unable to resist are perceived by the group to be at work. In general, I would argue that censorship tends to have limited success in shaping social mindscapes in the long term. These issues require a separate discussion, which for obvious reasons, cannot be carried out within the boundaries of the present contribution. For the use of the concept of "censorship," though having in mind, in the main, more heterogeneous groups with substantial inner strife, see for example, Mark S. Smith, *God in Translation. Deities in Cross-Cultural Discourse in the Biblical World* (Grand Rapids, MI: Eerdmans, 2008), 187–242 and works cited there.

23. Brettler, *God Is King*, 79. Esther was most likely not part of the repertoire of the Jerusalem-centered literati of the LPEH period, and in any case, the representation is not that of an Israelite/Judahite king.

To be sure, as in the case of YHWH's clothes, there are very few cases in which some reference is made to the royal robes of Israelite/Judahite kings. However, in these cases the royal garments are only mentioned for the sake of advancing some particular point in the narrative and no real attention is drawn to the clothes themselves (e.g., 1 Kgs 22:10, 30//2 Chr 18:9; cf. 1 Sam 18:4; 24:5; 2 Kgs 6:30). This lack of description contrasts with instances where the clothes of other figures, above all, the priests (e.g., Exod 28:1–43), but also even the royal princess (בַּת־מֶלֶךְ) are mentioned (see Ps 45:14–15).[24]

It is particularly worth stressing that the royal robes are absent in texts, stories, and sites of memories in which one might have anticipated them. For instance, the Queen of Sheba was a major site of memory. She was imagined and remembered as greatly impressed with the wisdom of Solomon, the house that he had built, the food of his table, the seating of his officials, and the attendance of his servants, *their clothing*, his valets, and his [Solomon's] burnt offerings that he presented at the house of YHWH (1 Kgs 10:4–5; 2 Chr 9: 3–4). All of the above took her breath away, but not Solomon's clothes? Why were the garments of the servants explicitly mentioned and evoked when readers re-visit this site of memory, but Solomon's garments are bracketed out, as though irrelevant to the story and not worth imagining and remembering? Or more generally, why would such a strong grammar of dis-preference on this matter characterize the world of the LPEH literati?

As usual in these cases, it is naïve to expect that the outcome of an exploration of the possible reasons for the fact that the clothes of YHWH or the Israelite king were not construed as particularly worthy of being recorded, remembered, or (through reading) imaginatively experienced time by the LPEH literati will lead us to a single, sufficient cause. More often, there is a particular constellation of factors, including both (a) facilitating, contingent social–cultural and political conditions, and (b) particular and historically contingent features of the ideological discourse

---

To be sure, there is a reference to what king David wore for a very particular occasion, but the reference is necessary and at the service of the plot and certainly has no bearing on royal garments (see 2 Sam 6:14b and cf. vv. 16 and 20). Similarly, one cannot learn anything about royal garments from 2 Kgs 6:30. Although in some narratives clothes may serve the plot (see, e.g., Mark Verman, "Royalty, Robes and the Art of Biblical Narrative," *SJOT* 30 [2016]: 30–43 and Ora Horn Prouser, "Suited to the Throne: The Symbolic Use of Clothing in the David and Saul Narratives," *JSOT* 71 [1996]: 27–37), not much about the clothes themselves can be learned from them. Even when some instances of, for example, transfer or tearing of clothes are worth remembering, the clothes themselves are not.

24. One may notice the lack of comparable detail to the king's clothes in this Psalm, except for the mention of their fragrance (v 9; cf. Prov 7:17 and notice the construction of "proper" gender roles). Despite the numerous visual references in the Psalm, including to the beauty of the king (v 3), no visual references to his clothes are made. It is possible that Ps 45 was read among the literati also in terms of YHWH and Israel/Jerusalem (cf. Isa 62:1–5; Ezekiel 16; 23).

of the group (which in turn are grounded in its general social mindscape). All these factors together contribute to the dominance of a particular (aspect of a) grammar of preferences (and dis-preferences), both in the textual repertoire as read and construed by the relevant community and in the shared social memory of the group strongly socialized through the reading and rereading of the mentioned repertoire.

In terms of "worldly" constraints as facilitating factors, two seem to deserve particular attention. The first concerns the lack of a local king and the second the lack of an iconic image of YHWH.

Turning to the first, the existence of an ad hoc conceptual realm including the human and the divine king, that is, king and King is beyond dispute and contributed to the ways in which YHWH was imagined. More directly relevant to the point discussed here, in Achaemenid visual art, clothes contributed to the depiction of the king (and at times, the crown prince as well), as separate from all others; in fact, "the Great King is the deity's [Ahuramazda] *doppelganger* ... (t) hey adopt the same hairstyle and beard shape, the same crown, the same type of garment, and they 'emit' the same *xvarnah* or 'brilliance' (in terms of luminosity or glory ...)."[25] But whether the literati were influenced by this Achaemenid tendency or just by the very existence of a conceptual realm of king and King, they still had no local Yehudite king and certainly, the literati could not have had any visual experience of his clothes.

In fact, if there was something in the "worldly" world that the vast majority of the literati and their readers could have seen and construed as potentially reminiscent of the "likeness" of a royal attire, this would have been the clothes of, in the big scheme of things, a relatively low-level local Achaemenid officer, the governor. (Very few literati would have ever seen the Satrap, never mind, the Persian king.) But imagining (and imaging) YHWH via the figure of the local Persian governor would have been problematic from an ideological and discursive perspective. Moreover, the Persian governor and the symbols projecting his (i.e., Achaemenid) power were, for the most part, bracketed out from the core repertoire and the shared mnemonic horizon of the LPEH literati (notice the lack of any direct reference to the building complex in Ramat Raḥel).[26]

---

25. See Emma Bridges, *Imagining Xerxes: Ancient Perspectives on a Persian King* (London/New York: Bloomsbury, 2015), 69–70 and bibliography. As for the citation, it is from Lloyd Llewellyn-Jones, *King and Court in Ancient Persia 559 to 331 BCE* (Edinburgh: Edinburgh University Press, 2013), 20–21.

26. The imagery of the royal garden in the Song of Songs might have been influenced by images of the garden that existed during the time of the literati in Ramat Raḥel. That said, Ramat Raḥel is not mentioned in the core repertoire of these literati (or even later literati; cf. Ezra-Nehemiah). The lack of any reference in this entire corpus to the impressive building complex of Ramat Raḥel that served as a seat and symbol of Persian control over Yehud and Jerusalem shows the existence and power of an ideological, generative grammar in which there was a strong dis-preference for mentioning Ramat Raḥel and thus for developing a mental map of the area in which Ramat Raḥel's dominant presence is not

There was, at least in theory, another potential source for something reminiscent of the "likeness" of a royal attire. Some features associated with kings in the ancient Near East were associated with ideal high priests of old within the discourse and memory world of the literati. Directly relevant to our topic here, the high priest of Exod 28 was imaged as clothed in ways that may recall a kingly figure.[27] That said, and from the perspective of "worldly" constraints as facilitating factors for the lack of references to YHWH's garments, it is clear that the actual garments of the high priest of a relatively small temple in a poor and marginal province of the Achaemenid Empire were unlikely to be considered an appropriate blueprint for imagining the clothes of the divine king of the entire world in all his glory. (Of course, the literati could still construe ideal high priests, but on this issue see below.)

As for the second observation, the aniconic character of the worship of YHWH in the Persian period meant that there was no divine statue, that clothes for the statue were not produced, displayed, controlled, stored, and that no ritual of deity dressing emerged.[28] It is in this context that it is important to note that while there was no statue of YHWH in Yehud or local kings, there were indeed priests serving in a temple in Yehud. Significantly, the core repertoire drew much attention to priestly garments, which were evidently considered worth thinking of and remembering (e.g., Exod 28:1–43; 29:5–9, 21, 29; 31:10; 35:19, 21; 39:1–31; 40: 13–15; Lev 6:10; 8:30; 10:6; 16:4, 23–24, 32; 21:10; Num 20:26, 28; Ezek 44:17–19; Ps 133:2).[29]

Although these facilitating conditions may have contributed to the development of the mentioned underlying, systemic dis-preference to imagine and remember YHWH's clothes, one must assume that other factors were at work as well for a variety of reasons. For one, social memory and shared imagination are not so easily "shepherded" or "constrained" by the "world as is," in any culture/society. Many of the references to the temple and temple ritual that existed within the literary repertoire of the literati and their social memory did not refer, at least directly, to institutions that existed in their times and the gates for hyperbolic imagery are

acknowledged (and contrast with the omnipresence of Jerusalem in this mental map). Ramat Raḥel was consistently considered not worth mentioning or remembering. From a social memory perspective, it is precisely the complete silence about this remarkable place, just by Jerusalem, in the literati's authoritative literature that speaks volumes and opens a window for historical reconstructions of their social mindscape.

27. See Nihan and Rhyder, "Aaron's Vestments in Exodus 28 and Priestly Leadership," and Nihan, "Le pectoral d'Aaron et la figure du grand prêtre dans les traditions sacerdotales du Pentateuque." See Exod 28 and cf. Sir 45:7–13; 50: 5–11.

28. On Mesopotamian rituals of clothing the divine statue, see note 4 above. Cf. the importance of the clothes of the high priest and of the storage of and control over these vestments in the late Second Temple period.

29. On priestly garments see Nihan and Rhyder, "Aaron's Vestments in Exodus 28 and Priestly Leadership" and Nihan, "Le pectoral d'Aaron et la figure du grand prêtre dans les traditions sacerdotales du Pentateuque." See also the contribution by Carmen Joy Imes in this volume and cited bibliography in all these works.

usually wide open in most societies (e.g., and directly relevant to our topic, Sir 50: 5–11). Moreover, Yehudite literati were not only able to but also successfully and repeatedly imagined, vicariously experienced, and certainly remembered multiple, utopian worlds that obviously had no counterpart in the "worldly" world, as even the most cursory browsing of the prophetic book collection that existed at the time clearly shows. Furthermore, at times, it was precisely the explicit and stressed "un-reality" of a site of memory that contributed much to its memorability (e.g., Ezek 40–48).[30]

Further, it is obviously the case that even without anthropomorphic statues of YHWH, these literati had no problem imagining YHWH (and YHWH's body-parts) in anthropomorphic terms and repeatedly imagined and remembered YHWH in roles such as the husband of Israel/Jerusalem or the mighty war hero.

In sum, if imagining and stressing social memories of YHWH's clothes or those of Israelite kings of old would have served an important purpose/s in their discourse, the lack of a statue and dressing divine rites or of a local king in Jerusalem would not have stopped them from developing them. The same is true for the realia of the Second Temple in the LPEH. Thus, one may assume that other factors would have also been at work.

To begin exploring these additional factors, it is worth stressing that although it is possible that in a relatively poor and "objectively" marginal society like the one in Yehud, in day-to-day life and aside from cultic activities—see above—there might not have been a very large disparity within the range of garments used by the free males who constituted "the community" or among the literati themselves,[31] it is still clear that they (and the entire culture of their *oecumene*) were very much aware of the (transculturally attested) symbolic value of clothes. Any potential explanation, no matter how partial, of the phenomenon discussed here should begin with the assumption that the literati worked within a system in which clothes carried symbolic value, not one in which this "universally" accepted social construction was categorically challenged and undermined.[32]

This being so and considering the effect that clothing and adornment causes among members of society, in particular, the development of inferences about the individual on the basis of his/her clothing,[33] it is noteworthy that although

---

30. Cf. Hanna Liss, "'Describe the Temple to the House of Israel': Preliminary Remarks on the Temple Vision in the Book of Ezekiel and the Question of Fictionality in Priestly Literatures," in *Utopia and Dystopia in Prophetic Literature*, ed. Ehud Ben Zvi, PFES 92 (Helsinki: Finnish Exegetical Society / Göttingen: Vandenhoeck & Ruprecht, 2006), 122–43.

31. Although, see the importance of prestige clothes in Prov 31:21–22 and how it may balance such images of the LPEH society.

32. Of course, as in all cultures, there are narratives and characterizations that exploit the point of a temporally limited lack of correspondence between true status and garments (e.g., 1 Kgs 14:2), but these narratives and characterizations only work within and actually enhance the common association of clothing and status.

33. Cf. Lennon, "Clothing and Adornment."

Solomon's clothes were not worth remembering, the fact that he "clothed" his servants in a particular way was worth remembering. Likewise, one may notice also that Moses' clothes are never mentioned, but that he clothed Aaron is mentioned (e.g., Lev 8:7).[34] Similarly, nothing is said about Pharaoh's garments in Gen 41, but certainly that he clothed Joseph in the context appointing him "overseer" over Egypt (v 42).

Although YHWH's clothes are not a site of memory, the repertoire of the literati asked them to notice and remember that YHWH clothed Adam and Eve (Gen 3:21), instituted the proper clothing of the priests (e.g., Exod 28; 39:1, and *passim*), clothed and adorned his wife (e.g., Ezek 16[35]) and even (through his רוח) "clothed" Gideon (Judg 6:34), Amasai (1 Chr 12:19), and Zechariah (2 Chr 24:20).

If clothing is understood as a way of "ordering," of shaping, and "creating" (or re-creating, when applicable) proper order, then it might well be that there was a preference for remembering acts of "clothing" subordinates over those of wearing of "clothes" by the hierarchically superior, "ordering" agent. This systemic preference would be consistent with and even constitute a particular expression of a general tendency among the relevant literati (and well-encoded in their core repertoire), namely to place much stress on memories of acts of creation (divine, or human royal with the support of the divine—e.g., building the temple) as didactic sites of memory from which the community may infer, construe, and remember about the ordering agent, so as to become socialized within the general ideology of the group.

Focusing on YHWH as creator and on proper human rulers as ordering agents rather than focusing on their own clothes as projections of their status, power, and proper agency is, in fact, very much consistent with the social mindscape of the literati of the LPEH period. This said, this shift in focus does not by itself demand that the clothes not be mentioned or remembered, nor does it preclude the possibility of additional factors at work, whether directly or indirectly.

Before addressing some of these potential additional factors, a general, systemic observation is in order. When social and mnemonic systems of preference converge, they tend to reinforce each other. In the present case, the existence of shared systemic dis-preference to turn the clothes of YHWH on the one hand

---

34. Moses was construed, in part, as a (quasi) monarchic figure. See, for example, Ian D. Wilson, *Kingship and Memory in Ancient Judah* (New York: Oxford University Press, 2017), 68–70; Thomas C. Römer, "Moses, the Royal Lawgiver," in *Remembering Biblical Figures in the Late Persian & Early Hellenistic Periods: Social Memory and Imagination*, ed. Diana V. Edelman and Ehud Ben Zvi (Oxford: Oxford University Press, 2013), 81–94; John Lierman, *The New Testament Moses: Christian perceptions of Moses and Israel in the Setting of Jewish Religion* (WUNT, 173; Tübingen: Mohr Siebeck, 2004), 79–89 and bibliography cited in these works.

35. Given the somewhat analogous character of clothes and footwear, it is worth noticing that YHWH is also imagined and remembered as one who also placed (high status) sandals in his wife's feet (see Ezek 16:10).

and of the human Israelite king on the other into important sites of memory discursively reinforced each one of these dis-preferences. This being so, facilitating factors which on the surface may work *only* in one of these cases, may ultimately end up serving as facilitating factors for the other case as well, and they contribute to positive feedback loops, even if they originally shared nothing in common.

For instance, in the case of human Israelite/Judahite kings, the mentioned systemic dis-preference likely resonated with the tendency to lessen the status of the king that is encoded and communicated by texts such as the law of the king in Deut 17:14–20. Moreover, the (related, but clearly separate) tendency toward an ideological "kingization"/Davidization of Israel (e.g., Isa 55:3) might have been supportive of a shift away from drawing attention to the royal attire of the kings of old. Clearly, none of this seems to hold any *direct* relation to the lack of a tendency to draw attention to YHWH's garments. After all, the literati could have construed "all Israel" as if they were all kings or priests (e.g., Exod 19:6), but not YHWH, and certainly YHWH's powers and status as king were not construed in any way as limited, unlike the human king in Deut 17:14–20.

Conversely, it is worth considering that lack of references to YHWH's clothes might have been consonant with an underlying desire to avoid a situation in which these clothes might be construed as quasi-deified or at least given or become associated with certain divine powers and capabilities.[36] This issue could have been

---

36. Transculturally, the paraphernalia of gods is often deified, quasi-deified, or given/become associated with certain powers and capabilities. This was true in the ANE, and for that matter in much later societies, and cf. the construction of relics of "sacred figures" and of their capabilities in many historical as well as present-day societies.

It is worth stressing that within the ideological discourse of the LPEH literati, the main "danger" was not that clothes were imagined to be able to "empower" the deity. Had they been able to imagine the clothes as such, were they to be removed, divine powers would be lost. One may compare and contrast this approach with the story of the descent of Inanna, in which (removed) garments stand for (removed) MEs, or moving in the realm of "humans," with the case of an individual who was once "clothed" with divine/YHWH's רוּחַ *rûaḥ*, but from whom it was later removed (cf. 1 Sam 16:13–14). Instead the likely potential concern from the perspective of the literati was that the clothes be empowered by their closeness or even direct contact with the divine body. The existence of such empowered clothes, outside YHWH, would not have been consonant with the ideological discourse of the LPEH literati. In fact, even the descent of Inanna/Ištar is to be understood within the frame of mythical narratives, and neither them nor performative ritual acts of investiture (or de-investiture) of garments should be understood as conveying the complete discourse and conceptual understanding of deities in the ANE. For instance, the Aššur who is the "creator of the creatures of heaven and earth, fashioner of the mountains, […] creator of the gods … [who] (even) a god does not comprehend" (from Assurbanipal's Hymn to Aššur; SAA 3.1, 15–28) or who is the "total sum of all the gods" is certainly not a deity whose power or rulership was conceptualized as depending on any garment or garment investiture. Aššur and his power, in fact, precede all and are the source of all in the world and cannot be

a concern consistent with some aspects of the social mindscape, ideology, and discourse of the LPEH literati.[37] But, to be sure, none of this has any *direct* bearing or explanatory power for the dis-preference that existed toward drawing attention to the robes of a human Israelite/Judahite king. Although none of these cases involves a concern that is relevant to matters of both YHWH and human king, indirectly and from a systemic perspective they functioned as facilitating factors to the success of the grammar of dis-preference discussed here, because each facilitated its success in one of these two spheres and the two were (partially) interconnected.

Finally, at times, multiple facilitating factors intersect. As an illustration, I will return to an issue mentioned but left unaddressed above, namely that although living in a poor province, the LPEH literati could still construe ideal high priests and certainly considered worth remembering their glorious garments, which to an extent carried some kingly connotations. Without entering into the details of the vestments of the high priest—an issue addressed by others in this volume and elsewhere[38]—the question might emerge of why the quite intense preoccupation with the vestments of the (ideal) high priest was not associated with a similar preoccupation for the vestments of the deity worshiped by the high priest?

To begin to address this question, it is worth stressing that there can be no doubt that the LPEH literati were well aware of the performative character of the garments of the high priest. Within their ideological world of memory and discourse, YHWH, through divine instructions and emissaries/servants beginning with Moses,[39] clothed them all, generation after generation (cf. Exod 29:29–30; Lev 21:10; Num 20:28; Ps 133:2), with a complex attire[40] that when donned properly

---

dependent on anything. Within this frame, Aššur is always king and never "becomes" king, unlike the divinely chosen, human Assyrian king, who needs at some point to become king, and thus a chosen delegate of the deity. Of course, again, this is one way among several used by neo-Assyrians literati in their attempts to approach and relate to the one whose essence and features the other gods could not comprehend, never mind them. Aššur is in all these aspects—and several others that cannot be discussed here—very much like the YHWH of the literati discussed here, though for them either Israel or the prophetic voices of old, as voiced and understood by the literati and thus indirectly, the literati themselves, or, from a certain perspective, the divine instruction (=tôrâ) itself or better a combination of them served as YHWH's delegates.

On several of these matters, including the Descent of Inanna and the light that it may shed on ancient Israel's approach to divine (or royal) garments, see also the chapter of Shawn W. Flynn in this volume, 33–36.

37. Cf. Ezek 44:19. Certainly, within the conceptual world of construed in this text, the relevant clothes have the power to and do transmit "holiness," but significantly, the same does not hold true for the priests themselves. To be sure, had the latter be the case, much trouble for the laity and the priests would have emerged.

38. See n. 29 and bibliography cited in the relevant works.

39. See Lev 8:7–9.

40. Including, of course, the breastpiece.

allowed the high priest to serve as an efficient "mediator" between Israel and YHWH.[41] Clearly, he cannot perform his normal roles without them.[42]

But all these considerations could only facilitate the development of a strong generative grammar of dis-preference for any kind of conceptual or visual association between the attire of even the ideal high priest (the other potential, but partial kingly figure in Yehud) and YHWH. Thus, for instance, YHWH's ability to rule the world was never construed in this discourse as dependent on proper clothing, nor was YHWH construed as one whose empowerment is associated with memories of earthly, even if sacred, buildings. YHWH empowers the temple/tabernacle but cannot be empowered by them. Similarly, YHWH does not need, for instance, Urim and Thummim or any other instrument to access knowledge. Moreover, YHWH could not have been construed as one who was clothed and thus empowered by someone else, above him hierarchically (see above).[43]

All this said, do any of the just aforementioned observations explain why YHWH's garments were not remembered? The answer is, of course, a clear "no." These observations only explain why there was a dis-preference to construe them

---

41. From a social memory perspective, it is worth noting that when the high priest was construed as donning these vestments, he becomes also symbolically associated with the tabernacle of old, and as such he becomes a personified "memorial" of it and the memories and conceptual and mnemonic realms associated with it. Cf. Nihan and Rhyder, "Aaron's Vestments in Exodus 28 and Priestly Leadership" and Nihan, "Le pectoral d'Aaron et la figure du grand prêtre dans les traditions sacerdotales du Pentateuque," and Baruch J. Schwartz who writes:

> the list of materials needed for the sanctuary (Exodus 25:1–7) includes the precious stones required for the ephod and breastplate. Further, the fabric portions of the garments were made of the same materials, and fashioned in the same manner, as the fabrics in the miškān itself, with those used to make the high priest's garments identical to those used in the most sacred sections of the miškān

(Baruch J. Schwartz, "The 'Garments' of the High Priest: Anthropomorphism in the Worship of God," available at http://thetorah.com/garments-of-the-high-priest-anthropomorphism-in-the-worship-of-god/).

Of course, the high priest serves also, though in a slightly different way, as a memorial of Israel (see the twelve stones and cited bibliography) before YHWH. It is precisely the intersection of multiple memorials carried by his body that makes him a suitable mediator. Exploring this and related matters goes, however, beyond the scope of this chapter.

42. Except for the case of the "purgation ritual" in the "Day of Purgation" (using Milgrom's terminology; see Lev 16:4, and then vv 23–24), but then again the point is that garments have performative roles to play.

43. And, of course, any construction of divine garments as carrying some form (even if derivative) of divine power would have raised the concerns mentioned above within the world of the literati (see above).

in a way that resembles and recalls those of the ideal high priest and vice versa. These observations constitute neither a sufficient nor a necessary reason for this dis-preference, but as all the others mentioned above might have facilitated the mentioned dis-preference, in this case at least by pre-empting the development of counter-tendencies.

To sum up, the present contribution does not conclude with a proposal of a set of causes that *necessarily* led to the development and dominance of a certain mnemonic dis-preference within a particular community. Given the complexity of any historical system and its chaotic tendencies, I have serious misgivings about historical determinism in general and, in this case, I would maintain that it is absolutely impossible to identify any single historical factor or a combination thereof the presence of which would be *sufficient* in itself to cause, *in deterministic terms*, the mentioned mnemonic dis-preference to become dominant.

Instead, the path I have taken is to explore various features of the ideological environment (and social mindscape) of the LPEH literati that separately or through their interaction would have been consonant with and supportive of the emergence of the mentioned dis-preference as dominant within the world of these literati. Given that this dominance is historically attested, it stands to reason that these features played some systemic role, small or large, separately or together, facilitating and furthering it.

To be sure, exploring these matters can only lead to preliminary conclusions. I hope this contribution elicits further discussion and study on this issue in particular and on the study of various implied, systemic sets of preferences and dis-preferences partially shaping and controlling the production of sites of memory and their relative social mindshare within the community of LPEH literati.

Let me conclude by noting that tendencies to bracket out certain matters in terms of memory often tend to create a "vacuum" as it were, which either the existing or successor societies eventually may end up filling. In this case, already within the literary corpus of the LPEH one notices the presence of the image of YHWH wrapped in light *as with* a garment (Ps 104:2[44]), which not only recalls a very long tradition about the luminosity of the deity (and often of the human king; cf. Moses in Exod 34:29) but also would become very important in the late Second Temple period and beyond,[45] and which, in turn would end up raising questions and memories about the radiance of characters such as Adam, Eve,

---

44. On Ps 104 see above.

45. In later rabbinic literature, light is often construed as the garment of YHWH at the time of creation (see, for example, Gen. Rab. 3:4) but other (symbolic) garments may be associated with the deity at different stages in the story of past and future Israel (see, for example, Pesiq. Rab. 37).

Abel, Enoch, Abraham, Sara, various angels, and even Satan. But these issues and, to be clearly distinguished from them, the case of Daniel 7 demands a separate discussion, addressing groups later than the LPEH literati, each with its own memories and grammars and thus stands well beyond the scope of this particular contribution.[46]

---

46. I would like to thank all the participants of seminar out of whose discussions this volume emerged for their comments. I would like to thank, in particular, Shawn W. Flynn and Carmen Joy Imes for dealing with matters related to those discussed in this chapter at the seminar and in this volume. I hope readers will find helpful to see how these contributions interact, directly and indirectly, with each with other. I want to express also my gratitude to Sara Koening for her written response to a previous version of this chapter, to Christophe Nihan and Julia Rhyder for supplying me with copies of the essays mentioned above when I was writing this chapter, and to Tony Finitsis for organizing the seminar, editing this volume, and commenting on a previous version of this chapter.

SELECT BIBLIOGRAPHY

Aaron, David H. "Shedding Light on God's Body in Rabbinic Midrashim: Reflections on the Theory of a Luminous Adam." *HTR* 90 (1997): 299–314.

Adelman, Rachel. "From Veils to Goatskins: The Female Ruse in Genesis." *Journal of Textual Reasoning* 6.2 (2011): np. http://jtr.shanti.virginia.edu/volume-6-number-2/from-veils-to-goatskins-the-female-ruse-in-genesis/

Appadurai, Arjun. *The Social Life of Things: Commodities in Cultural Perspective.* Cambridge: Cambridge University Press, 1988.

Asher-Greve, Julia and Deborah Sweeney. "On Nakedness, Nudity, and Gender in Egyptian and Mesopotamian Art." Pages 125–76 in *Images and Gender: Contributions to the Hermeneutics of Reading Ancient Art*. Edited by Silvia Schroer. OBO 220. Fribourg: Academic Press/Göttingen: Vandenhoeck & Ruprecht, 2006.

Bahrani, Zainab. "The Iconography of the Nude in Mesopotamia." *Notes in the History of Art. Essays on Nudity in Antiquity in Memory of Otto Brendel* 12.2 (1993): 12–19.

Baizerman, Suzanne, Joanne B. Eicher, and Catherine Cerny. "Eurocentrism in the Study of Ethnic Dress." Pages 123–32 in *Visible Self: Global Perspectives on Dress, Culture and Society*. Edited by Joanne B. Eicher, Sandra L. Evenson, and Hazel A. Lutz. New York: Fairchild Publications, 2008.

Barkay, G., A. G. Vaughn, M. J. Lundberg, and B. Zuckerman. "The Amulets from Ketef Hinnom: A New Edition and Evaluation." *BASOR* 334 (2004): 41–71.

Barnes, Ruth and Joanne B. Eicher. *Dress and Gender: Making Meaning in Cultural Contexts*. Cross-Cultural Perspectives on Women, Vol. 2. Oxford: Berg, 1993.

Batten, Alicia J. "Clothing and Adornment." *Biblical Theology Bulletin* 40.3 (2010): 148–59.

Batten, Alicia J., Carly Daniel-Hughes, and Kristi Upson-Saia. "What Then Shall We Wear?" Pages 1–20 in *Dressing Judeans and Christians in Antiquity*. Edited by Alicia J. Batten, Carly Daniel-Hughes, and Kristi Upson-Saia. Burlington, VT: Ashgate, 2014.

Bertman, Stephen. "Tasseled Garments in the Ancient East Mediterranean." *BA* 4 (1961): 119–28.

Bledstein, Adrien Janis. "Tamar and the 'Coat of Many Colors.'" In *Samuel and Kings, A Feminist Companion to the Bible*. Edited by A. Brenner. Sheffield: Sheffield Academic Press, 2000.

Cifarelli, Megan and Laura Gawlinski. *What Shall I Say of Clothes?: Theoretical and Methodological Approaches to the Study of Dress in Antiquity*. Boston: Archaeological Institute of America, 2017.

Cohen, Norman J. *Masking and Unmasking Ourselves. Interpreting Biblical Texts on Clothing and Identity*. Woodstock, VT: Jewish Lights/Skylights, 2012.

Colburn, Cynthia S. *Reading a Dynamic Canvas: Adornment in the Ancient Mediterranean World*. Newcastle, UK: Cambridge Scholars, 2008.

Cras, Alban. *La Symbolique Du Vêtement Dans La Bible: Pour Une Théologie Du Vêtement*. Lire La Bible. Paris: Cerf, 2011.

Edwards, Douglas. "Dress and Ornamentation." *Anchor Bible Dictionary* 2 (1992): 232–38.

Eicher, Joanne B. and Mary Ellen Roach-Higgins. "Definition and Classification of Dress: Implications for Analysis of Gender Roles." In *Dress and Gender: Making Meaning in Cultural Contexts*. Edited by Ruth Barnes and Joanne B. Eicher, Cross-Cultural Perspectives on Women, Vol. 2, 1–28. Oxford: Berg, 1993.

Foster, Benjamin R. "Clothing in Sargonic Mesopotamia: Visual and Written Evidence." Pages 110–45 in *Textile Terminologies in the Ancient Near East and Mediterranean from the Third to the First Millennia BC*. Edited by C. Michel and M.-L. Nosch. Ancient Textiles Series 8. Oxford/Oakville: Oxbow Books, 2010.

Gaspa, Salvatore. *Textiles in the Neo-Assyrian Empire: A Study of Terminology*. Studies in Ancient Near Eastern Records 19. Berlin: De Gruyter, 2018, esp. pp. 186–235.

Gawlinksi, Laura. "Theorizing Religious Dress." In *What Shall I Say of Clothes? Theoretical and Methodological Approaches to the Study of Dress in Antiquity*. Edited by Megan Cifarelli and Laura Gawlinski. Selected Papers on Ancient Art and Architecture, Vol. 3, 161–78. Boston, MA: Archaeological Institute of America, 2017.

Germer, Renate. "Flowers." *OEAE* 2 (2001): 541–44.

Grenfell, Alice. "The Rarer Scarabs, etc., of the New Kingdom." Pages 113–36 in *Recueil de Travaux Relatifs à la Philologie et à l'Archéologie Égyptiennes et Assyriennes*. Fascicules 3–4. Edited by Gaston Maspero. Paris: Librairie Honoré Champion, 1910.

Guralnick, Eleanor. "Neo-Assyrian Patterned Fabrics." *Iraq* 66 (2004): 221–32.

Guralnick, Eleanor. "Fabric Patterns as Symbols of Status in the Near East and Early Greece." Pages 84–114 in *Reading a Dynamic Canvas: Adornment in the Ancient Mediterranean World*. Edited by Cynthia S. Colburn and Maura K. Heyn. Newcastle, UK: Cambridge Scholars, 2008.

Harlow, Mary. "Dress and Identity: An Introduction." Pages 1–5 in *Dress and Identity*, Edited by Mary Harlow. BAR International Series 2356. Oxford: Archaeopress, 2012.

Harris, J. S. "The Stones of the High Priest's Breastplate." Edited by John MacDonald. *ALUOS* 5 (1963): 40–62.

Haulotte, Edgar. *Symbolique du Vêtement Selon la Bible*. Collection Théologie 65. Paris: Aubier, 1966.

Hebdige, Dick. *Subculture: The Meaning of Style*. New York: Methuen, 1979.

Houston, Mary G. *Ancient Egyptian, Mesopotamian & Persian Costume*. Mineola, NY: Dover, 2002.

Huddlestun, John R. "Divesture, Deception and Demotion: The Garment Motif in Genesis 37–39." *JSOT* 98 (2002): 47–62.

Keller, Sharon R. "Aspects of Nudity in the Old Testament." *Notes in the History of Art. Essays on Nudity in Antiquity in Memory of Otto Brendel* 12.2 (1993): 32–36.

Laver, James. *Costume in Antiquity*. London: Thames and Hudson, 1964.

Lennon, S. J. "Clothing and Adornment: Social Psychology Perspectives." Pages 320–26 in Vol. 1 of *Encyclopedia of Body Image and Human Appearance*. Edited by Thomas Cash 2 vols. London: Elsevier, 2012.

Ludwig, Tiffany and Renee Piechocki. *Trappings: Stories of Women, Power and Clothing*. New Brunswick, NJ: Rutgers University Press, 2007.

Lutz, Henry F. *Textiles and Costume among People of the Ancient Near East*. Leipzig: Hinrichs, 1923.

Mace, Arthur C. "The Murch Collection of Egyptian Antiquities." *BMMA* 6 (1911): 1–28.

Matsushima, Eiko. "Divine Statues in Ancient Mesopotamia: Their Fashioning and Clothing and Their Interaction with Society." Pages 209–19 in *Official Cult and Popular Religion in the Ancient Near East*. Edited by Eiko Matsushima. Heidelberg: Winter, 1993.

Matsushima, Eiko. "Eleven Neo-Babylonian Texts Relating to the Lubuštu (Clothing Ceremony)." Pages 235–43 in *Essays on Ancient Anatolia and Its Surrounding Civilizations*. Edited by Prince Takahito Mikasa. Wiesbaden: Harrassowitz, 1995.

Matsushima, Eiko. "Some Remarks on the Divine Garments: kusitu and nahlaptu." *Acta Sumerologica Journal* 17 (1995): 233–49.
Matthews, Victor. "The Anthropology of Clothing in the Joseph Narrative." *JSOT* 65 (1995): 25–36.
Matthews, Victor. *More Than Meets the Ear*. Grand Rapids: Eerdmans, 2008.
McKay, Heather. "Clothing, Adornment and Accouterments." Pages 238–52 in *Samuel, Kings and Chronicles, I: Texts@Contexts*. Edited by Athalya Brenner-Idan and Archie C.C. Lee. London: Bloomsbury T&T Clark, 2017.
Nelson, Milledge Sarah. *Women in Antiquity: Theoretical Approaches to Gender and Archaeology*. Lanham: Alta Mira, 2007.
Neufeld, Dietmar. "The Rhetoric of Body, Clothing and Identity in the *Vita* and Genesis." *Scriptura* 90 (2005): 679–84.
Nihan, Christophe and Julia Rhyder. "Aaron's Vestments in Exodus 28 and Priestly Leadership." *Debating Authority. Concepts of Leadership in the Pentateuch and the Former Prophets*. Edited by Katharina Pyschny and Sarah Schulz BZAW 507. Berlin/New York: de Gruyter, 2018.
Noegel, Scott B. "Scarlet and Harlots: Seeing Red in the Hebrew Bible." *HUCA* 87 (2016): 1–47.
Nosch, Marie-Louise and C. Michel Nosch, eds. *Textile Terminologies in the Ancient Near East and the Mediterranean Area from the 3rd to the 1st Millennium BC*. Ancient Textiles 8. Oxford: Oxbow, 2010.
Oppenheim, A. Leo. "The Golden Garments of the Gods." *JNES* 8 (1949): 172–93.
Prouser, Ora Horn. "Suited to the Throne: The Symbolic Use of Clothing in the David and Saul Narratives." *JSOT* 71 (1996): 27–37.
Riefstahl, Elizabeth. *Patterned Textiles in Pharaonic Egypt*. Brooklyn: Brooklyn Institute of Arts and Sciences, 1944.
Roach-Higgings, Mary Ellen, and Joanne B. Eicher. "Dress and Identity." *Clothing and Textiles Research Journal* 10 (1992): 1–8.
Rollason, Will. "Counterparts: Clothing, Value and the Sites of Otherness in Panapompom Ethnographic Encounters." *Anthropological Forum* 18 (2008): 17–35.
Ross, Robert J. *Clothing: A Global History: Or the Imperialists' New Clothes*. Cambridge: Polity, 2008.
Rozier, Emily J. "Fashion." Pages 415–30 in Vol. 1 of *Handbook of Medieval Culture: Fundamental Aspects and Conditions of the European Middle Ages*. Edited by Albrecht Classen, 3 vols. Berlin: de Gruyter, 2015.
Schellenberg, Annette. "More than Spirit: On the Physical Dimension in the Priestly Understanding of Holiness." *ZAW* 126 (2014): 163–79.
Schwartz, Baruch J. "The 'Garments' of the High Priest: Anthropomorphism in the Worship of God," http://thetorah.com/garments-of-the-high-priest-anthropomorphism-in-the-worship-of-god/
Silverman, Eric Kline. *A Cultural History of Jewish Dress*. London [etc.]: Bloomsbury, 2013.
Smith, Sidney. "The Babylonian Ritual for the Consecration and Induction of a Divine Statue." *JRAS* 1 (1925): 37–60.
Sørensen, Marie Louise Stig. "Gender, Things, and Material Culture." In *Women in Antiquity: Theoretical Approaches to Gender and Archaeology*. Edited by S. M. Nelson, 75–106. Lanham: Alta Mira, 2007.
Taylor, J. E. "Imagining Judean Priestly Dress: The Berne Josephus and Judaea Capta Coinage." In *Dressing Judeans and Christians in Antiquity*. Edited by Alicia J. Batten, Carly Daniel-Hughes, and Kristi Upson-Saia. Burlington, VT: Ashgate, 2014.

Tranberg, Hansen Karen. "The World in Dress: Anthropological Perspectives on Clothing, Fashion, and Culture." *Annual Review of Anthropology* 33 (2004): 369–92.

Tsevat, Matitiahu. "The Husband Veils a Wife (Hittite Laws, Sections 197–98)." *Journal of Cuneiform Studies* 27.4 (1975): 235–40.

Turner, Terence S. "The Social Skin." *HAU: Journal of Ethnographic Theory* 2 (2012): 486–504.

Vearncombe, Erin K. "Adorning the Protagonist: The Use of Dress in the Book of Judith." In *Dressing Judeans and Christians in Antiquity*. Farnham, Surrey, England; Burlington, VT: Ashgate, 2014.

Verman, Mark. "Royalty, Robes and the Art of Biblical Narrative." *SJOT* 30 (2016): 30–43.

Vogelsang-Eastwood, Gillian. *Pharaonic Egyptian Clothing*. Studies in Textile and Costume History 2. Leiden: Brill, 1993.

Vogelzang, M. E. "Meaning and Symbolism of Clothing in Ancient Near Eastern Texts." In *Script Signa Vocis: Studies about Scripts, Scriptures, Scribes, and Languages in the Near East, Presented to J. H. Hospers by His Pupils, Colleagues and Friends*. Edited by L. J. Vanstiphout, K. Jongeling, F. Leemhuis, and G. J. Reinink. Groningen, The Netherlands: Forsten, 1986.

Winner, Lauren. *Wearing God: Clothing, Laughter, Fire, and Other Overlooked Ways of Meeting God*. New York: HarperOne, an Imprint of HarperCollins, 2015.

Zawadzki, Stefan. *Garments of the Gods: Studies on the Textile Industry and the Pantheon of Sippar according to the Texts from the Ebabbar Archive*. OBO 218. Göttingen: Vandenhoeck & Ruprecht, 2006.

INDEX OF PRIMARY SOURCES

BIBLICAL SOURCES

Genesis
24:65	96
37	90
37–50	90
37:3	100
38:1	90
38:7	91
38:10	91–2
38:11	92
38:12	93
38:14	93
38:15	93–4
38:19	95
38:20–22	94
39	51
39:1	90
41	177

Exodus
22:25–26	16
25:8	38
28	51, 55, 175
28:4	31
28:6–43	31
28:12	56
28:33–34	17
28:36	68–70
29	51
29:44–46	54
39:1–31	31
39:28	155
39:30	68–70

Leviticus
8	51
8:7–9	31
8:9	68–70
22:2	58

Numbers
6:23–27	60
6:24–26	83
6:27	61, 84
15	67
15:37–41	66-7, 78, 84
15:38	72
15:39	72
16–17	78
16:1–17:5	158
16:1–17:15	78
16:3	78
17	77
17:1–15	79

Deuteronomy
6:8–9	84
11:18–19	84
17:14–20	178

1 Samuel
9:1–2	113–14
10:23–24	113–14
13–15	111
16–31	110
17	118
17:32–40	114–16
18:1–4	116–18
18:10–11	118–19
19:9–10	118–19
19:23–24	119–20
22	120–1
26	118
28	121–3
31	123–4

2 Samuel
6	125, 130, 138, 139
6:16	133, 138
8	137

13	98	59:19	153
13:1	98–9	60:1–22	151
13:2	98–9	61	153–4, 159
13:9d–18	102–3	61:1–3	151, 155, 156
13:18	100–1, 104	61:1–10	159
13:19	105	61:4–10	155, 158
13:20	105, 106	61:4–11	151, 156, 157
13:21	102	61:8	153
		61:9	152
1 Chronicles		61:10	143, 145, 151, 152, 153, 154, 155, 156, 158
15	125, 130		
15:27	138	61:11	156
15:29	138	62:1–5	156
26:4–8	132	62:1–12	151
		63:1–3	168
Esther			
8:15	172	Jeremiah	
		3:3	96
Psalms		13:22–26	17
45:8	156		
45:9	172	Lamentations	
60:10	169	1:9	17
96:6	26		
108:10	169	Ezekiel	
132	21	1	170
		16:8	169
Proverbs		40–48	158
6:20–26	84	44	158
31:10–31	3–6	44:18	155
31:25	9		
		Daniel	
Isaiah		7	182
6:1	24		
6:1–4	167	Hosea	
20:2–4	133	4:14	95
22:20–25	157		
22:21	157	Amos	
45	153	2:8	16
45:8	153		
54:4	97	Nahum	
54:17	153	3:5	17
55	153		
55:1–4	154	Judith	
55:3	153, 178	10:23	96
53:10	154		
54:17	154	Hebrews	
55:1–5	154, 157, 158	9:4	77
55:5	154		
59:17	144	Dead Sea Scrolls	
59:17	150, 153	4Q374	83

Index Of Primary Sources

Ancient Near Eastern Sources
Amulet T-S K 1.127 83–4
Assyrian coronation hymn 129
Babylonian ritual text 20
Black Obelisk 146–7
Book of the Dead ch.81 75
Descent of Ištar 21–4
Enūma eliš 25–6
Epic of Baal and Anat 68–9
Hittite Marriage Laws 96
Middle Assyrian Law 96
Nabu-apla-idina Stone Tablet 14–15
Nineveh ritual tablet 19
Stela of Ikhernofret 48–9
Stela of Tanetperet 74
Tell Fakhariyeh inscription 148–9
Uruk Vase 127
Yavneh Yam letter 16

INDEX OF SUBJECTS

Achaemenid 174, 175
actant 91
Ahimelech 120, 121
Ahuramazda 128
anthropomorphic terms 161, 176
anti-elect 111, 112, 124
apotropaic 64
Ashtoreths 123
Ashur-nasir-pal 43
Aššur 77
Assurbanipal 22, 146
atef-crown 74

band 32
Bathsheba 136, 140
Black Obelisk 146, 147
bloody garments 168
botanical imagery 73
breastpiece 30, 32, 33–4, 35, 36, 37, 39, 55, 56, 57, 62

Calvin, John 105
celestial imagery 73
chitōn astragalōtos 100
chitōn karpōtos 100
chitōna poikilon 100
Clayton, Francis 107
cognitive psychology 139
communalization 70, 153, 158
constellations 66, 73
covenantal faithfulness 71, 80
crimson 4–6

Dagon 19
Darius I 15
date palm 87
Day of Atonement 30, 58
diadem 30, 35, 36, 37, 51, 58, 59, 68, 156
dress 2–3

Ea 23
Ebabbar *lubuštu* 14
Eighteenth Dynasty 40
el-Amarna 20
Enaim, Petah 93
Endor 122
enthronement ritual 130
Enūma eliš 25, 26
epattu 33
ephod 30, 32, 33, 35, 36, 57, 58, 121, 122, 126, 132, 138, 147, 149
Ereshkigel 22

fabula 91
fashion 108

garment of splendor 156
garments of salvation 154, 158
Greek fertility rituals 130

Hezekiah 81
Hittite festivals 126
ḥōšēb 31

iblal 15
Inanna 22, 127
ipantu 33
Ištar 21–5

Jehu 15, 146

kallatu kutumtu 96
kĕtōnet passim 100, 105, 106
Khorsabad 77
kilt 39, 146
kilt/*ibbaru* 15
King Sargon II 146
kingization/Davidization 178
Korah 78
kusītu 15, 49

Index Of Subjects 191

lamaḫuššu-garment 19, 20, 27
Late Persian period 126
linen ephod 121, 125, 132, 138, 141, 149
Lord of Abydos 49

maḥəttâ 79
manacles 71
Marduk 24, 25, 26, 28
Marduk-Nadin-Akhe 43
Melammu 26
menorah 79
mīs pî 13, 19, 20, 23, 25, 27, 50
mišnepet 68
Muricidae/murex 5–6, 9

nakedness 36, 52, 119, 120, 133, 169
Necromancer 122
Neferetum 75
New Kingdom 39
niglal 15

Obed-edom 131
ordering agent 177
ordination ritual 54
ŏrēg 31
Othering 112, 116, 122

pala 14, 15, 16, 17, 25, 28
phallic display 132
phallic power 131
Pharaoh Rameses III 39
Pharaoh Seti 41
pit pī 19
Pussumtu 96

qĕdēšā 95
Queen of Sheba 173

rite of passage 52–4
robe 36, 101, 104, 116, 145–59
rōqēm 31
rosette 42, 63, 64, 66, 68–70, 73, 75, 76, 77, 79, 80, 81, 82, 85

rosette-stamped-seals 81
royal garment 42, 43, 147, 148, 170, 172, 173

sacerdotal garment 147
sacerdotal vestment 148
sacred tree 76
sacred vestments 30
šakattu 15, 16
sandals 165, 169
šaqītu 16
Sargonic period 13
Sargon II 43
sash 30, 32, 36, 37, 39, 40, 146, 157
Second Temple era 126
Shalmaneser III 146
Shamash 14, 20
shul 17, 18, 25
simla 16, 17
Sippar 49
sisiktu 82
ṣiṣṣatu 72

Tabernacle furnishings 37–8, 54
tassels 43, 63–4, 66–7, 70–4, 77–8, 80, 82, 84, 85–6
tefillin 83
Tell Fakhariyeh 146, 148
Thebes 40
Tiglath Pileser III 147
tropologically 150
tunic 29, 32, 35, 36, 37, 40, 41, 42, 43, 48, 101, 146, 157
turban 30, 32, 35, 36, 57, 59, 62, 68, 70, 152, 154, 155, 156

Uriah 137, 140
Urim and Thummim 33, 57, 62, 180

widow's garment 95
woman of substance 3–4, 9

www.ingramcontent.com/pod-product-compliance
Lightning Source LLC
Chambersburg PA
CBHW052043300426
44117CB00012B/1959